Missions and Pueblos of the Old Southwest

Their Myths, Legends, Fiestas, and Ceremonies, with some accounts of the Indian Tribes and their Dances; and of the Penitentes

by
EARLE R. FORREST

The Rio Grande Press, Inc.
GLORIETA, NEW MEXICO · 87535

© 1979
The Rio Grande Press, Inc.,
Glorieta, N.M. 87535

First edition from which this edition was reproduced
was supplied by
INTERNATIONAL BOOKFINDERS, INC.,
P. O. Box 1
Pacific Palisades, Ca. 90272

1. New Publisher's Preface
2. New Introduction by Dr. Richard N. Ellis

Library of Congress Cataloging in Publication Data

Forrest, Earle Robert, 1883-
   Missions and pueblos of the Old Southwest.

   (Beautiful Rio Grande classics)
   Bibliography: p.
   Includes index.
   1. Spanish missions of the New Southwest.
2. Southwest, New--History--To 1848. 3. Indians of
North America--Southwest, New. 4. Indians of North
America--Southwest, New--Dances. I. Title.
F799.F66 1979   979   79-468
ISBN 0-87380-175-X

A RIO GRANDE CLASSIC
First Published in 1929

1990

GLORIETA, NEW MEXICO · 87535

Publisher's Preface

After founding The Rio Grande Press in April 1962, we selected *Missions and Pueblos of the Old Southwest* as one of our first six titles for reprinting. Although our research indicated that the copyright had expired in 1957, we learned from the copyright office that author Earle R. Forrest still lived, spending his summers at his home in Washington, Pa., and his winters in San Marino at the home of his daughter, Mrs. (Margaret Forrest) Thomas P. Brown, Jr. After a great deal of difficulty, we finally reached Mr. Forrest and subsequently spent several hours talking with him between his planes at O'Hare airport in Chicago. He said he was pleased that we wanted to reprint his book, and he readily gave us permission to do so.

Our Beautiful Rio Grande Classic edition came along, finally, in October 1962. We ran a second printing in the summer of 1965, and half of that run was destroyed when a water pipe burst in our inventory room and partially submerged many skids of books—of which this title was one. Our last copies were sold in 1967 and the book has remained out of print since then. In the meantime, during our move from Chicago to New Mexico, we lost the printing negatives but not the cover design stamping dies.

Moreover, our two previous editions were simply facsimile printings, neither of them containing any new material. Hence, we present here a *new edition* rather than a new printing. Besides our own Publisher's Preface, we have a "mini-review" of the book in an Introduction by our friend Dr. Richard N. Ellis of the history faculty of the University of New Mexico. Dr. Ellis describes this book perfectly; it is oriented towards newcomers and visitors who have relocated or visited in New Mexico and Arizona. It is not strictly speaking a scholarly book by a scholar, but it is pristine source material (and hence, citable by researchers) some of which was gathered while the two states were still territories. The many photographs by the author are visual documentations of a long-gone period in time.

Who was Earle R. Forrest?

He was born in Washington, Pa., on June 29, 1883, the son of Joshua Rhodes and Marybelle Boyle Forrest. Earle grew up at a time when the American west was fast becoming a legend instead of a frontier. Mr. Forrest told us that even as a boy, he was impatient to see real live Indians ". . . out west". He wanted very much, he told us during our visit, to follow the footsteps of a literary predecessor in the Southwest—author Charles Lummis—and to a great extent, as he grew older, that is just what author Forrest did. He walked—literally— over almost all of New Mexico and Arizona when it was relatively safe for a White man to do so.

He earned a B.S. degree at Washington and Jefferson College in 1908, and did some post-graduate work during 1908 and 1909 at the University of Michigan. He married Margaret Bingham on his 26th birthday, June 29, 1909. Sources indicate one daughter, Margaret Isabel, was born of this marriage before Mrs. Forrest passed away.

Among several other jobs, author (and sometime cowboy) Forrest did some time as a newspaper reporter, which may be what influenced him to take up the nomadic roaming in the Southwest that he undertook after the death of his wife. He was a prolific writer. Some of his volumes: *A History of Washington County (Pa)*, this title, *California Joe, Noted Scout and Indian Fighter, Lone War Trail of Apache Kid, Arizona's Dark and Bloody Ground, Patrick Gass, Lewis and Clark's Last Man*, and *Snake Dance of the Moqui Indians* (he seems to have borrowed the title from an earlier work bearing the same words by John Gregory Bourke).

He was 79 years old when we met him, tall, thin, slightly stooped, alert and bright but with a hearing problem. Still active, amiable and friendly, our visit was all too brief. He had much to tell, but between planes, no time to tell it. We were saddened when we learned he had passed away on August 26, 1969.

Missions and Puebles of the Old Southwest is not a *great* book, bibliographically speaking, but it is a *very good* book to *read*. Author Forrest's intense love affair with the history of the American Southwest comes through clearly. Any reader who shares that feeling will find this book and its photographs engrossing and fascinating; it is a classic study of a classic time—it is to contemporary readers a warm and intimate glance backward to a place and an era one can know about now only in books like this.

This is our 119th Beautiful Rio Grande Classic, considering that it is an amplified version of our earlier printing. Because of the new material herein, this edition has a new Library of Congress catalog number and a new ISBN number, and it has been cataloged this time (CIP) in production.

It is our pleasure to bring this fine book back for those of the younger generations who somehow have developed an interest in American history (a subject too much ignored these days), and for those of the older generations who would like but cannot find a first edition or a copy of our 1962/1965 editions.

Go ahead, enjoy!

Robert B. McCoy

La Casa Escuela
Glorieta, NM 87535

Introduction

First published in 1929, *Missions and Pueblos of the Old Southwest: Their Myths, Legends, Fiestas, and Ceremonies, With Some Accounts of the Indian Tribes and Their Dances: and of the Penitentes* was a popular account of highlights of southwestern history. Earle R. Forrest was a Pennsylvanian who had spent a number of years in the Southwest soon after the turn of the century. His work as a ranch hand in southwest Colorado and in Arizona, particularly in the San Francisco Peaks region near Flagstaff, acquainted him with the region and its people at a time before it was inundated by tourists. The Southwest that Forrest knew was isolated and sparsely settled. Railroads did traverse the area, but they were few in number. Roads did exist, but they were a far cry from modern paved highways. Automobiles were rarely seen, and travel was by horseback or by wagon.

Today we speed along interstate highways, forgetting what travel was like seventy or even fifty years ago. We fail to remember that a trip by wagon from Santa Fe to Espanola took several days, or that even by the late 1920s an auto trip from Albuquerque to Santa Fe would be a day's journey. When cowboy Earle Forrest rode from the Flagstaff area to view the Snake Dance at the Hopi villages in 1906, he joined a trader at Canyon Diablo, the nearest railpoint, and made the remainder of the trip on horseback in two days.

The Southwest was changing in 1929 when Forrest's book was published. Tourism had already become a big business, and a fascination with southwestern Indians drew many visitors from other portions of the United States. Forrest had observed these changes and, indeed, had frequently returned to the Southwest as a tourist. Automobiles & roads made historic sites accessible; also Indian villages and geological marvels that hitherto had been seen by only a few outsiders. By 1929 it was relatively easy for a traveler to visit Taos Pueblo, the Hopi villages, Tumacacori, Canyon de Chelly, (pronounced 'dooshay'), or the Painted Desert. The influx of visitors brought changes which Forrest noted. The Hopis, for example, inaugurated a prohibition on the taking of pictures during the Snake Dance. It is perhaps ironic that Forrest, whose book was geared to a popular audience and to tourists in particular, also reflects a nostalgic interest in the Southwest that he had known as a cowhand. "What little was left of the old frontier," he wrote, "has vanished before the modern tourist, who, during the last ten or fifteen years, has invaded many a corner of the old Southwest."

When Herbert Eugene Bolton reviewed *Missions and Pueblos of the Old Southwest* for the *American Historical Review,* he commented, "There is much to praise in the book. It is well written and beautifully illustrated . . . . The Indian dances are described with the touch of one who has seen them. Some of the outstanding episodes of history are well told." Bolton went on to indicate that it was a tourist's guide to Southwestern antiquities. He was correct, for Forrest had determined to write a book ". . . to be helpful to the tourist and visitor to the old Pueblos and missions, as well as to form an authentic record for the student of Southwestern history."

Forrest obviously organized his book with the tourist in mind. His chapters described a series of convenient journeys to historic sites of Hispanic and Indian heritage. He covered such topics as missions, churches and chapels of Santa Fe and missions in geographical regions such as southern Arizona, from Santa Fe to San Juan, or from Albuquerque to Jemez. His interest was in Spanish missions and Indian ceremonials, and he included appendices listing Spanish mission names, annual fiesta dates of New Mexico pueblos, and ceremonies held by the Hopis.

Like so many, Forrest was fascinated by the Spanish and Indian heritage in the Southwest. Perhaps because he knew New Mexico and Arizona, or perhaps in reaction to the attention devoted to Spanish missions in California he chose to limit his coverage to the former two states. Forrest had great admiration for Spanish missionaries who risked their lives to penetrate the Southwest to spread their religion, and he presents a very favorable description of their activities.

If Forrest was impressed with Eusebio Francisco Kino, Francisco Garces, and other lesser known priests, he was also attracted to native ceremonies. Although denied permission, he surreptitiously took photographs of such events. He admired the Hopis (who preserved so much of their traditional culture) and wrote of them, ". . . They love their own way better than anything civilization has to offer, and they preserved until recent times the strange beliefs of their fathers almost as pure as when Coronado's conquistadores first found them in 1540." He admired the determination of traditional Hopis to preserve their culture and religion and was critical of the attitude of missionaries in Hopi country. "They do not understand the native point of view, and did not seem to want to," he wrote. ". . . All Hopi rites were regarded as institutions of the devil; yet the missionaries failed to show these Indians where Christianity would be better than the religion they have known since the beginning of time."

There are a number of factual errors in the text, For example, Santa Fe was not founded in 1605, nor did Dominguez and Escalante reach Los Angeles on their famous expedition in 1776. However, the book was well written and undoubtedly was of great benefit to tourists in the 1930s; it remains useful for that purpose. Those interested in visiting Spanish mission sites such as the "cities that died of fear"—Abo, Quarai, or Gran Quivira east of New Mexico's Manzano Mountains, which have now been designated state or national monuments, will appreciate the historical sketches in *Missions and Pueblos of the Old Southwest*. The photographs which interested Herbert Bolton continue to be useful as a historical record and for comparison with the present. The photograph of the Mission San Jose de Tumacacori in southern Arizona depicts a marked contrast to the partially restored site which today is a national monument. Modern readers can still enjoy this excellent "tour" book of the Southwest.

Richard N. Ellis, Ph.D.,

University of New Mexico
Department of History

Missions and Pueblos
of the
Old Southwest

SAN XAVIER DEL BAC MISSION

The finest Spanish mission in North America. Photograph taken by author before restoration

Missions and Pueblos of the Old Southwest

Their Myths, Legends, Fiestas, and Ceremonies, with some accounts of the Indian Tribes and their Dances; and of the Penitentes

by
EARLE R. FORREST

The Arthur H. Clark Company
Cleveland, U.S.A: 1929

Copyright, 1929, by
THE ARTHUR H. CLARK COMPANY

To my wife
and daughter, Peggy
comrades of my wanderings

Contents

Preface	15
I. The Trail of the Padres	25

The First Padres – List of Spanish Priests murdered in New Mexico.

II. The First Missions	33

San Bartolomé at old Puaray – San Gabriel Mission – Oñate founds the first Spanish settlement – The site of San Gabriel Mission located.

III. Missions, Churches and Chapels of Santa Fé	41

San Miguel – Our Lady of Light – San Francisco Church and Saint Francis Cathedral – Guadalupe Church – Rosario Chapel – Agua Fria Church – Old Cemetery Chapel – Ortizea Chapel – Chapel of the Vigiles.

IV. From Santa Fé north to San Juan	59

Tesuque – Pojoaque – Nambé – Chimayó – San Ildefonso – Santa Clara – Santa Cruz.

V. From San Juan to Taos	77

San Juan – Popé – Rebellion of 1680 – Picuris – Taos Pueblo – Battle of San Geronimo Mission – Fernandez de Taos – Los Ranchos de Taos.

VI. From Santa Fé to Pecos and south of Santa Fé	97

Pecos Church – San Cristóbal – San Lazáro – Santa Cruz de Galisteo – San Marcos – Cienega – San Pedro del Cuchillo.

VII. From Santa Fé to Albuquerque	111

Cochití – Santo Domingo – San Felipe – Sandiá – Santa Ana.

VIII. From Albuquerque to Jemez	131

Albuquerque – San Felipe Church – Santa Ana Pueblo – Sia – The Jemez Missions, San José, San Diego, and San Juan.

IX. The Cities that Died of Fear	141

Quarai – Tajique – Chililí – Abó – Gran Quivira, or Tabira.

X. From Albuquerque south to Socorro	151

The Isleta Missions, San Antonio and San Agustin – The legend of Padre Padilla's coffin – Nuestra Señora de Belen – San Luis Obispo de Sevilleta – Santa Ana – Nuestra Señora del Socorro – San Pascual – San Antonio de Senecu.

10 MISSIONS AND PUEBLOS OF OLD SOUTHWEST

XI. FROM ALBUQUERQUE WEST TO ZUÑI 161
    San José de Laguna – A curious lawsuit over a painting – San Estévan Rey de Acoma – Cebolleta.

XII. THE SEVEN CITIES OF CIBOLA 169
    The myth of the golden cities – Coronado's Expedition – Hawikuh, the first city – Kechipauan – Halona – Zuñi – Thunder Mountain – Inscription Rock.

XIII. THE PENITENTES OF NEW MEXICO . . . 195

XIV. THE HOPI MISSIONS IN ARIZONA 207
    The Hopi Missions – San Bernardino de Awatobi – San Francisco de Oraibi – San Buenaventura de Mishongnovi – San Bartolomé de Shongopovi – Walpi or Kisakobi.

XV. THE SOUTHERN ARIZONA MISSIONS 229
    The southern missions – Padre Eusebio Francisco Kino – San Gabriel de Guevavi, the first mission – The Pima Rebellion of 1751 – Lost Spanish mines – San José de Tumacacori – Pete Kitchen's famous pioneer road – San Xavier del Bac – San Ignacio de Sonoita – Jamac – Santa Gertrudes de Tubac – San José and San Agustin del Tucson – San Cayetano de Calabazas – San Luis de Bacuancos – Arivaca – San Francisco de Ati – San Serafin – The treasure of San Bernardino ranch.

XVI. THE DANCE FOR RAIN AT COCHITÍ . . . 265

XVII. THE LAND OF THE SNAKE DANCE . . . 277
    The last old-time Snake Dance at Oraibi – The founding of Hotevilla – Lost on the Little Colorado – The Mishongnovi Snake Dance of 1907 – The Oraibi Flute Dance of 1907 – A visit to Hotevilla – The Mishongnovi Flute Dance of 1908 – The Oraibi Snake Dance of 1908.

Appendix I: SPANISH MISSION NAMES WITH THEIR ENGLISH EQUIVALENTS 333
    II: ANNUAL FIESTA DATES OF THE PUEBLOS OF NEW MEXICO 337
    III: CEREMONIES HELD BY THE HOPI INDIANS OF ARIZONA 339
    IV: DATES OF THE SNAKE AND FLUTE DANCES AT SOME OF THE HOPI PUEBLOS . . . 347

BIBLIOGRAPHY 349

INDEX 355

Illustrations

[All reproduced from original photographs taken by the author unless otherwise stated]

SAN XAVIER DEL BAC MISSION . . . . *Frontispiece*
    The finest Spanish mission in North America; erected between 1783 and 1797. Photograph taken by the author before the restoration.

RUINS OF THE FOUNDATION AND PART OF THE WALL OF OLD SAN GABRIEL CHURCH 35
    Built in 1598 at San Gabriel settlement, this is all that is left of the first church – the oldest building built by Europeans in North America.

SAN MIGUEL CHURCH, SANTA FÉ, NEW MEXICO . . 43
    Built by Don Juan de Oñate between 1605 and 1608, this is the oldest place of religious worship still in use in North America.

THE ALTAR AND INTERIOR OF SAN MIGUEL CHURCH . 47
    This is typical of all the New Mexico missions.

CHAPEL OF OUR LADY OF THE ROSARY 51
    Known as Rosario chapel, Santa Fé, New Mexico; originally built by General de Vargas after the reconquest of 1692. The present building was erected on the same spot in 1807.

HEAD OF THE DE VARGAS PROCESSION, SANTA FÉ, NEW MEXICO 55
    This ceremony, instituted by De Vargas after the reconquest, is still observed by the Mexican population of Santa Fé.

SAN ILDEFONSO MISSION 65
    Built shortly after 1696, this shows the building as it appeared before remodeling in recent years. Courtesy of the United States Department of the Interior.

SANTA CLARA MISSION BEFORE THE BUILDING FELL . . 69
    This great church, one of the fine examples of Franciscan missions in the state, was erected after the reconquest in 1692, and stood until a few years ago, when the building crashed to the ground during remodeling repairs.*

12 MISSIONS AND PUEBLOS OF OLD SOUTHWEST

RUINS OF SAN GERONIMO MISSION, TAOS, NEW MEXICO . 85
    Erected shortly after 1600, this church was battered down by American artillery on February 3, 1847. This is the shrine of indian heroism and martyrdom, where one hundred and fifty were killed and great numbers wounded. The Taos mountains are in the background.

OLD MISSION OF LOS RANCHOS DE TAOS, NEW MEXICO . 93
    Erected in 1772, it is still in use.

RUINS OF PECOS CHURCH TODAY 101
    The arch over the doorway at the side is the only arch found in any of the old missions of New Mexico.

SANTO DOMINGO MISSION, SANTO DOMINGO PUEBLO, NEW MEXICO 113
    While this building was erected in modern times, after 1885, the type of architecture is the most typical of the early New Mexico missions now found in the state. The church erected in 1700 was destroyed by the flood of 1885.

RUINS OF THE SECOND MISSION FOUNDED AT OLD SAN FELIPE 117
    Built in 1694 on the Black mesa near Bernalillo, New Mexico; the village was abandoned shortly after 1700.*

THE PRESENT MISSION AT SAN FELIPE PUEBLO, NEAR THORNTON, NEW MEXICO 121
    Erected shortly after 1700.*

SANTA ANA MISSION, SANTA ANA PUEBLO, NEW MEXICO . 125
    Believed to have been erected shortly after 1694.*

RUINS OF SAN DIEGO DE JEMEZ MISSION . . . 137
    Founded in the seventeenth century at ancient Gyusiwa pueblo. This is one of the finest mission ruins in New Mexico.*

MISSION OF SAN AGUSTIN AT ISLETA PUEBLO BEFORE IT WAS REMODELED 153
    This shows its original appearance; erected in 1709.*

MAIN ALTAR OF LA CONCEPCION MISSION AT ANCIENT HAWIKUH 175
    Made after the excavations in 1919 by Jesse L. Nusbaum for the Hendricks-Hodge Hawikuh expedition, of the Museum of the American Indian, New York. At the foot of this altar Fray Pedro de Avila y Ayala was slain by Apaches in the raid of August 7, 1670. This view is looking south. Note the adobe altar at each side of the steps, the main altar is beyond the steps, beneath which the skeleton was found. Photo by courtesy of Frederick W. Hodge, Esq.

ILLUSTRATIONS

CANAQUE DANCE, OR DANCE OF THE WHITE MASKS, AT
ZUÑI PUEBLO, NEW MEXICO 181
    This dance is held only once every four years, and by a strange coincidence it comes during the presidential year. Photographs are forbidden and are only taken at great personal risk. This photograph was taken in 1912 by James C. Harvey, Esq., of Santa Fé, New Mexico. Courtesy of Mr. Harvey.

RUINS OF THE ZUÑI MISSION AT ZUÑI PUEBLO, NEW MEXICO 185

A PENITENTE MORADA, OR HOUSE OF WORSHIP . . . 197

PROCESSION OF THE PENITENTES TO THE CALVARIO CROSS
FOR THE CRUCIFIXION ON GOOD FRIDAY . . . 201
    A rare old photograph, the only one of a Penitente procession known to be in existence. Photographs of this procession are absolutely barred. The photographer is unknown.

RUINS OF SAN BERNARDINO MISSION AT OLD AWATOBI,
ARIZONA 217
    Erected in 1629, this is the oldest building in Arizona built by Europeans. It was destroyed in the Rebellion of 1680 and never rebuilt.*

RUINS OF SAN GABRIEL DE GUEVAVI MISSION IN SOUTHERN
ARIZONA 241
    Founded between 1687 and 1691 by Father Kino. From a rare old photograph in the possession of the author.

RUINS OF SAN JOSÉ DE TUMACACORI MISSION IN SOUTHERN
ARIZONA 245
    Founded by Father Kino about 1692; once a magnificent church. Photograph by Buehman, Tucson, Arizona.

THE INTERIOR OF SAN XAVIER DEL BAC MISSION . . 249

THE DANCE FOR RAIN AT COCHITÍ 273
    This ancient tribal dance takes place in the public plaza, in the shadow of the christian church of another race. Photographs are not now permitted to be taken.

THE DANCE PLAZA AT ORAIBI, ARIZONA, DURING THE
GREAT SNAKE DANCE OF THE HOPIS IN 1906 . . 287
    This was the last of the old-time Snake dances ever held at Oraibi, and such a picturesque assembly of indians will never be seen again under similar circumstances in all the Southwest.

THE LAST OLD-TIME SNAKE DANCE OF THE HOPI INDIANS
EVER HELD AT ORAIBI, ARIZONA, 1906 . . . 293

THE HOPI SNAKE DANCE AT MISHONGNOVI, ARIZONA,
IN 1907 311
 Even today the pueblos of the Middle mesa are seldom visited by white people during the ceremony.

THE HOPI FLUTE DANCE AT ORAIBI, ARIZONA, IN 1907 . 315
 The ceremony of the Cakwalenya, or Blue Flute society in the village plaza.

THE HOPI FLUTE DANCE AT MISHONGNOVI, ARIZONA, IN
1908 323
 This shows the complete ceremony of both the Cakwalenya, or Blue Flue, and the Macilenya, or Drab Flute societies on the first terrace before the village was reached on the march from Toreva Spring.

[* Courtesy of the Bureau of American Ethnology]

Preface

This volume is the result of many years study and personal observations of the missions and Spanish history of the old Southwest. Geographically the Southwest includes Texas, New Mexico, Arizona, and California; but historically speaking the old Spanish Southwest is New Mexico and Arizona, for these states had been explored and settled many long years before either Texas or California.

My interest in and studies of the indian pueblos, missions, and ruins of this section began more than twenty-five years ago, when as a cowboy I rode the cattle ranges of the great Southwest. I was little more than a boy then, out from decorous old East in search of adventure; and the opportunities for a study of the ancient civilization of that little-known land, afforded by my wanderings with cow outfits, were almost without limit; for on every hand were the remains of this ancient civilization; ruins abandoned long before the coming of the first Europeans into that land nearly four hundred years ago, as well as of the Spanish period which extended down to the early years of the nineteenth century.

I had always associated missions with California, but when I saw San Xavier del Bac, the finest in North America, and heard some of its history my interest was aroused. Then when I stood before the great ruin of San José de Tumacacori, magnificent in its loneliness amid the mesquite, and a cowboy comrade pointed out an adobe wall that had once been San Gabriel de Guevavi, now almost lost in the sage and cacti, and again when I beheld the ruins of the ancient Hopi city of Awatobi and its crumbling mission almost gone, I realized that this southwestern land had a wonderful story to tell that our English histories do not contain.

My interest continued and year after year I returned during my vacations from college and after graduation, and with the historical background I then had I spent many more years visiting and revisiting these ancient missions and the ruins of the earliest settlements in this country. When you are with a cow outfit the opportunities for visiting and discovering remote places inaccessible to other travelers are almost without limit, and I made the most of my advantages.

You cannot go into any corner of the old Southwest, no matter how remote, without bumping into some padre or adventurous Spaniard who was there hundreds of years ago. It is well known that the Grand Canyon was discovered by Cárdenas in 1540; but not many people, even today, know that carved on the stone walls of Inscription House, a cliff dwelling in northeastern Arizona, is the name of Carlos Arnius, 1661. With the exception of a few wandering cowboys, prospectors, and indian traders, this region was practically unknown to Americans until within the last fifteen years. Again we find that in 1776 the first trail across the Grand Canyon was discovered by Padre Garcés; and so the story of padre and conquistadore might be continued indefinitely.

In this volume I have given first-hand information on these missions and pueblos which has not hitherto been available. I have used every care to present the facts with historical exactness, checking my personal records and observations with published material.

Our popular histories have taught us to think only of California when we speak of missions, and no mention is ever made of the fact that more than a century and a half before the first mission had been founded in the Golden State, Spanish padres had carried the Cross into the deserts of New Mexico and Arizona. My investigations have brought out the fact that the story of the missions of those states is one of the most romantic and tragic in American history. Many long-forgotten missions, only mentioned in old records, have been brought to light, and the complete narrative is here presented for the first time.

From the founding of the first New Mexico mission, known as the Mission of Friar Ruiz, at old Puaray pueblo in 1581, down through two hundred years forty-eight others were established in New Mexico and eighteen in Arizona. Before July 6, 1769, the date Father Junípero Serra founded San Diego de Alcalá, the first of the California missions, forty-eight had been established in New Mexico and sixteen in Arizona; but many of them were in ruins long before 1769. During the ten years following 1598, the year that mission work was really started on an extensive scale, eight thousand indians were converted, and by 1617 there were between eleven and fourteen thousand neophytes. In 1630 there were thirty-three missions and in 1680, the year of the great Pueblo rebellion, there were forty. Sixteen of the New Mexico missions are still in use, mostly for the indians; twenty-six are in various stages of ruin, and the remaining seven have disappeared utterly from the face of the earth. Arizona has one mission still in use, nine are in ruins, some of which are almost gone, while all trace of the remaining eight has completely vanished.

Unlike California, the history of these Southwestern missions was written in the lifeblood of the padres. It is impossible for anyone, no matter of what denomination, to go over the records of those times without gaining a great admiration for those Spanish priests. Their story is one of the marvels of American history. Voluntarily they left their own fair land across the sea, never to return, and buried themselves in the unknown deserts of our present Southwest to gain converts for their religion. They not only endured the dreary solitude and suffered the hardships of the wilderness for long years, but they constantly faced death from the raiding Apaches, Navajos and Comanches, and sometimes at the hands of their own neophytes. Between 1540 and 1680 twelve priests are known to have been murdered by the natives, and in the Rebellion of 1680 no less than twenty-one, found martyrs' graves; yet in spite of all this the padres continued to come year after year.

It is a mistaken idea that Spain abandoned New Mexico and Arizona after Coronado failed to find the reputed wealth of the fabled Seven Cities of Cibola, for the Spaniards were colonizers and explorers as well as gold hunters. Other expeditions followed Coronado, but nothing permanent was accomplished until Oñate came in 1598, and established the first European colony in the Southwest. That event, which marks the first permanent settlement of New Mexico, was nine years before the English were at Jamestown, ten years before Champlain, the great French explorer, founded Quebec, and twenty-two years before the pilgrims landed at Plymouth Rock. An important discovery in New Mexico history was made by the author some years ago when he identified the foundation of old San Gabriel Mission, dedicated at this settlement September 8, 1598.

Reared in a protestant community of the East, where ideas are slow to change, I first went to the Southwest with the idea firmly planted in my mind that the Spaniards had treated the indians with great cruelty, and that the padres had converted them to the catholic religion at the point of the sword. Imagine my surprise when I learned that there was no truth in this; that it was simply the teachings of people who either did not know the facts, or had concealed them.

Contrary to the popular belief those old-time Spanish conquistadores were not cruel to the indians. It is true that the invaders fought the aborigines when they were opposed; but so did the English. However, the Spaniards did not treat them like a conquered nation, but gave them every opportunity and helped them. The priests did not take the sword with them into the desert; their only weapon was the Cross, and many of them paid with their lives before the indians understood this new religion. The priests, one generation after another, treated the native religion with a tolerance not known today among most protestant missionaries. The result is that practically all of the indians of New Mexico who have been converted to the christian religion are catholics; but the priests of long ago and those of today never frowned upon the native rites, and the Pueblos still hold many of their own religious ceremonies in connection with the new religion.

Governor Otermin did hang indian prisoners in the plaza at Santa Fé just before his retreat in 1680; but we must remember that a mere handful of Spaniards were fighting for their lives against Pope's Pueblo legions. It is also true that one hundred sixty-six years later Colonel Sterling Price and his invading American army battered down the walls of the Taos church with artillery, killed one hundred fifty natives and afterwards publically hanged fifteen of the leaders of the Taos indians, all because they had opposed the American occupation.

It is also true that the Spaniards swept down on camps of the Apaches, Navajos and Comanches, and killed many indians; but this was only after those tribes had raided Spanish settlements and the more peaceable Pueblo towns and carried off women and children into captivity. The Apaches, Navajos, and Comanches were never conquered by the Spaniards. They were natural hunters; and man has always been the most dangerous game in the world to hunt, for a man hunt produces more thrills than a grizzly bear hunt. The Apaches, Navajos and Comanches wanted war, and they did not care who they fought. First it was the surrounding tribes — Pueblos, Hopis, Pimas, and Papagos; then it was the Spaniards and later the Americans; and they never quit fighting down through three centuries until they were completely subjugated by the Americans. And yet, in view of all this, protestants in the East who do not understand, to put it kindly, still believe that the Spaniards were cruel because Spain is a catholic nation. The record of those times show that the indians prospered better during two centuries and a half of Spanish rule than under seventy-five years of American regime. I will just ask my readers to remember at this point that I am a protestant.

In the days of my earlier study of the indian pueblos, missions and ruins the only means of access were often by saddle and packhorse; and many times I carried my entire camp equipment, such as it was, strapped to my saddle, depending upon trading-posts and indian villages for shelter and supplies. That was long before roads had been laid out to many points of present day interest, and we followed desert trails, or simply found our own way like pioneers of old. In the solitude of the desert I could work upon and study these missions and ruins without interruption.

Today I cannot help but marvel at the ease with which the modern traveler can visit places in a few hours that were a matter of days twenty years and more ago; for a journey that required a week on horseback in those times is now made in a day. This has had its effect on the life and customs of the old Southwest, for the great army of tourists that has come with the automobile has changed the indian's ideas and character. Instead of greeting the white visitor with friendship, he now looks upon him with contempt, simply tolerating him for the dollars that he will leave behind. Even the children have changed, and instead of gazing shyly at the white visitor like scared rabbits, they set upon you in crowds, begging for nickels and dimes. What little was left of the old frontier has vanished before the modern tourist, who, during the last ten or fifteen years, has invaded many a corner of the old Southwest. But even this has its compensations, for the automobile has made it possible for thousands of persons to visit sections that in former days were as inaccessible to them as the North pole. Yet those of us who knew the old Southwest cannot help but lament its passing.

The Southwest that I knew long ago was entirely different from the Southwest of today. The modern traveler will never know many of the things that I enjoyed in those earlier days. He can never know the thrills of riding, sometimes alone, sometimes with only one comrade, into a land where few white people had ever been; of the chances of discovering something new; of camping on the desert far from human habitation, often without water and with but little food; of finding some new ruin or pictograph concealed in some unknown canyon; of visiting indian dances when you were one of five or ten white persons present. That was the Southwest as I first knew it.

Within the past few years the automobile has invaded those little known sections of the old Southwest. In the badlands along the Little Colorado river, not far from the main road from Flagstaff to Tuba City, out on the Painted Desert, is Tappan spring. Half a century ago some cattle rustlers discovered this place, built corrals and a stone house, the ruins of which still stand, and made it their headquarters, where they carried on their business in safety until ferreted out by cowboys from some of the outfits that had lost stock. Thereafter it was used occasionally as a camping place for wandering cowboys, or by branding outfits, and few people even knew of its existence even until recent years. Today the main road from the Grand Canyon to Cameron Bridge passes along the rim, and the spring is pointed out to every tourist; but none of those guides know its history. Along this same road, a few miles from Tappan spring are a few petrified tree trunks, which road builders claim to have discovered a few years ago, and they gave the place the name of Melgosa Petrified Forest. I first saw them a quarter of a century ago, but they were really discovered by cowboys probably fifteen years before that time.

The dinosaur footprints near the Tuba City road across the Painted Desert were known to every cowboy and indian in that section long years ago; but it took a modern scientist to identify them. We thought they were the tracks of some prehistoric bird. I mention these to show how the West has been invaded by the automobile.

The Southwest should have a special appeal to every American, for it had a civilization as ancient as that of Europe, while the indians, Spaniards and Mexicans of New Mexico, Arizona and California furnished an early population as picturesque as can be found in any section of the world; but it is only within the past few years that Americans are "discovering" – or shall I say "rediscovering"? – this land of enchantment. The manners and customs of the early people of the Southwest, their dances, fiestas and other ceremonies held at frequent intervals throughout the year, cannot be excelled in interest and are seldom equalled by any other race.

The ruins of the great Southwest, both prehistoric and Spanish, have a charm and individuality, a historical background, an intensely interesting population, and a setting which surpasses and even antedates the ruins of Europe. I have endeavored in this volume to present this material in such form that it will interpret and present the historical facts in such a way as to be helpful to the tourist and visitor to the old Pueblos and missions, as well as to form an authentic record for the student of Southwestern history.

EARLE R. FORREST

January, 1929

I. The Trail of the Padres

The First Padres – List of Spanish Priests murdered in New Mexico.

Winding north from the City of Mexico across two thousand miles of wild, rugged mountains and sun-blistering deserts where men go mad for a drink of water, is a trail which dates back to the ancient civilization of America; a trail marked by the bones of Spanish priests and the ruins of missions they built to save the souls of the heathen indians of the Southwest. Such is "The Trail of the Padres," the most historic, the most romantic, the most pathetic in all the world; christened long years ago in the life-blood of those Spanish fathers of old as they carried the word of God into the unknown desert lands.

Those in quest of ancient and unusual places have overlooked this "trail," and know little of it except in a vague, mythical way. Yet white men had followed it for many years before the pilgrim fathers landed at Plymouth; and for nearly two centuries before the Declaration of Independence was signed it was the only route from old Mexico to what is now New Mexico and Arizona.

This trail of the Padres is like an octopus with a thousand tentacles. It begins at the City of Mexico, but it has no end. Its many branches penetrate to every corner of the old Southwest, where ancient churches and ruins stand silent and lonely far out on the desert, monuments of an historic past. Those crumbling walls were ruins long years before the California missions were built. Each has its romance, its tale of suffering and martyrdom.

The history of this trail is the greatest romance of all time. Before the Spaniards came that way it was the main route from the north to the south; and it was old when the Aztecs followed it on their great migration from ancient Aztlan in the north down to the valley of Mexico where Cortez found them three centuries later. Then came the priests of Coronado's expedition in 1540 and 1542, who sowed the first seeds of christianity in the desert, which bear fruit even to this day.

The first European pioneer of this highway was Fray Marcos de Niza, who, guided by the negro slave, Estévan, set out from Mexico in 1539 in search of the fabled "Seven Cities of Cibola." Estévan went ahead to announce the coming of the father, and boldly entered the Zuñi nation where no European had ever been. But he paid the price of his daring with his life; for he was killed by the natives of old Hawikuh pueblo, the first of the "Seven Cities," the ruins of which still stand on the Zuñi reservation in western New Mexico; and this blood of a negro slave was the first that baptized "The Trail of the Padres."

Fray Marcos pressed on until he came within sight of Hawikuh before he turned back; but he never entered it. The stories he afterwards told of the fabled riches of the "Seven Cities" set all Mexico mad with gold lust, and in 1540 Coronado set out at the head of the greatest exploring expedition America has ever known. Although he failed to find the reputed wealth of the southwestern indians, he opened a new country to Spanish settlement.

Spain was slow in colonizing this new land. When

Coronado failed to find gold the officials of the crown lost interest, and it remained for the padres to blaze the way; but nearly forty years passed before another attempt was made to explore the mysterious land to the north. Then a few Franciscan priests, sent out by the church to carry the Cross and Rosary to the heathen nations discovered by Coronado, trudged across the blistering deserts where water holes were days apart, and founded a mission at old Puaray pueblo, on the Rio Grande river, in what is now Sandoval county, New Mexico.

During the next two hundred years forty-nine missions and visitas were founded in New Mexico and eighteen in Arizona. Of the New Mexico missions sixteen are still used for worship, twenty-five stand in ruins in various stages of dilapidation and decay, prey to the desert's whims, but no trace is left of the others. The story of the Arizona missions is even more tragic; for only one – San Xavier del Bac – is still in use. Of the others, eight have been swept from the face of the earth, and nine are in ruins.

The history of those old-time padres is something to marvel at today. In defiance of the desert and the opposition of the natives, in spite of suffering and murder, a total of eight thousand indians were converted to the christian religion in New Mexico between 1598 and 1608; and in 1617 there were eleven missions and fourteen thousand converts. This was increased to thirty-three missions by 1630; and in 1680, the year of the great Pueblo rebellion, there were forty.

Before July 6, 1769, the date Fray Junípero Serra founded San Diego de Alcalá, the first of the California missions, forty-eight missions had been established in New Mexico and eight in Arizona; but many of these were in ruins in 1769, having been destroyed in the indian wars that had swept the Southwest.

Fray Juan de Padilla, the first christian martyr in the Southwest, was one of the priests who accompanied Coronado in 1540 and 1542. When the expedition started back to Mexico, Padre Padilla set out for Gran Quivira, to remain there as long as he should live. His lifework was cut short, for he was murdered on November 30, 1542, by plains indians when he announced his intentions of going to another tribe. According to a local tradition his body was carried back to Isleta and buried under the church floor; and to this day a strange legend is told of how the old padre rises from his grave.

Fray Juan de la Cruz Escalona, another priest of the Coronado expedition who remained in New Mexico, was murdered in 1542 in one of the pueblos of the province of Tigeux.[1]

The next priests who went to New Mexico in search of souls to save were Agustin Rodriguez, known as Fray Ruiz, Francisco Lopez, and Juan de Santa Maria, who crossed the deserts from old Mexico in 1581, escorted by only eight soldiers commanded by Francisco Sanchez Chamuscado, and seven indian servants. After the escort departed all three were killed at Puaray.

The following is the list of the other priests murdered before the Rebellion of 1680:

Fray Francisco Letrado, the missionary at Hawikuh, one of the fabled "Seven Cities of Cibola," was shot to death with arrows on February 22, 1632, while on his knees with a crucifix in his hands.

Fray Martin de Arvide, killed February 27, 1632, near Halona by five Zuñi indians from Hawikuh, while on his way to the Zipia.

---
[1] English Tigua.

Fray Domingo de Saraoz was poisoned by the indians at Santa Ana in 1631.

Fray Pedro de Miranda was killed at Taos, December 28, 1631.

Fray Francisco Porras was poisoned by the Hopi indians at old Walpi, Arizona, June 28, 1633.

Fray Pedro de Avilia y Ayala was killed by the natives at Hawikuh on August 7, 1670.

Fray Alonzo Gil de Avila, was killed in a sudden attack of the Apaches on Senecu pueblo, January 23, 1675. A large number of the inhabitants of this village were killed at the same time.

In the great Pueblo rebellion that swept all Spaniards from the Southwest in 1680, no less than twenty-one Franciscan priests were murdered, martyrs to the cause of christianity in that desert land. This was the greatest loss the order ever suffered at one time. Planned and carried out by Pope, of San Juan, ably assisted by Catiti, of Santo Domingo; Jaca, of Taos, and Tacu, of Picuris, it came upon the Spaniards like a bolt out of a clear sky. August 13, was the day selected, but on the eighth two indians of Tesuque revealed the plot to Governor Otermin at Santa Fé, and on the tenth the leaders struck. Only those Spaniards escaped who had fled to the capital. Otermin, with the handful of survivors, returned to old Mexico; and for twelve years New Mexico was left in the hands of the Pueblos.

The following is the list of priests murdered on that fatal August 10, 1680:

Fray Juan Bautista Pio, killed at Tesuque while in search of his converts who had deserted the pueblo when he went there to hold mass.

Fray Juan Bernal and Fray Domingo de Vera, killed at Santa Cruz de Galisteo.

Fray José de Truxillo, killed at San Bartolomé de Shongopovi, one of the present Hopi villages, in Arizona.

Fray Fernando de Velasco, who had been stationed at Pecos for thirty years, was overtaken and murdered within sight of Galisteo, to which place he was hastening to warn his superior of the revolt.

Fray Tomas de Torre, killed at Nambé.

Fray Luis de Morales and Fray Antonio Sanchez de Pro, killed at San Ildefonso.

Fray Mathias Rendon, killed at San Lorenzo de Picuris.

Fray Antonio de Mora, killed at San Geronimo de Taos.

Fray Manuel Tinoco, killed at San Marcos.

Fray Francisco Antonio Lorenzana, Fray Juan de Talaban, and Fray José Montes de Oca, killed at Santo Domingo.

Fray Juan de Jesus Maria, shot with an arrow while at the altar of San Diego de Jemez.

Fray Lucas Maldonado, killed at San Estévan de Acoma.

Fray Juan de Val, killed at Purisima Concepcion de Halona.

Fray José de Figueroa, killed at San Bernardino de Awatobi, the ruins of which still stand on the Painted Desert, on the Hopi indian reservation, Arizona.

Fray José de Espeleta and Fray Agustin de Santa Maria, killed at San Francisco de Oraibi. This was at old Oraibi pueblo, until recent years the largest of the Hopi towns in Arizona.

In another revolt against Spanish rule on June 4, 1696, four more priests were added to the list. Fray Francisco Corvera, in charge of San Ildefonso, was visited by Fray Antonio Moreno, from Nambé. That night the indians fastened the doors and windows of the church and convent, set fire to the buildings, and both priests perished.

On that fatal day Fray Antonio Carbonelli from Taos, was visiting Fray José de Arizu at San Cristóbal pueblo, when both were murdered.

An account of the indian missions of New Mexico would be incomplete without mention of some of the early Spanish churches and chapels, which were closely associated with the early history of the country. Some of the best known and more important have been included.

With Santa Fé as headquarters many of the old missions and churches can be reached; while the others can be visited from Albuquerque, with the exception of Laguna, Acoma, and far-off Zuñi. These can be reached on the journey west by either train or automobile.

II. The First Missions

San Bartolomé at old Puaray – San Gabriel Mission – Oñate founds the first Spanish settlement in the Southwest – The site of San Gabriel Mission located.

SAN BARTOLOMÉ MISSION AT OLD PUARAY [Saint Bartholomew] In 1581 three priests, Agustin Rodriguez, Francisco Lopez and Juan de Santa Maria, escorted by Francisco Sanchez Chamuscado with only eight soldiers and seven indian servants, crossed the deserts to New Mexico for the salvation of heathen souls. They stopped at old Puaray pueblo, "the village of the worm," where they founded the first mission in the state, on a bluff overlooking the Rio Grande river in front of the present town of Bernalillo. Puaray was the principal Tigua settlement when Coronado passed through the land. He spent the winter of 1540 and 1541 in the province of Tiguex; and Puaray was one of the villages in which the indians fortified themselves during a fifty-day siege by Coronado's men.

These padres named their church San Bartolomé, but it is generally known as the Mission of Friar Ruiz, so-called after Agustin Rodriguez, known as Friar Ruiz, the leader of the trio. Its career was short, for soon after the departure of Chamuscado with the escort, the natives decided that they wanted none of the white man's religion, and so they killed the three daring priests.

In 1598, when Don Juan de Oñate visited that section he discovered on a wall at Puaray a partially effaced native painting representing the murder of these three padres; and in February, 1614, Estevan de Perea, commissary of the province, discovered what he identified as the remains of Friar Lopez and removed them to the new church at Sandía.

Nothing daunted, other priests came and went with the passing years, and the mission at Puaray maintained a precarious existence until about 1711, when it was totally destroyed by the natives and the pueblo abandoned.

The ruins of historic Puaray, the site of the first mission in New Mexico, can be reached from the nearby town of Bernalillo, on the Santa Fé railroad, or by a good automobile road from Albuquerque or Santa Fé.

SAN GABRIEL MISSION [SAINT GABRIEL] On a gravelly bluff at the junction of the Rio Grande and Chama rivers, opposite Chamita station on the Denver and Rio Grande railroad twenty-five miles northwest of Santa Fé, is the site of old San Gabriel, the first Spanish settlement in the Southwest and the first capital of New Mexico. In 1598, nine years before the first permanent English settlement was established at Jamestown, Virginia, and twenty-two years before the pilgrims landed at Plymouth Rock, Don Juan de Oñate, whose name is indelibly stamped in New Mexico's history, crossed the deserts from old Mexico with a company of soldiers and settlers, and stopped at old Yugeuingge, the "village of the ravine," on the west bank of the Rio Grande. This was a Tewa village, opposite the present San Juan pueblo, which tradition places near the site of Chamita station. The indians voluntarily gave up their pueblo to the Spaniards, and went to San Juan.

There Oñate established his colony, which thus became the first Spanish settlement in the entire South-

SAN MIGUEL CHURCH, SANTA FÉ, NEW MEXICO
Built by Don Juan de Oñate between 1605 and 1608

THE FIRST MISSIONS 37

west and the headquarters of the provincial government of New Mexico, which embraced what is now the states of New Mexico, Arizona, and the western part of Texas. For their courtesy in receiving the inhabitants of Yugeuingge, who had abandoned their homes to the strangers, the Spaniards bestowed upon the people of San Juan the name of San Juan de los Caballeros (Saint John of the Cavaliers); and to this day the visitor at San Juan pueblo may read this legend printed on a board above the doorway of the governor's residence.

Beside ancient Yugeuingge Don Juan de Oñate built the city of San Francisco de los Españoles; and on September 8, 1598, thirty-three years to the very day after Saint Augustine, Florida, the oldest city in North America, was founded by this same race of pioneers, San Gabriel chapel was consecrated by the Father-commissario, having been built in exactly two weeks by the Royal Ensign, Peñaloza, under the padres directions. This, an important event to those early Spaniards was fittingly observed with an elaborate ceremony, and a week of festivities and sports, in which the indians joined, followed the dedication. An important feature was a dramatic spectacle representing a battle between Spaniards and Moors, in which the former, aided by Saint James, were victorious.

The name of the little settlement was soon changed from San Francisco to San Gabriel, but the reason is unknown. During the next six or seven years, while the Spaniards remained there, many indians from the surrounding country were baptized in the mission. But the existence of San Gabriel was short. For some cause not known today Oñate abandoned the place in 1605, and founded the present city of Santa Fé, which has been the seat of government in New Mexico from that day to this.

San Gabriel was the headquarters of all missionary work in New Mexico from 1598 until its abandonment in 1605. Immediately after the chapel was completed the country was divided into provinces, each in charge of a priest. Fray Francisco de San Miguel was assigned to the Pecos district, which included seven pueblos east of that town, and the Salinas country east to the great plains. Fray Juan Claros went to the Piros pueblos, which covered the country as far as Socorro and San Antonio. Fray Juan de Rosas was placed in charge of the province of the Queres, Santo Domingo, Cochití, San Felipe, San Marcos, and San Cristóbal. Fray Cristobal de Salazar was appointed to the Tewas district, including San Gabriel, San Juan, Santa Clara, San Ildefonso, Nambé, and Tesuque. Fray Francisco de Zamora was assigned to Picuris, Taos, and the surrounding country. Fray Alonzo de Lugo was given Jemez, Sia, and a number of pueblos in that vicinity. Acoma, Zuñi, and the province of Tusayan, now known as the Moki or Hopi country in Arizona, were given to Fray Andres Corchado. Pedro Vergara and Juan de San Buenaventura, the two lay brothers, remained with Father Martinez, the commissario at San Gabriel, to aid in the work there.

San Gabriel is today one of the ghost cities of the old Southwest. Even the spot upon which it stood is a matter of some dispute among historians. Benjamin M. Read, of Santa Fé, in his *History of New Mexico,* places the location on the east side of the Rio Grande, while the late Colonel Ralph E. Twitchell, in *Leading Facts of New Mexican History*, says that it was on the west bank of that stream. Local tradition, handed down

THE FIRST MISSIONS

from one generation to another, also places it on the west side of the river, as already stated, on the bluff at Chamita station.

After a personal visit to the locality, the author is of the opinion that Colonel Twitchell is correct. This site is one mile west of San Juan pueblo and four miles from San Gabriel ranch, at Alcalde. The buildings of the original Spanish settlement vanished long ago; and the site was later taken possession of by Mexicans who built a town there; but they, too, have gone, and at present only the adobe walls of half a dozen houses remain like specters of the past, at what might have been the capital of New Mexico, on this sandy waste, barren of vegetation, wind swept in winter and baked by the desert sun in summer.

The best evidence that this is the site of San Gabriel settlement is found in the ruins of the old mission, which are still visible. At one corner the walls stand about two feet high, while the foundation of the entire building is easily traced. This little section of adobe wall is all that is left of the oldest building erected by Europeans in North America; and it should be preserved before it has entirely disappeared. In this ruin the author picked up pieces of pottery of the same type used by the indians of that section when the Spaniards first visited New Mexico.

This interesting spot may be reached over the Denver and Rio Grande railroad from Santa Fé to Chamita, or by automobile from the capital thirty miles to interesting old San Juan pueblo, where a fine modern church has taken the place of the ancient mission which is described in another chapter.

III. Missions, Churches and Chapels of Santa Fé

San Miguel – Our Lady of Light – San Francisco Church and Saint Francis Cathedral – Guadalupe Church – Rosario Chapel – Agua Fria Church – Old Cemetery Chapel – Ortizea Chapel – Chapel of the Vigiles.

The capital of New Mexico contains only one indian mission, ancient San Miguel; but several other churches and chapels erected in the city during the long centuries of its existence are of such importance in connection with the early religious history of New Mexico that an account of the missions would not be complete without including them.

SAN MIGUEL CHURCH [Saint Michael] Old San Miguel church, the pride of Santa Fé, erected by Don Juan de Oñate between 1605 and 1608, bears the distinction of being the oldest place of religious worship still in use in North America. There have been long periods when it stood in ruins; but it was always repaired, and today, more than 320 years after it was built, it is still used. Ancient San Miguel is as old as the town itself; for Oñate started its erection almost immediately after he founded Santa Fé. Its history reads like a romance. Built for the salvation of souls, it has been the center of many a bloody conflict from the first Pueblo revolt in 1680 down through the centuries to that day when General Kearney entered the city in 1846 with his "Army of the West"; and later when the Confederates captured Santa Fé in 1862.

This church was the first in the ancient pueblo of Analco for the indians surrounding the capital city, as well as for some Tlascalans, who had been brought by the conquistadores from old Mexico. It served the parish until the Spaniards were driven out in 1680, and when the rebellious Pueblo indians took possession of the town only the roof of the edifice was destroyed. Thus it stood, prey to the sun and winds until 1692, when General Diego de Vargas, the "Napoleon of the Southwest," crossed the deserts from old Mexico, and captured the city. The church was repaired by him and used until 1710, when it was fully restored by the Marquis de la Peñuela, as shown by an ancient Spanish inscription on the main beam supporting the gallery. Translated into English this reads: "The Marquis of Peñuela rebuilt this building the Royal Ensign Don Augustin Flores Vergara his servant, A.D. 1710." In 1830, Don Simon Delgado, one of the prominent men of Santa Fé a century ago, placed the third roof on the old church.

The next calamity occurred during the great storm of 1872, when the tower was blown down; and for fifteen years New Mexico's most historic building stood in a state of dilapidation and decay; but in 1887 it was repaired as now seen.

An old tradition tells us that General de Vargas is buried under the floor; and the ancient cemetery in the rear, inclosed by a high adobe wall, is filled with hundreds of unmarked graves of Spanish conquistadores and pioneers, padres and indian neophytes, all sleeping peacefully together.

The old mission bell of San Miguel, just inside the doorway, is the largest and the second oldest in North America. It weighs 780 pounds, and the date on the side

Ruins of the Foundation and part of the Wall of old San Gabriel church
Built in 1598, this is all that is left of the oldest building constructed by Europeans in North America

shows that it was cast in August of 1356. On each side of the ancient altar are two faded paintings of the Annunciation, the work of Giovanni Cimabue, an Italian artist, in 1287.

A description of San Miguel would not be complete without mention of the old one-story adobe house, standing in a state of utter ruin on the north side of the church. The people of Santa Fé say that it is the oldest house in the United States, claiming it as a part of ancient Analco, the pueblo that occupied the site of Santa Fé. For many years this statement was accepted without question; but when the second story was removed in 1902, because of the building's dilapidated condition, and the first floor was repaired, it was discovered that only about eighteen inches of the foundation was of Tewa workmanship, the remainder of the structure being of Spanish construction; but the fact remains that it was, until very recent years, the oldest inhabited building in a civilized community in the Southwest. In 1885 two old indian women, who claimed to be lineal descendants of the original occupants, were living there. Today it stands deserted, in ruins, a relic of Santa Fé's historic past.

CHURCH OF OUR LADY OF LIGHT – The Castrense. Built by Governor Antonio del Valle during his term of office from 1754 to 1760, this was another of the historic churches of old Santa Fé. The Castrense, as it was called, was erected for the garrison of the city, and by his act Governor del Valle made himself popular with the army, as there had never been a military chapel in the capital prior to that time. It stood in the center of the public square on the south side of the plaza until it was razed in 1859 by Don Simon Delgado, who erected his home on the site.

A noted feature of the interior of this church was its great stone reredos carved from native stone by artists from old Mexico. This was the largest and most artistic work of the kind in New Mexico, and nothing like it was ever attempted in the Southwest either before or since that time. The entire altar end of the building, eighteen feet wide by fourteen feet high, was completely filled, and for a century this was the pride of all New Mexico.

Fortunately, when the building was razed the reredos was removed to San Francisco church, which stood on the present site of Saint Francis cathedral, where this wonderful example of old Spanish stone work is preserved to this day, extending across the entire width of the chancel recess. It was carved in three sections with barabesque columns between. Above a life-sized statue in the center is a mounted figure of Saint James killing the Saracens. At the top are Saint Joseph with the Virgin Mary and the child Jesus. On one side are two figures, one of Saint Anthony of Padua with the Holy Child and a tree, and the other of Saint Ignatius with a book and standard. Opposite these are Saint John Nepomuceno with a cross and palm, and Saint Francis Xavier baptizing the indians by pouring water from a shell. It is doubtful if its equal can be found in all North America.

After the American occupation the Castrense was deserted, and in 1851, when Judge Baker held the first term of court in the new territory he attempted to use the old church for this purpose. Public feeling was very strong against such an act, and Donaciano Vigil, the secretary and governor under the provisional government, refused to take the oath, protesting against the use of the church for civil purposes on the grounds that

THE ALTAR AND INTERIOR OF SAN MIGUEL CHURCH
This is typical of all the New Mexico missions

it was sacred and that the bones of his ancestors were buried there. When the judge ordered his arrest, the officer in command of the troops said to Vigil; "Stand firm and these troops and their cannon will sustain you." Then Judge Baker very wisely transferred his court to the old Palace.

SAN FRANCISCO, THE PARISH CHURCH, AND SAINT FRANCIS CATHEDRAL. The history of these two buildings is so closely associated that they will be described together. The first parish church that stood on the ground now occupied by Saint Francis cathedral was erected in 1627 by Padre Alonzo de Benavides; but in the Rebellion of 1680 it was practically destroyed and was not rebuilt until 1713. This building was used from that time until the cathedral was completed; but it is a fact worthy of mention that the old church was not disturbed during the construction operations, and while work was in progress services were held in the ancient edifice. The east end of the old adobe church still remains in the walls of the cathedral.

In 1759, after Governor del Valle erected the Church of Our Lady of Light he removed the remains of Friar Ascencion Zarata from the ruins of San Lorenzo church at Picuris, and those of Friar Geronimo de la Llama from the deserted mission at Quarai; and on August 31, 1759, he buried both in one coffin in the wall of the gospel side of the parish church of San Francisco. On this coffin, which remains in the section of the old church still standing as a part of the cathedral, is a Spanish inscription. Translated into English it reads: "Here rest the bones of the venerable P. Fray Geronimo de la Llama, an apostolic man of the Order of Saint Francis. These bones were unearthed from the ruins of the old mission of Quarac [Quarai] in the province of Las Salinas, on April 1, 1759."

The inscription to Father Zarata reads: "Here rest the bones of the venerable Fray Ascencion Zarata, an apostolic man of the Order of Saint Francis. These bones were exhumed from the ruins of the church of San Lorenzo of Picuris May 8, 1759; and the remains of the two venerable missionaries were transferred to this parish of Santa Fé, and buried on August 31, of the same year."

The cornerstone of Saint Francis cathedral was laid on July 14, 1869. This magnificent edifice is a monument to the noted Bishop Lamy, who went to New Mexico in 1850. As already related the large stone reredos removed from the Church of Our Lady of Light in 1859 still remains in the cathedral.

The towers of Saint Francis have never been completed, and never will. An excellent view of the city may be obtained from the belfry if you can induce the sexton to let you climb the old stone steps and the ladder into the loft which has been the abode of generation upon generation of pigeons during the past half century.

CHURCH OF OUR LADY OF GUADALUPE. An old tradition says that this church was erected in 1640; but according to some authorities it was built by De Vargas after the reconquest in 1692. Those who support the first date claim that it is carved on one of the beams supporting the old choir gallery, but is now concealed by the plaster cornice. Be that as it may Guadalupe church is very old. For many years it was used but little; but the coming of the railroad in 1880 brought an era of prosperity which the congregation still enjoys. At that time it was a plain adobe structure, open for re-

CHAPEL OF OUR LADY OF THE ROSARY
Known as Rosario chapel, Santa Fé, New Mexico

ligious services but once a year, December 12, the festival day of "Our Lady of Guadalupe."

With the advent of the railroad in 1880 and the discovery of minerals in Los Cerrillos shortly thereafter, came a number of English speaking catholics who demanded a church. Accordingly, the Reverend James H. Defouri was placed in charge; the building was remodeled, the interior decorated and a new altar built. Thus it stood until the roof and tower were destroyed by fire in 1922, but the damage was repaired immediately and today it is one of the most beautiful catholic churches in New Mexico.

Among its interesting relics of other days is an old painting of "Our Lady of Guadalupe," showing her as she is supposed to have appeared to the poor peon, Juan Diego, where Guadalupe church now stands near the City of Mexico, when, tradition says, she filled his zarape with roses as a sign to the bishop that she wanted a shrine erected to her on that spot.

The English speaking congregation vanished long years ago; and a visit to this old church on Sunday is a rare treat that should not be missed; for it is typical of Spanish America. A peon or two may be seen squatted on the floor near the door, and in the congregation the high and the low touch elbows as they listen to the sermon of the black-gowned padre, who preaches in Spanish. Students of this language of the Southwest will learn much by attending the services; for the father speaks slowly and distinctly so that all can hear and understand.

ROSARIO CHAPEL [Our Lady of the Rosary] One of the most interesting of the old churches at Santa Fé is Rosario chapel, originally built after the reconquest by General Don Diego de Vargas Zapata Lujan Ponce de

León. This is the full name of General de Vargas, the conqueror of the Southwest, as it appears in the old Spanish records; but he is usually known in history by the shorter General Don Diego de Vargas. Rosario chapel stands in the old Spanish graveyard, west of the town and about a mile from the plaza. Nearby is the United States military cemetery where many soldiers of the Mexican, Civil, and Indian wars in New Mexico are buried.

The story of the founding of Rosario chapel is one of the most interesting of the reconquest. When General de Vargas reached Santa Fé on September 12, 1692, with his little army he found the indians entrenched in the old Palace, and the whole town walled and fortified. He camped on a hill about a mile away, and, according to one version, made a vow to build a chapel on the spot for the glorification of "Our Lady of the Rosary" if he should be victorious in the impending battle. Another story is told that a small figure of the Virgin Mary, carried by the Spanish troops, suddenly became so heavy when this spot was reached that the entire army could not lift it. This was taken as a good omen. The statue was left there, and the town was captured the next day.

True to his vow De Vargas erected a chapel on the spot to shelter the mystic statue. This was the origin of the De Vargas procession, which is still held by the Spanish population of Santa Fé in June of each year. If you are fortunate enough to be in the city at this time you will see a small statue of the Virgin, which is claimed to be the original of De Vargas, carried in the procession from Rosario chapel to the cathedral, and the next Sunday taken back with great ceremony.

The original chapel built by De Vargas became so

HEAD OF THE DE VARGAS PROCESSION, SANTA FÉ, NEW MEXICO
This ceremony is still observed by the Mexican population of Santa Fé

MISSIONS AND CHAPELS OF SANTA FÉ

dilapidated with the passing years that a new building was erected on the spot in 1807, and this remains unchanged by time. The congregation increased during the early years of the present century, and in 1914 an addition was erected.

AGUA FRIA CHURCH [COLD WATER] During his march of reconquest in New Mexico in 1692, De Vargas erected small sanctuaries at many of his camping places. One of these was at Agua Fria, five miles west of Santa Fé; and, according to local traditions, the church which still stands there in an excellent state of preservation was one of these original chapels. Some of the scenes of Margaret Hill McCarter's interesting narrative of the old Santa Fé trail, *Vanguards of the Plains*, are laid around it.

THE OLD CEMETERY CHAPEL. On the high hill north of Santa Fé, near the old Spanish garita on the road to Fort Marcy, are the ruins of an old chapel said to have been erected about 1776. In front of it, surrounded by a crumbling adobe wall, is the old Spanish cemetery used as a burial ground until the American occupation. Not a single grave is marked by headstone or mound; but the bones of many of the distinguished citizens of the old Spanish times rest there, unmarked and unknown today. Among them are those of Desiderio Montoya, Antonio Abed Montoya, Juan José Esquibel, and José Vigil, the four leaders of the Revolution of 1837, who were executed at the nearby garita on January 24, 1838.

THE ORTIZEA CHAPEL. The Ortizea family, one of the wealthiest and most influential of a century ago, erected a chapel on Lower San Francisco street, at the west corner of Sandoval street. It was razed many years ago, and the present large stone building at the point where San Francisco street narrows, was built on the spot.

CHAPEL OF THE VIGILES [Holy Trinity] In the early years of the last century Juan Bautista y Alarid, acting governor of New Mexico who received General Kearney when he took possession of Santa Fé in August, 1846, erected a small chapel at the west side of the plaza. After the American occupation, Manuel Alvarez, who then owned the building, moved it to his ranch at Tesuque.

IV. From Santa Fé north to San Juan

Tesuque – Pojoaque – Nambé – Chimayó – San Ildefonso – Santa Clara – Santa Cruz.

TESUQUE [The cottonwood-tree place] The original Tesuque of the early Spaniards stood three miles east of the present village, which is nine miles north of Santa Fé, near the main road to Taos; and the old mission, founded early in the seventeenth century, was in charge of a visiting priest from the capital. Old Tesuque is of special interest in connection with the Rebellion of 1680; for it was there that the first blood was shed on the evening of August 9, when a Spaniard named Cristobal de Herrera was murdered. It was from Tesuque on that same day that two indians, Catua and Omtua, hastened to Santa Fé, giving the Spaniards the first warning of the great revolt planned by all of the Pueblo tribes, and when the leaders learned that their plot was known they decided to strike the blow on August 10 instead of the thirteenth, the date originally set.

On August 10, when Father Pio, who had charge of the Tesuque mission, boldly went from Santa Fé to hold mass in spite of the warning he found the village deserted. The padre started in search of his converts; but when he found some of them hiding in a nearby wash they murdered him – the first martyr of 1680. The one soldier who had accompanied him escaped on his horse.

The old pueblo was abandoned in 1680, and after the reconquest in 1694, the present village was founded. The church which stands there today was built about seventy years ago. It was long a visita of Pojoaque; but it is now served by a priest from Santa Fé. The annual fiesta takes place on November 12.

POJOAQUE. Two missions were located at this village, San Francisco (Saint Francis) and Nuestra Señora de Guadalupe (Our Lady of Guadalupe). Soon after 1600 San Francisco mission was established by the Franciscans at the small village of Pojoaque; but the original church was probably destroyed when the inhabitants abandoned the pueblo after the Rebellion of 1680. The village remained deserted after the revolt until 1706, when it was resettled with five families by order of the governor at Santa Fé. A new mission named Nuestra Señora de Guadalupe was founded, and the present church erected. In 1760 it was reduced to a visita of Nambé, but was made the seat of a mission again in 1782, with Nambé, and Tesuque as visitas.

This mission ceased to exist long years ago, and in 1900 the last of the few remaining indians abandoned the village; but Mexican families moved in and still occupy the buildings. The ancient church and adobe houses, which have changed but little with the passing years, give it the picturesque touch of the old Spanish days; but most travelers pass it by without knowing of its existence. Old Pojoaque and its ancient mission stand on a hilltop eighteen miles north of Santa Fé, on the main highway to Taos; but the village is concealed from view of the passing automobile by a curve in the road as it winds around the base of the hill. An annual fiesta is held by these natives on December 12.

NAMBÉ MISSION. One of the first missions in New Mexico after the settlement of San Gabriel, was founded by Friar Cristobal de Salazar at Nambé, a Tewa pueblo on the Nambé river, twenty-five miles north of

Santa Fé and a few miles east of Pojoaque. This village was bigger at that time than it is today, and a large church was erected to accommodate the many inhabitants; but the population has been greatly reduced since the Spanish times by the many executions for witchcraft. Nambé is the native name and is believed to refer to a round hill or round valley.

The Nambé people joined in the Rebellion of 1680, murdering their priest, Friar Tomas de Torres, and destroying the church. On April 23, 1695, De Vargas placed the mission work in charge of Friar Antonio de Acevedo, who was succeeded a year later by Friar Antonio Moreno. On June 4, 1696, while the new priest was visiting Padre Corvera at San Ildefonso the indians of that place set fire to the convent during the night and both missionaries perished.

About 1696, a new building was erected and the mission prospered until by 1729 the converts had increased to such numbers that Governor Juan Domingo de Bustamante erected at his own expense the great church which stood until modern times. An inscription carved in Spanish on a large square beam supporting the gallery told the story of the building of this edifice. Translated into English it reads: "This church was erected, at his own cost, by Senor General Don Juan Domingo de Bustamante, he being governor and captain-general, 1729, A.D." In 1782 Nambé was reduced to a visita of Pojoaque.

Several years ago many of the ancient missions of New Mexico were remodeled, and the spirit of those times seemed to have been to change the old buildings to the modern type, more suitable for a New England village. As a result many priceless relics were lost by the erection of new roofs and towers, which greatly changed their appearance; and the historic mission at Nambé was entirely destroyed by this spirit of modernization. The old flat roof was removed and a new one erected; but the walls were weakened by the work, and during a great storm in 1909 the entire building collapsed.

The beautiful scenery at the falls of Nambé, near the pueblo, and the excellent trout fishing attract many to this section, which has become a popular picnic ground for residents of Santa Fé. The annual festival is held on October 4.

THE SANTUARIO OF CHIMAYÓ. One of the most interesting spots in all New Mexico is the little Mexican village of Chimayó, home of the famous Chimayó blankets, sold in every curio store in the West. It is nestled in a beautiful valley in a secluded section in the foothills of the western slope of the Sangre de Cristo range, forty-five miles north of Santa Fé. In this remote spot is found the Church of Santuario; not an indian mission, for the people there are all Mexicans, contented and happy in their solitude, living at peace with themselves and the rest of the world; but no other spot in the entire Southwest is better known or held in greater reverence. This is a shrine for the miraculous cure of disease. Several such places are found in southern Europe, and in Mexico is the sacred spring of Guadalupe, near Mexico City; but the Santuario of Chimayó is the only place of its kind within the United States.

Any day the visitor may see the lame, the halt, and the blind, who have traveled from far distant points to secure its precious, healing earth as their last hope for health. In automobiles, in wagons, in ancient vehicles of all descriptions; on foot, on horseback and on burros, they come, all according to their stations in life, from Colorado on the north to far-off Chihuahua on the south; aged men and women, deformed and sick children, all inspired with faith and the last hope.

Just when or in what manner the virtues of the sacred earth of Chimayó were discovered is not known; nor can we say when the pilgrimages began, but it was far back in the dim past. In 1816, one Bernardo Abeyta, who was well favored with worldly possessions, erected a church with massive walls three feet thick, as a shrine for the pilgrims; and this is still standing.

A small amount of sacred earth from this spot is brewed into a drink; and it is claimed that if you have implicit faith a single spoonful will often effect a cure. Although the actual benefits derived are questioned by the skeptical, there are many persons throughout the entire Southwest who claim to have been restored to health by its magic influence. Pilgrims from a distance usually carry back a small quantity of the earth for future use; and often when the invalid is unable to make the long journey some friend will secure a supply.

It is related that in early times priests who made the pilgrimage to Chimayó would carry back a quantity of the holy earth with which to appease storms. To accomplish this a small portion was thrown into a fire, and the magical smoke thus produced would subdue the most violent tempest. No charge was ever made for the earth, and nothing was asked in the way of donations; but the voluntary offerings received at the church went to the support of the owner.

The Santuario of Chimayó was the cause of one of the most bitter battles between a catholic priest and an individual ever waged in New Mexico. When Bernardo Abeyta died he bequeathed the property to his only daughter, Señora Carmel Chavez, who kept it in a good state of repair, and during the passing years added much to its appearance. A warm welcome was extended to all visitors; the Santuario became a very popular place in which to give thanks for the blessings of the sacred earth, and Señora Chavez received considerable revenue from the voluntary contributions of the pilgrims. The Mexican padres had been friends of her family for generations; and these amicable relations were continued by the French priests brought to New Mexico by Bishop Lamy. The owner of Santuario had always donated liberally to her religion.

A day came when all this was changed. A young priest, in charge of his first parish, was sent to Chimayó, and it is said that he felt his own importance very much. Almost immediately he demanded that Señora Chavez should deed the Santuario chapel to the Catholic church. In vain she protested, explaining that it was private property, built by her father and handed down to her; that it was her only support and without it she would be penniless. The young autocrat was obdurate, and when she declined to comply with his demands he threatened to bring the wrath of the church down upon her head. But Señora Chavez came from a race of pioneers who had gained an independent spirit by fighting the desert and Apache indians for generations. She had inherited a will of her own from those old Spanish dons, and she would not be bullied. Finally, the priest excommunicated her, and went so far as to refuse to either baptize, marry, or bury any member of the Chavez family; but even this drastic step did not shake the brave woman's determination. The Catholic church did not approve of this action, and when the story reached the ears of the bishop the young man was re-

SAN ILDEFONSO MISSION

As it appeared before remodeling in recent years

moved. And since that time complete harmony has reigned between the owner and her religion. After Señora Chavez's death the property was left to her daughter, Maria de los Angeles Chavez.

SAN ILDEFONSO [SAINT ALFONSO] One of the most interesting pueblos in the upper Rio Grande valley is old San Ildefonso, eighteen miles north of Santa Fé, on the road to the famous Rito de los Frijoles. This village is the home of Julian (pronounced Hulean) and Marie, his wife, best known of all the pottery makers, and manufacturers of the famous black pottery of San Ildefonso.

When Oñate first visited this pueblo in 1598 and gave it the name of Bove, it stood about a mile from its present location. Little was known of it before that time. Even the exact date of the founding of the mission is uncertain, but it was early in the seventeenth century; for it was standing there in 1617, and from that year until 1680, Santa Clara and San Juan were visitas of San Ildefonso.

In the Pueblo revolt of 1680 these indians murdered their priest, Fray Luis de Morales, and his assistant, Antonio Sanchez de Pro, while they were holding service at the altar. Father Morales had been at San Ildefonso for some years and was loved by all his converts; but his life could not be spared for the leaders of the rebellion had decreed that all Spaniards must die.

Just before reaching the village the visitor passes the famous Black mesa of San Ildefonso, where, according to local tradition, the indians still keep burning the fire that is never allowed to die. Several terrific battles of the reconquest were fought at this mesa. When De Vargas marched against the northern tribes in 1694, the Tewas intrenched themselves on its summit, which was impregnable to the inferior arms of that time. Nothing daunted, the Spaniards, with only one hundred men, assaulted the stronghold on March 4, depending upon two pieces of artillery to strike terror to the indians. The cannon burst, but the conquistadores fought valiantly all day, with a loss of twenty-five wounded. The Tewas repelled every charge of their enemies, losing fifteen killed and many wounded. After another unsuccessful assault the next day, De Vargas settled down to a siege. Driven to desperation by the scarcity of water, several hundred indians charged the Spaniards, but after a terrific battle they were driven back to the mesa's top. Finally, on the nineteenth, De Vargas was compelled to abandon the siege because his ammunition and provisions were very low, leaving the indians in possession of the field with a loss of forty killed and a great number wounded.

After the declaration of peace in 1694, the mission was reëstablished; but the inhabitants of San Ildefonso took part in the uprising of 1696, and on the night of June 4, set fire to the convent. Fray Francisco Corvera, the priest in charge, and Fray Antonio Moreno, the missionary from Nambé who was visiting the former, perished in the flames, which destroyed both church and convent.

De Vargas marched against San Ildefonso and once more the indians fled to the Black mesa; but this time the Spaniards were more successful, and after the fourth assault on their stronghold the Tewas surrendered.

The mission burned in 1696 is still marked by a mound of earth; but a new church was built near the site in the center of the pueblo. This building remained unchanged by time until recent years, when the spirit

Santa Clara Mission before the building fell
One of the fine examples of Franciscan missions in New Mexico

of innovation got in its destructive work, and the ancient edifice was remodeled as seen today. Among its furnishings are several old paintings, some of which are on elk and buffalo skins, used in early times on account of the scarcity of canvas.

The annual festival is held January 23, the saint's day of San Ildefonso.

SANTA CLARA [SAINT CLAIRE] Santa Clara, a Tewa pueblo, the native name of which is K'hapoo, meaning "where the roses grow near the water," stands on the west side of the Rio Grande river, two miles south of the town of Española on the Denver and Rio Grande railroad, and about twenty-four miles north of Santa Fé. The inhabitants of this village claim that their ancestors lived in the artificial caves excavated in the pumice cliffs of Puyé and Shufinno, two of the most interesting of the ancient ruins in the Santa Fé region.

The first mission was built between 1626 and 1629 by Fray Alonzo de Benavides, as a visita of San Ildefonso. There was no resident priest at Santa Clara in 1680; and the people joined in the great Rebellion, destroying the church, the site of which is now marked by a mound of earth.

After the reconquest a new church and monastery were erected; and at intervals during the next hundred years Santa Clara was changed from a visita to a mission and back again until 1782, when it became a permanent mission with San Ildefonso as a visita.

This great church, one of the finest examples of the early Franciscan missions in New Mexico, was built of adobe, 135 feet long, cruciform in shape, and with a large entrance eight feet wide and ten feet high. The two massive doors were divided into ten deeply indented squares in which were engraved escutcheons.

These large doors were only opened on special occasions, but cut in one was a smaller entrance, three by six feet, for daily use. In the priest's quarters were rude native carvings of animals; and stored away in several old wooden chests were some ancient ecclesiastical vestments and old documents, which probably contained much valuable historical information, but the indian guardian of later times refused to permit an examination of them.

This great building was so massive that no one ever dreamed it would not stand for all time to come; and some twenty years ago when the destructive hand of the modern spirit reached Santa Clara, the work of remodeling the ancient edifice was started. The old roof was removed with its supporting timbers, and during a terrific storm the walls fell, the same as at Nambé; and this historic landmark was utterly destroyed.

The annual festival on August 12, is a tabla dance followed by horse races.

SANTA CRUZ [HOLY CROSS] At the little Mexican village of Santa Cruz, on the east side of the Rio Grande thirty miles northwest of Santa Fé, is the largest and finest church of the Spanish era left in New Mexico. It was built for the early settlers, but christian indians living in that vicinity were in charge of the priest at Santa Cruz; and it is therefore closely associated with the mission history of New Mexico.

The fertile land in that section attracted some of the colonists brought from old Mexico by Don Juan de Oñate in 1598; but they had no organized government until after the reconquest, and the priest at San Juan pueblo, or San Gabriel, had charge of the religious welfare of the people. In the Rebellion of 1680 the Spaniards were either killed or driven out of the valley.

During the twelve years of Pueblo rule the Tanos abandoned the villages of San Cristóbal and San Lázaro, east of Santa Fé, because of the continual warfare waged against them by their neighbors, the Pecos, and settled on the site of the present Santa Cruz, where they remained until ordered out by De Vargas.

Santa Cruz has the distinction of being the first town settled in New Mexico after the founding of Santa Fé ninety years before. In 1694, sixty-six new families arrived at the capital, and De Vargas decided to establish a new villa to accommodate them. He selected the fertile lands at Santa Cruz, and ordered the Tanos to move, but gave them time to find a new location; and so the actual settlement did not take place until April 21, 1695, when the colonists left Santa Fé. The full name, or title of the new town, was "La Villa Nueva de Santa Cruz de los Españoles Mejicanos del Rey Nuestro Señor Carlos Segundo," meaning in English, "The New Town of Holy Cross of the Spanish Mexicans of the King Our Master Carlos II"; but the old Spanish records generally refer to it as "La Villa Nueva de Santa Cruz de la Cañada," or "The New Town of Holy Cross of the Canyon."

A priest, Fray Antonio Moreno, accompanied the settlers to care for their spiritual welfare, and under his direction a church was erected. This was evidently only a temporary affair; for it was in a very dilapidated state in a few years, and on June 15, 1733, upon petition of the people of Santa Cruz, the governor gave them permission to build a new house of worship at their own expense.

In compliance with this concession the present great church, the largest in all New Mexico, was erected. Cruciform in shape, it contains two chapels, one to Our

Lady of Carmel on the north side, and the other to San Francisco. In the chapel of San Francisco known locally as the chapel of the Penitentes, is a small statue of Saint Francis, three and one-half feet high, said to be the finest example of Spanish wood carving of the seventeenth century period found in the state. In a niche in the wall of the church is an image of Christ in the tomb, and nearby is a figure of Our Lord and another of Our Lady of Carmel.

From the very beginning in 1695 down through the years to the American occupation, Santa Cruz was one of the important towns in New Mexico; but since 1846 it has remained a quiet, interesting Mexican hamlet. During the old Spanish days it was headquarters for the northern district of the province; and under Mexican rule from 1822 to 1846 it was of much political importance.

In the Revolution of 1837, Santa Cruz was the scene of an important battle between Mexican federal troops and the insurrectionists. Juan José Esquivel, alcalde of the villa, was one of the leaders of the revolt, and on August 7, 1837, Governor Perez marched against Santa Cruz with two hundred troops from Santa Fé, the majority of whom were indians. When he met the rebel army near the village many of his own men deserted at the first fire from the enemy. A few remained loyal, but in the first charge by the insurgents they were routed with a loss of seven killed and many wounded. Governor Perez with twenty-three others managed to escape to Santa Fé, only to be assassinated the next day as he was riding through the streets of the capital. His head was cut off and carried as a trophy to the rebel encampment.

Another battle was fought at Santa Cruz during the

Mexican war, when the American army under Colonel Sterling Price, advancing to Taos to avenge the death of Governor Bent, defeated a large force of indians under Montoya, Chavez, and Tafoya on January 24, 1847. The Americans lost two killed and several wounded, while the enemy suffered thirty-six killed.

V. From San Juan to Taos

San Juan – Popé – Rebellion of 1680 – Picuris – Taos Pueblo – Battle of San Geronimo Mission – Fernandez de Taos – Los Ranchos de Taos.

SAN JUAN MISSION [SAINT JOHN] The Tewa pueblo of San Juan, thirty-five miles north of Santa Fé and three miles from the main road to Taos, is in the center of the oldest European civilization in America; for at the junction of the Rio Grande and Chamita, just one mile west of the village, is the site of old San Gabriel settlement and the ruins of the ancient mission which have been described in another chapter.

Before the coming of the Spaniards the San Juan people had occupied three other pueblos, – Pioge, Sajiuwingge, and Pojiuuingge, all in ruins today. The first stood at the site of the present village of Los Lucero, in the southeast part of Rio Arriba county, while the ruins of both Sajiuwingge and Pojiuuingge are at La Joya, ten miles north of San Juan.

When Don Juan de Oñate reached New Mexico in July, 1598, with his colony he found this tribe living in two villages, one the present San Juan and the other at Yugeuingge, a mile away on the west bank of the Rio Grande, where he founded San Gabriel. The Tewas received the Spaniards in the most friendly manner. The people of Yugeuingge voluntarily gave up their pueblo to the whites and were taken in by their kinsmen at San Juan; and for this courtesy Don Juan conferred upon that village the name of "San Juan de los Caballeros," meaning "Saint John of the Cavaliers."

The date of the erection of the first church is unknown. As already related a mission was built at San Gabriel in 1598, and it is more than probable that this was used by the converts of San Juan until 1605, the year the Spaniards settled Santa Fé. There is no record of a mission at San Juan pueblo between 1605 and 1680; and it is reasonable to suppose that the church at San Gabriel was used. This supposition is borne out by the fact that San Juan was the home of Popé, the instigator of the rebellion; and there was no priest at the village in 1680.

The fact that this pueblo was the home of Popé makes it of special interest today. The leader of the great rebellion was a Tewa medicine man who made his first appearance in history in 1675, when he headed a delegation that visited the Spanish governor at Santa Fé in behalf of forty-seven indians accused of witchcraft. He was unsuccessful, and the prisoners were executed, and this might be said to have been the principal cause of the revolt.

In all history there is no plot equal to the great Pueblo rebellion of 1680. Like all medicine men, Popé was shrewd; and he quietly spread his doctrines of independence from Spanish domination, and the restoration of the old order. In this he was ably assisted by Catiti of Santo Domingo, Tupatu of Picuris, and Jaca of Taos; and so quietly did they work during the five years following the execution just related that the Spaniards gained no knowledge of what was going on. During those years Popé traveled among the various pueblos of the Rio Grande until he had worked the indians into a state of rebellion; and in all that time there was no leak, no traitors among them until five days before the date upon which the blow was to have been struck. To no woman was the secret confided; and with his own hands Popé killed his brother-in-law, Nicholas Bua, whom he suspected of treachery.

Runners were sent to far distant tribes. Even the Hopis in Arizona, hundreds of miles away, were included; but for some unknown reason the Piros of the lower Rio Grande were not asked. There were approximately 2400 Spaniards in New Mexico at that time, and Popé planned to rise up on August 13, 1680, and massacre every person of white blood.

The first intimation the Spaniards received of the plot was on August 9, when Catua and Omtua of Tesuque turned traitors and warned Governor Otermin at Santa Fé. The news of this treachery was quickly carried that day to the leaders, and by means of that strange secret of communication used by all North American tribes, which no white man has ever been able to fully explain, orders were flashed throughout the Pueblo empire to strike the blow the next day. How this was accomplished has never been known, but it could not have been done more thoroughly by a modern radio broadcasting system. All we know today is that notice of the change in the date from the thirteenth to the tenth was sent out in a single day to every tribe in the plot, even to the far-off Hopi; and every pueblo, from Pecos on the east to Oraibi on the west, hundreds of miles away in Arizona, arose on August 10, and four hundred Spaniards were massacred.

All that saved Santa Fé from destruction was the warning received the day before. Three thousand warriors were sent against the capital, and the Spaniards were besieged in the old Palace. In a sortie on the twentieth, one hundred whites suddenly attacked the indians with great fury, killing two hundred and capturing forty-seven, who were promptly hanged in the plaza. The next day Governor Otermin began his retreat to old Mexico; and for twelve years the Pueblo indians reigned supreme as in the days before the coming of the Spaniards.

The old order was restored, and everything possible done to wipe out all trace of the hated white race and its religion. The churches were burned and every object of christianity destroyed. Every indian who had been converted and baptized was washed in yucca suds to remove the stains of christianity, while the Spanish language was absolutely prohibited.

Dressed in ceremonial garb, Popé traveled from one pueblo to another, monarch of the indian empire; but his power went to his head, and he ruled with a greater despotism than any Spaniard. Death was the penalty for those who refused to obey his orders; and he seized the most beautiful women of his kingdom as wives for himself and his subordinate chiefs.

Taking advantage of the poor defense of the towns as a result of the absence of the Spaniards, the Navajos, Utes and Apaches, hereditary enemies of the Pueblos from the beginning of time, resumed their destructive raids. Drought came on, and internal dissension finally brought on civil war. Santa Domingo, Cochití, Acoma, Laguna, and other Keresan tribes on the south joined the Pecos from the east and the Taos from the north, and marched against the Tewas and Tanos. Popé was deposed and Tupatu elected in his place. He ruled the Tanos and Tewas, but the other tribes refused to recognize his authority, and in 1688 Popé was again chosen leader, but he never lived to see the restoration of

Spanish power in the land, for he died before the coming of De Vargas in 1692.

After the reconquest a large church, probably the first at San Juan pueblo, was erected. Built of adobe, long and narrow, this was one of the best and most picturesque of the old Spanish missions of New Mexico; and its destruction was a calamity for which there is no excuse. It could easily have been preserved; for empty ground for a building site is the cheapest thing they have at San Juan. Nevertheless this ancient church was demolished in 1913 to make room for the present brick edifice.

Both San Juan and the nearby pueblo of Santa Clara were visited by a great pestilence in 1782, and five hundred of the inhabitants died in two months.

San Juan is one of the most prosperous and progressive of the upper Rio Grande pueblos. Industrious and well governed, the people are noted for their hospitality to strangers. Much of this is due to the Reverend Camilo Seux, the last of the young priests brought from France by Bishop Lamy. For many years he was in charge of the mission at San Juan, and devoted his life to his people; and coming from an old French family of wealth, he gave liberally to his congregation and its church.

He began his work by making some much needed repairs to the old building. Then he improved the plaza in front, and at the gate erected a beautiful statue of the Virgin Mary, a real work of art made in France and brought across the sea and desert to San Juan. It was dedicated April 9, 1888, as shown by the Spanish inscription carved on the base: "A La Madre de Dios. El Padre Camilo Seux Abril 9 de 1888."

The next year he erected the Chapel of Our Lady of Loudres, one of the finest in all New Mexico and often called an architectural jewel set in the desert. The beautiful red volcanic rock used in its construction is found west of the Rio Grande. The cornerstone was laid in 1889, and the formal dedication took place on June 19, 1890. His next donation was a new parish house modeled after the style of the old Spanish convento, large enough for the needs of the local padre and for the accommodation of all visiting priests; for Father Seux always kept open house.

The one great blunder committed at San Juan was the destruction of the fine old Spanish mission, which had stood for more than three centuries, merely to make room for a new brick church, designed along modern lines. This was another gift of Padre Seux in 1913 when the old church which could have been so easily preserved, was ruthlessly torn away and the present edifice erected on the spot. While it is a fine, substantial building and would be a credit to any New England town or some other eastern village, the style of architecture is very incongruous out there in the sun baked desert, surrounded by adobe indian houses centuries old. It is so strangely out of keeping with its surroundings in a land where everything is Spanish, that it strikes a harsh, discordant note, and leaves an unpleasant thought of what would otherwise be an ideal visit to old San Juan.

The annual festival, held on June 24, is one of the most interesting of any of the pueblos, the ceremonies alternating each year from a tabla dance to races and indian games. After more than three centuries the people of San Juan are still very proud of their title of "Los Caballeros," and extend as warm a welcome to the visitor at the festival as they did to the first Spaniards under Oñate.

SAN LORENZO MISSION AT PICURIS [SAINT LAWRENCE] This pueblo was first visited by Coronado in 1540, and he gave it the name of Acha; but, although several expeditions were in that locality later, we find no further record of Europeans stopping there until after the organized mission work was started in 1598, when it was assigned to Fray Francisco de Zamora. A church was probably built soon afterwards, and in 1620 it was in charge of Fray Martin de Arvide, who was murdered in the Zuñi country, on February 27, 1632. San Lorenzo was an important mission, and in 1629 the resident priest had charge of a number of smaller neighboring villages.

Tupatu of Picuris led his people in the Rebellion of 1680; and after they murdered their priest, Fray Matias Rendon, and burned the church, they killed every Spaniard in the vicinity. The Picuris warriors then marched to Santa Fé and joined in the attack on Governor Otermin. For some reason, probably fear of Spanish retribution, the village was deserted after the rebellion and De Vargas found it in ruins in 1692. He induced the people to return and build a new pueblo; but in 1704 they abandoned it on account of some superstition, and fled to Quartelejo, a Jacarilla Apache settlement. Two years later they returned to their former home.

On May 8, 1759, Governor Del Valle exhumed the bones of Fray Ascencion Zarate from the ruins of the old mission at Picuris, and they were buried with those of Friar Geronimo de la Llama in the church at Santa Fé; and to this day they remain in the walls of the cathedral. The details of this have been related in the chapter on Santa Fé.

The ancient church at Picuris is one of the few old missions left in New Mexico. An interesting feature of the interior decoration is the gridiron representing the instrument of torture upon which San Lorenzo, the patron saint of Picuris, was slowly burned to death. In the wall near the door is a human skull, covered with an old cloth; but its story has long since been lost in the archives of the past. Among the furnishings are two statues, one of San José and the other of Our Lady of Carmen; and in each of the transepts is a rude altar carved out of solid masonry.

Picuris is situated in the mountains forty miles north of Santa Fé, and on this account it is seldom visited by tourists, for the road is bad. But this isolation has been its salvation, and it has been demoralized very little by outside influence. A peculiar feature is found in the manner of its construction, the walls being built of adobe mud poured into molds, the same as concrete today. This is the only modern pueblo in New Mexico in which this ancient method was used; but it is found at Casa Grande, Arizona, the greatest of all prehistoric ruins in the United States.

The people of Picuris were always warlike; and today, among the cherished relics of the past are a number of scalps taken from enemies in the olden days. They are kept in the tower of the "scalp house," and are only taken down on festival days to be carried in the procession. The annual festival, which is well worth the long journey, takes place on August 10.

SAN GERONIMO MISSION AT TAOS [SAINT JEROME] With its jagged belfry outlined against the blue sky as a monument to the indians who died within its crumbling walls before the guns of the avenging Americans, the ruins of the ancient mission of San Geronimo de

Ruins of San Geronimo mission, Taos, New Mexico

The shrine of indian heroism and martyrdom. The Taos mountains are in the background

Taos are the most historic in all New Mexico. This is the shrine of indian heroism and martyrdom, where one hundred fifty were killed and great numbers wounded in that terrible battle of February 3, 1847. No more picturesque setting for an indian mission could be found in all the world. Within the shadow of the Taos mountains which tower high above it, and the five-story pueblo immediately behind it, this ancient ruin has a background that is unsurpassed. From that fatal August 10, 1680, when the two priests were murdered, San Geronimo mission was a storm center of revolt until its massive walls were battered down by American artillery over two centuries later.

Taos with its twin pueblos five stories high is the greatest aboriginal communal dwelling in the United States. It has been known to Europeans since 1540 when Hernando de Alvarado, a captain in Coronado's army, explored that section. The next year came Francisco de Barrionuevo, another of Coronado's officers, who called it Braba, seemingly an indian name mispronounced by the Spaniards; but the early conquistadores christened it Valladolid after the Spanish city of that name. The Tewa name is Towih, and from this the Spaniards who came after Coronado coined Taos.

In July, 1598, Oñate visited Taos, and when New Mexico was divided into mission districts that same year this pueblo was assigned to Fray Francisco de Zamora. The padre began his work immediately and one of the first missions built in his province was the great church which now stands in picturesque ruin. Oñate had applied the saint name of San Miguel, but Zamora christened the new mission San Geronimo.

In 1629, Fray Benavides reported that 2500 indians had been baptized at Taos; but in spite of this Fray

Pedro de Miranda, the missionary, was killed December 28, 1631, together with Luis Pacheco and Juan de Estrada, two soldiers acting as his guard.

Taos was the central point from which Popé of San Juan, leader of the Rebellion of 1680, sowed the seeds of discontent against Spanish authority; and the inhabitants took a prominent part in the revolt. Fray Antonio de Mora, the missionary in charge at that time, had been in New Mexico for nine years. He was assisted by Juan de la Pedroza, a lay brother; and on August 10, both were murdered together with nearly every Spaniard in the Taos valley.

When De Vargas marched against Taos in October, 1692, the inhabitants fled to the mountains, and nothing was accomplished. He returned on July 3, 1693, but the indians again escaped; and when his attempts to negotiate with them failed, he sacked the pueblo. When peace was restored in 1694, missionaries were sent to Taos; but the inhabitants joined in the revolt of June 4, 1696, in which five priests and twenty-one other Spaniards were killed. De Vargas marched to the pueblo in September, and finding the indians fortified in a canyon, he laid siege to the stronghold, forcing them to surrender a month later. From that time peace reigned between the people of Taos and the Spaniards; but during the next century the pueblo was frequently raided by Utes and Comanches.

Inflamed by Mexicans who had refused to recognize American authority in New Mexico, the Taos indians rebelled in January, 1847, and on the night of the nineteenth murdered Governor Charles Bent while he was asleep in his residence at the nearby village of Fernandez de Taos, and eight other Americans were slain after a two-days' battle at Turley's Mill, twelve miles away.

On February 3, Colonel Sterling Price arrived at Fernandez de Taos with an avenging army of three hundred twenty American troops. The indians, numbering nearly seven hundred, fortified themselves in the old mission, the Alamo of Taos pueblo. The next day the Americans assaulted the indian stronghold, but the Taos warriors fought with a heroism born of desperation. Finally, Colonel Price brought his artillery into action, and at close range the walls of the ancient church were battered down by a furious cannonade. The indians fled to the pueblo and then to the mountains in the rear, leaving one hundred fifty dead and many wounded as the price of that day's fighting. The Americans lost seven killed and forty-five wounded, among the latter being Captain Burgwin who afterwards died.

Before Colonel Price would treat with the defeated indians he demanded the surrender of Tomas and fourteen other leaders of the insurrection, and very reluctantly the Taos warriors delivered their chiefs into the hands of their conquerors, who hung them on February 7 – martyrs to the cause of their people.

More than half a century passed before the peace of Taos was broken again. Finally, driven to desperation by the encroachments of whites upon their land, the natives threatened another rebellion in May, 1910; but it was speedily quelled without loss of life by the arrival of the New Mexico militia.

The ruins of the historic old mission at Taos, built three centuries and a quarter ago, stand today in picturesque grandeur, changed but little since the American cannon reduced its massive adobe walls to piles of sun-baked mud. Originally there were two towers, but only one stands today, the other having been destroyed in the battle. Within the ruined walls of the church and patio numerous little crosses mark the graves of christian converts of the twin pueblos, who have long used the sacred spot as a burial ground.

The little Catholic church now at Taos, plain without any of the picturesque beauty of the early missions, was erected in the early sixties.

Taos lies eighty-five miles north of Santa Fé, from which it can be reached by private automobile, or a daily stage. If the trip is made by private conveyance other interesting missions and pueblos may be visited along the way, by making slight detours, such as Tesuque, Pojoaque, San Ildefonso, Nambé, Santa Clara, San Juan, the site of old San Gabriel settlement, Picuris, Ranchos de Taos, and Fernandez de Taos.

The annual festival of San Geronimo is held at Taos on September 30; but numerous other public ceremonies occur during the year.

FERNANDEZ DE TAOS. Three miles from the twin pueblos of Taos is the village of Fernandez de Taos, a Spanish settlement which dates back to the conquistadores. In the early days of the Santa Fé trade, both before and after the American occupation, this was one of the most important towns in the territory, and during the forties and fifties it was the New Mexico headquarters of that famous coterie of old-time traders, trappers and indian fighters of which Kit Carson, Charles and William Bent, and Ceran St. Vrain were the leaders.

The residence of Kit Carson from 1858 to 1868, and

the house in which Governor Charles Bent was murdered are among the old historic buildings untouched by time; while in the old cemetery are the graves of Kit Carson and his wife, inclosed by an iron fence erected in 1908 by the Grand Lodge of New Mexico, Ancient Free and Accepted Masons. Carson died May 23, 1868, at Fort Lyons, Colorado, and his body was brought back to his old home at Taos.

This village was founded at a very early date. In 1680, it had a Spanish population of seventy; but only two escaped the rebellion, Don Fernando de Chaves and Sergeant Sebastian de Herrera, who, after many thrilling adventures and narrow escapes succeeded in reaching Isleta, where they joined Governor Otermin on his retreat from Santa Fé.

The town was settled again after the reconquest, and it grew and prospered until it bid fair to rival the capital. The decline set in after the coming of the railroad to Santa Fé, and for many years it was little more than a Mexican hamlet; but after the Denver and Rio Grande railroad reached Taos junction, twenty-five miles away, and with the advent of the automobile a new prosperity set in. A modern hotel has just been completed where the best accommodations can be secured, and the regular automobile stage line has placed it within easy access of Santa Fé.

Old Taos was raided frequently by both Utes and Apaches. In December, 1761, the Apaches attacked the town, killing many inhabitants and carrying away fifty women captives. Governor Manuel Urrizola with eighty soldiers pursued the hostiles, and by a surprise attack at Conejos completely annihilated them, killing about four hundred.

After San Geronimo mission was founded at Taos pueblo another church was built by the Spaniards at Fernandez de Taos, and frequently one priest had charge of both. This was in use until 1806, when a larger edifice was erected and used until recent years. This was in charge of Padre Martinez from 1826 until 1856; and after the murder of Governor Charles Bent and other Americans on the night of January 19, 1847, he saved the lives of others by giving them a safe refuge in his home.

Padre Martinez was one of the most progressive men of his time. Besides conducting a school he brought a printing press to Taos and established the first newspaper in the Southwest, as well as publishing several books. He was removed as pastor by Bishop Lamy in 1856, but he was so beloved that many of his people refused to leave him as long as he lived. His chapel is still standing, but since his death it has been used for other purposes. A new church was erected in 1914.

LOS RANCHOS DE TAOS. One of the finest of the early New Mexico missions left in the state is the great church at Los Ranchos de Taos, about a mile from Fernandez de Taos. It was built in 1772 for a number of Pueblo indians living there at that time; but they are all gone and it is today used as a place of worship by the Mexican population in that vicinity. This building is of adobe, one hundred eight feet long inside, with massive walls and two huge towers above the entrance. The patio in front is inclosed by a high adobe wall. The roof beams rest on carved supports imbedded in the walls. The altar of French design is the only modern thing about the church, but the reredos in the rear

OLD MISSION OF LOS RANCHOS DE TAOS, NEW MEXICO
Erected in 1772, it is still in use

has been unchanged by time. The furnishings include several old paintings on canvas and wood, the latter by native artists; and a large statue of Christ, very old, stands in the chancel.

This old mission, surrounded by the quaint little Mexican village of Los Ranchos de Taos, is one of the most picturesque in all New Mexico. It stands today just as it was a century and a half ago, unchanged by time. Many of the old houses erected by the Pueblos are still standing; and if you have an imagination it is easy to drift back across the gap of years and picture a black-robed priest and his indian neophytes gathered in the ancient church; but the padre sleeps in the churchyard under one of the little crosses you see, and his dusky converts have been gone these many years.

VI. From Santa Fé to Pecos and south of Santa Fé

Pecos Church – San Cristóbal – San Lázaro – Santa Cruz de Galisteo – San Marcos – Cienega – San Pedro del Cuchillo.

PECOS CHURCH. One of the most interesting mission ruins in all New Mexico is Pecos church, a noted landmark on the old Santa Fé trail during all the years of its existence. From the days of 1804 when Juan Bautista Lelande, followed in 1805 by James Pursley, the first of that great army of prairie traders, crossed the American desert to Santa Fé with their pack trains, down through all the years that the commerce of the entire Southwest was hauled across the plains in prairie schooners drawn by ox teams, this ancient ruin was known to every trader, merchant, and trapper who traveled the old trail. The great American desert is no more, and the Santa Fé trail is only a memory; but Pecos church still stands as a monument to the historic past. It is located about thirty miles southeast of Santa Fé and forty-five miles west of Las Vegas, and may be reached over a good automobile road that was once the Santa Fé trail between these two cities.

Nearby are the ruins of ancient Pecos pueblo, the Cicuye of Coronado and the conquistadores, but called Tshiquite, or Tziquite, by the natives. Pecos was discovered by Europeans when Coronado visited the pueblo in 1540, at which time it was the largest in all

New Mexico, with a population of nearly 2,500. The old Spanish chronicles describe it as having two great communal dwellings, as at modern Taos, each four stories high, the one containing 585 rooms and the other 517 rooms, with five plazas and sixteen kivas.

In 1582, Antonio de Espejo and Fray Bernardino Beltran set out with an expedition from Mexico to find the three priests, – Agustin Rodriguez, Francisco Lopez, and Juan de Santa Maria, who had accompanied Chamuscado to New Mexico in 1581 and were murdered at old Puaray after their escort left. After learning the fate of these padres, Espejo continued on as far as Pecos.

The next expedition to New Mexico was a party of colonists led by Castaño de Sosa, late in 1590. Several scouts sent ahead by the commander reached Pecos in December, cold and hungry, and were well received by the natives. The next day they very foolishly left their arms in one of the houses, believing there was no danger, while they went through the village; but they were suddenly attacked and driven out, glad to escape with their lives.

Those old-time Spaniards were endowed with a courage hard to understand today. With only nineteen soldiers and seventeen indian servants, Sosa marched against an unknown pueblo of nearly 2,500 inhabitants. When he reached Pecos on December 31, he found the natives strongly entrenched and determined to resist the invaders. In vain he tried to persuade them that he came in peace, but they answered him with showers of stones and arrows. He must either retreat or fight, and Sosa was no coward. How many men today would attack a well fortified village of unknown strength, with a force of only nineteen soldiers and seventeen native followers, who might desert at any moment? Yet Sosa did this very thing; and with the aid of two brass cannon he gained a foothold in the village after a desperate battle, when the natives were then glad enough to ask for peace.

Sosa went as far north as Taos, seeking a site for his proposed settlement, and then came back down the Rio Grande to the vicinity of the present Santa Fé, where he met a party from Mexico with orders for his arrest on the charge of making explorations without authority from the viceroy. Thus ended the first attempt to plant a colony in New Mexico.

The next visitor to Pecos was Don Juan de Oñate, who was welcomed by the natives July 24, 1598; and when New Mexico was divided into districts the following September, this pueblo and a number of others to the east were assigned to Fray Francisco de San Miguel, who founded the first mission. The old records of the Pecos mission were destroyed in the revolt of 1680, and little is known of its early history; but the data available establishes the fact that the great church standing in ruins today was started in 1617 and probably completed by 1620; for in that year Fray Alonzo de Benavides reported "a monastery and a very splendid temple of distinguished workmanship and beauty" at Pecos.

Fray Fernando de Valasco, the priest at Pecos in 1680 and a missionary of thirty years service in New Mexico, was one of the martyrs of the great rebellion. On the night of August 9, he was warned by Juan Ye, one of his faithful converts, and early the next morning he set out for Galisteo to carry the warning to Father

Bernal, his superior. He was overtaken within sight of his destination and murdered, but whether by his own converts, or by natives of Galisteo is not known. Five hundred warriors from Pecos then marched to Santa Fé and joined the other tribes in the attack on Governor Otermin.

During the twelve years of Pueblo rule the people of Pecos were continually at war with the Tanos and Tewas; but when De Vargas marched into New Mexico in 1692, they took no active part against him. In fact, Juan Ye, then governor of Pecos, joined De Vargas and acted as mediator in the campaign against Taos. The ruined church at Pecos was restored by De Vargas after the reconquest, and for a number of years it was the center of missionary work in that district.

The decline of Pecos brought on by disease and the disastrous raids of the Apaches and Comanches from the plains, set in during the early years of the eighteenth century. By 1750 the population had dwindled down to less than a thousand, and in 1760 it was five hundred ninety-nine. Driven to desperation by the constant raids, the people of Pecos resolved as a measure of defense to carry the war into the enemy's country; and an army composed of practically every able-bodied warrior in the pueblo marched away, but was ambushed by the Comanches, and, according to an old tradition still told in that section, only one man escaped.

In 1760 the mission still survived, with Galisteo as a visita; but by 1782 the population had fallen away to such an extent that it was abandoned, and the people were served by a priest from Santa Fé. The final blow came in 1788, when smallpox ravaged the town, leaving one hundred eighty survivors; and from that time until

RUINS OF PECOS CHURCH TODAY

This great church on the old Santa Fé trail has been called the most historic mission ruin in New Mexico

1805 more were carried off by disease until only one hundred four were left.

Thus reduced by disease and raids, the disheartened survivors struggled on, not knowing what else to do. Their descendants now living at Jemez tell a pathetic tradition of the sacred fire in the innermost kiva, which was never allowed to die during all the long years of the pueblo's existence. The people believed that the greatest of misfortunes would visit them if the flame went out for a single instant; and so those few survivors kept it alive until, in 1838, only seventeen were left, seven men, seven women, and three children, in what was once the largest pueblo in all New Mexico. In the year just mentioned, when it seemed as if they had only a short time to live, a delegation arrived from Jemez, sixty miles away, and invited them to that town. And so, after having been kept burning all those centuries, no man knows how long, the sacred fire was permitted to die, and Pecos was left to the mercy of the elements.

One of their most prized possessions was a picture of the Virgin painted on a wooden slab, which they carried with them to Jemez, where it remained until 1882, when Honorable L. Bradford Prince purchased it from Agustin Pecos, one of the seventeen, and removed it to Santa Fé.

The last survivor of the seventeen members of the Pecos tribe who abandoned the pueblo in 1838 was this same Agustin Pecos, or Se-sa-fwe-yah (his indian name), who died at Jemez on July 20, 1916 at an advanced age. At the time of the migration to Jemez he was a child and he recalled distinctly his childhood in old Pecos. José Miguel Pecos, or Zu-wa-ng, an uncle of Agustin, who died at Jemez in 1902, was a young man at the time Pecos was abandoned, and he was next to the last survivor.

Several blood descendants of the seventeen survivors of Pecos still live at Jemez; and to this day a small statue of the Virgin taken from the church when the village was deserted, is given the place of honor in the annual festival held in memory of the ancient pueblo of their fathers.

During the years following the abandonment of the village many pilgrimages were made back to the old home by the survivors of this once mighty tribe. Somewhere near Pecos is a sacred cave known only to the descendants of those indians. It is known that they opened it in August, 1904, during a visit to their ancestral home, and when they found that nothing had been disturbed they sealed it again and departed. What this cave contains, or where it is located is a secret no white man knows. The Mexicans in that vicinity claim that these pilgrimages were discontinued about 1910; but in 1915, when Phillips Academy, of Andover, Massachusetts, sent its first expedition to explore the ruins, two carved wooden prayer sticks were found at a shrine near the pueblo. Their appearance gave the impression that they had not been there more than a year.

An interesting bit of New Mexican history of later date is to be found at old Pecos. During the Texas-Santa Fé expedition of 1841, the north building of the abandoned pueblo was used for a few days in October, 1841, by the Mexicans as a prison for General McLeod's Texans captured by Governor Manuel Armijo. In 1846, General Kearney camped there with his Army of the West, during his march to Santa Fé, and Colonel Emory, an officer of that expedition, made an interesting drawing of the old church as it appeared at that time.

Beginning with 1915, Phillips Academy, of Andover, Massachusetts, has sent several field expeditions to Pecos, all in charge of Doctor Alfred Vincent Kidder. The ruins of the ancient pueblo that have been excavated are among the most interesting in New Mexico, and much valuable material has been collected.

In the rear of the old church is the only arched doorway found among all the missions of New Mexico. The walls of the entire building have been repaired under Doctor Kidder's direction, and reinforced at the foundation with concrete.

SAN CRISTÓBAL [SAINT CHRISTOPHER] San Cristóbal, one of the cities that died of fear, was once the principal Tano pueblo, but it was abandoned long centuries ago because of constant raids by the Apaches and the later hostilities of the neighboring Pecos. The ruins of this village are between Pecos and Galisteo, and about twenty-three miles southeast of Santa Fé, not far from Lamy on the Santa Fé railroad.

The date the mission was established is not known, as little mention of it is found until after the reconquest, beyond the fact that it was a visita of Galisteo and had no resident priest prior to 1680.

This pueblo was constantly exposed to Apache raids, and after the Rebellion of 1680, when the Pecos tribe declared war on the Tanos, the inhabitants of San Cristóbal and the neighboring town of San Lázaro were forced to abandon their homes. Going about thirty miles northwest of Santa Fé, the San Cristóbal people established a new village under the same name, two miles east of the present Santa Cruz.

When Santa Cruz was founded in 1695, De Vargas compelled them to return to their former home, where the mission was re-established and placed in charge of Fray José de Arizu. On June 4, 1696, the day of the second uprising, Fray Antonio Carbonelli, the missionary from Taos was visiting Fray Arizu at San Cristóbal, and both were murdered. In fear of the wrath of De Vargas, they abandoned their pueblo again, and most of them fled to the Hopi country in Arizona, where their descendants are still living.

SAN LÁZARO [SAINT LAZARUS] San Lázaro, from which the Tanos were driven by the Pecos after the Rebellion of 1680, stood on the south side of the Arroyo del Charro, twelve miles southwest of the present Lamy, Santa Fé county. Little is known of the history of this mission beyond the fact that it actually existed. It was established about 1629, and prior to 1680 was a visita of San Marcos. After the great rebellion the neighboring Pecos tribe made war on San Lázaro, and drove the inhabitants out. Migrating north of Santa Fé, they settled at the site of the present Santa Cruz, where they remained until 1695 when they were forced by De Vargas to seek another location. At the present time there is little to be seen at the site of the original pueblo.

SANTA CRUZ DE GALISTEO [HOLY CROSS OF GALISTEO] Like Pecos, Galisteo is another once strong pueblo that was abandoned because of the inroads of disease and raids of the Comanches and Apaches, the survivors moving to Santo Domingo, where their descendants still live. The ruins of this deserted city, one of the most important of ancient New Mexico, stand twenty-two miles south of Santa Fé, from which they may be reached by automobile. A little Mexican hamlet a mile and a half away takes its name from the old pueblo.

Galisteo was first visited by Europeans when Coronado passed through the country in 1541, and called it Ximena; but it was never afterwards known by this name. At that time the pueblo contained thirty houses; but it grew during the next century, for in 1680 the mission had eight hundred neophytes, and, according to Bandelier, the population at one time was about a thousand.

The mission of Santa Cruz was founded at Galisteo, probably about 1617, the same year as Pecos. However, this is not definite, but the old records show that it was there in 1629. By 1680, the year of the great rebellion, this was an important mission with eight hundred converts and San Cristóbal as a visita.

It will be remembered that on the night of August 9, 1680, Fray Fernando de Velasco, the priest at Pecos, was told by Juan Ye of the impending revolt; and early the next morning he set out for Galisteo to carry the warning to his father superior, but was overtaken within sight of his destination and killed. Fray Manuel Tinoco from San Marcos, was also hastening to warn the priests at Galisteo, but was slain a short distance from that pueblo. And so Fray Juan Bernal and Fray Domingo de Vera, the two missionaries at Galisteo, were both murdered in spite of these efforts to save them.

After the Spaniards were driven out of New Mexico in 1680, the Tanos of Galisteo deserted their village and took possession of the old Palace at Santa Fé, which they converted into a pueblo. There De Vargas found them well fortified in 1692, but in the battle of September 13, the Spaniards drove them from their stronghold.

Ninety of the inhabitants of Galisteo returned to their old home in 1706, and the Spanish governor designated it as "Nuestra Señora de los Remedios de Galisteo," but it was sometimes called Santa Maria de Galisteo. This pueblo never flourished again. For three-quarters of a century it remained a small village, prey to the raids of the two greatest enemies of the Pueblo indians – the Comanches and disease. The number of inhabitants increased slightly; for in 1712 there were one hundred ten, and in 1748 fifty families lived there, but in 1782 there were only fifty-two souls left. The final blow came between 1782 and 1794, when the village was almost wiped out by smallpox, and the few survivors removed to Santo Domingo, where their descendants still live.

SAN MARCOS [SAINT MARK] Eighteen miles southwest of Santa Fé, reached by a road that is good except in the rainy season, are the ruins of old San Marcos pueblo, the site of a Franciscan mission before the Rebellion of 1680. According to Adolph Bandelier, the noted authority on New Mexican ethnology, this was a Tano village called Cuâkâ, or Kuakaa by the natives. During the early Spanish times Cuâkâ was a large pueblo; but little is known of its early history, or the mission erected there, for it was abandoned after 1680 and never resettled.

It was named San Marcos by Gaspar de Sosa in 1591; but the date of the erection of the mission is unknown, as the early records were destroyed. At the time of the

Rebellion of 1680 it had six hundred neophytes with both San Lázaro and Cienega as visitas, which shows that the pueblo was of considerable size. Sometime during the day or night of August 9, 1680, Fray Manuel Tinocco, the missionary at San Marcos, learned in some manner of the impending revolt, and early the next morning he started to warn Padres Bernal and Vera at Galisteo, but was murdered before he reached his destination. Thus ends the history of the mission. When De Vargas came on the reconquest in 1692 he found San Marcos in ruins, with only a few of the walls standing, and no attempt was ever made to resettle it.

CIENEGA. Cienega, which stood in the Santa Fé river valley, twelve miles southwest of Santa Fé, was another of the pueblos abandoned after the great rebellion and never again inhabited. Its size is not known definitely, but Bandelier informs us that it contained less than one thousand. This was a Tano village called Tziguma before the coming of the first conquistadores, meaning "the lone cottonwood tree"; but the early Spaniards gave it the name of Cienega, or "marsh." Sometime in the seventeenth century a mission was established there, but very little of its early history is known beyond the fact that it was a visita of San Marcos in 1680. The pueblo was abandoned before 1692, and in 1695 De Vargas made an unsuccessful attempt to resettle it.

SAN PEDRO DEL CUCHILLO [SAINT PETER OF CUCHILLO] Paako, an ancient Tano pueblo near the old mining camp of San Pedro forty miles south of Santa Fé, is the site of a Spanish mission which was very short lived. Little is known of the history of either

Paako or the mission, and they were evidently of little importance. The ruins today show that the village was of the communal type with houses two stories high and containing three circular kivas. The early Spaniards gave it the name of San Pedro del Cuchilla when the mission was established in 1661, and from this the present mining camp takes its name; but its existence was short, for the pueblo was deserted before 1670. The cause is not known, but was probably due to raids of the Apaches and the inroads of disease. These ruins are not located on any regular road and are hard to reach, but the journey may be made in good weather from either Santa Fé or Albuquerque.

VII. From Santa Fé to Albuquerque

Cochití – Santo Domingo – San Felipe – Sandiá – Santa Ana.

SAN BUENAVENTURA DE COCHITÍ [SAINT GOOD FORTUNE OF COCHITÍ] One of the most interesting and pleasant journeys to be made from Santa Fé is to Cochití pueblo, especially on July 14, the date of the annual festival, or Rain Dance, which is described in another chapter. While this village is not as large as some others in the Rio Grande valley it has a charm all of its own. The people are very hospitable, not at all like the surly inhabitants of Santo Domingo, and they always extend a warm welcome to visitors. Cochití, which is far enough removed from the beaten path to be overlooked by the tourist unless on fiesta day, stands on a picturesque site on a broad plain about thirty feet above the Rio Grande, and thirty miles southwest of Santa Fé.

Cochití contains everything that goes to make an interesting pueblo; an ancient catholic mission in charge of a priest from Peña Blanca, two large kivas where the members of the Turquoise and Calabash clans still strive to keep alive the religion of their fathers in spite of the fact that most of these indians are catholic, and a picturesque plaza in the center of the village. To those who have read *The Delight Makers*, Adolph Bandelier's wonderful story of ancient indian life in New Mexico before the coming of the first Spaniards, Cochití will be especially interesting, for this noted southwestern explorer lived there many years, and the scenes of his historical romance are laid around the Cochití people in their ancient home at Tyuonyi.

Before going to Cochití you should visit those wonderful ruins of prehistoric Tyuonyi, in the Rito de los Frijoles, the greatest circular communal house in all the Southwest, discovered by Bandelier about forty years ago. It is forty-eight miles west of Santa Fé, in the bottom of Frijoles canyon, a spot that will charm your soul with its wild, rugged beauty.

The tribe settled at the site of the present Cochití before the Spanish era, for Don Juan de Oñate discovered this pueblo in 1598; but the earliest home of which there is a definite record was at ancient Tyuonyi and in the cliff and cave dwellings in the talus cliffs of the Rito de los Frijoles. The trail of their wanderings during the centuries is marked by the ruins of their villages. From Tyuonyi they drifted to the Potrero de las Vacas, then to ancient Haatze, and finally to Kuapa in the Cañada de Cochití, where the tribe divided, one branch founding the present San Felipe. The Cochití people settled at Potrero Viejo, where they built Hanut Cochití; but in a short time they moved to a spot seven miles southeast where Cochití stands today.

The mission of San Buenaventura was established at Cochití at a date unknown, but probably early in the seventeenth century, or about the time of the founding of Nuestra Señora de la Asuncion monastery and mission at the neighboring pueblo of Gipuy (Santo Domingo). Little is known of the early history of San Buenaventura mission. No priest was killed there on that fatal August 10, 1680; but an old tradition is still told of how the padre's life was saved by the indian sacristan of the church, who warned him the day before.

SANTO DOMINGO MISSION, SANTO DOMINGO PUEBLO, NEW MEXICO
Erected in modern times, but typical of the early New Mexico missions

Aided by this faithful convert, the priest, disguised as an indian, escaped by going to the river with a water jar at dusk. He then crossed and made his way to San Felipe, but what finally became of him is not known.

The Cochití took a prominent part in the revolt; but fifteen months later they fled before the army led by Governor Otermin in his unsuccessful attempt to reconquer New Mexico. With their kinsmen from San Felipe and Santo Domingo, together with the Tewas from San Marcos, and some Tiguas from Picuris and Taos to the north, they took refuge at the Potrero Viejo above the Cañada de Cochití, where they remained until the Spanish alarm subsided in 1683.

At the approach of De Vargas in 1692, the people of Cochití, joined by those from San Felipe and San Marcos, again fled to the Potrero Viejo. This massive rock towers seven hundred feet above the canyon, and on its summit they built a strong fort, called Cieneguilla by the Spaniards. De Vargas marched against them, and they all returned peacefully to their pueblos without a battle; but the Cochití went back to their Gibraltar on the Potrero Viejo as soon as the Spaniards departed.

On April 12, 1694, De Vargas marched to the Potrero with seventy Spanish soldiers and twenty colonists, reinforced by one hundred friendly warriors from San Felipe, Santa Ana and Sia; and at midnight of the sixteenth assaulted the rock, driving the Cochití from their stronghold with a loss of twenty warriors killed and three hundred women and children taken prisoners, and seventy horses and one thousand sheep captured. The next day De Vargas's force was weakened when his indian allies returned to their homes. Taking advantage of this, the Cochití, by a surprise attack liberated one hundred fifty of the captives before the Spaniards could rally and repulse the indians, who lost only two warriors killed. De Vargas then destroyed the fort, and returned to Santa Fé with a large quantity of corn and about one hundred fifty captive women. These were liberated when the Cochití warriors returned to their pueblo on the Rio Grande.

The mission, destroyed in 1680, was standing in ruins, but a new church, thirty-four feet wide by one hundred feet long, was built by De Vargas in 1694 on the same spot, where it remains to this day. This building was a fine example of the early Franciscan mission; but the exterior has been remodeled in recent years so that it bears little resemblance to the original. The interior is still typical of the old-time indian mission. Over the entrance is a wide gallery, reached by a ladder. The walls are decorated with the stations of the cross, and the old tin candlesticks were brought up from Chihuhua before the American occupation.

San Buenaventura, the patron saint of Cochití, must have been a man of many personalities; for none of the three statues of this "santos" in his mission bear the slightest resemblance to each other. Because it has represented their patron saint for many generations, the oldest is held in great veneration and love by all of the indians, in spite of the black beard and hard, almost sinister expression of the face. The figure is only about eighteen inches high, and is adorned with the usual robe and several strings of beads around the neck. Another of the statues was carved from wood many years ago by an indian from old Mexico. The smooth, oval face has a pleasant expression, while a halo around the head adds to the saintly appearance. The most modern and the largest of the three was made in France and pre-

RUINS OF THE SECOND MISSION FOUNDED AT OLD SAN FELIPE
Built in 1694 on the Black mesa near Bernalillo, New Mexico

sented to the mission in 1901 by the Sisters of Mercy at Santa Fé. It is a fine piece of French workmanship. With its smooth, thoughtful face it is a marked contrast to the other two.

A large painting of San Buenaventura adorns the center of the wall above the altar, while the Nativity, the Transfiguration, the Last Supper, and three scenes of the Crucifixion form the reredos. All are ancient cracked with age and covered with the dust of years. The ceiling of the chancel is decorated with moons, horses, and other figures, in red, yellow and black, the work of indian artists.

The modern destructive spirit which has ruined several of New Mexico's ancient missions reached out its hand to Cochití, and a few years ago the exterior of the old edifice was so altered that it looks more like a visitor from some eastern hamlet. This is the only discordant note in an otherwise perfect indian pueblo. The old flat roof and picturesque Franciscan belfry have been replaced by corrugated iron and a high pointed steeple. The balcony was removed from the outside and the entrance was inclosed by an adobe porch with three arches, the only attempt at adornment.

The most interesting time to visit Cochití is on July 14, the date of the annual festival of San Buenaventura held in connection with the Rain Dance. During the morning, mass is held in the old mission by a priest from Peña Blanca. The service is typically indian, and when you enter the church you step back across the centuries to the old Spanish days. Kneeling in the nave, which is without seats, the men on one side and the women on the other, are the indian neophytes with bowed heads listening to the black-gowned padre as in the days of old, while an indian choir sings at intervals from the gallery above. It is a picture that once seen will never be forgotten.

NUESTRA SEÑORA DE LA ASUNCION MONASTERY [OUR LADY OF THE ASCENT OF THE HOLY VIRGIN] When Don Juan de Oñate explored the upper Rio Grande valley in 1598, he selected old Gipuy as the site for the monastery of the advocation of Nuestra Señora de la Asuncion. This Gipuy was the second pueblo of that name. The first, located a mile and a half east of the present Thornton, Sandoval county, was washed away by the Rio Grande prior to 1591, and the second was built four miles west, almost on the site of the present Santo Domingo. In 1591, Castaño de Sosa visited the latter pueblo and named it Santo Domingo. Both the pueblo and the monastery were entirely destroyed by the great flood of 1605, and no trace of either remains.

SANTO DOMINGO [SAINT DOMINIC] After the destruction of the second Gipuy and the monastery in 1605, the natives built another village on the Rio Grande, which they named Huashpatzena. In 1607 a church was erected by Fray Juan de Escalona, which became his sepulcher; for he died there and was buried within its walls.

In the Rebellion of 1680, the three priests in charge, Francisco Antonio Lorenzazana, Juan de Talaban, and José Montes de Oca, were murdered on August 10, and their bodies, clad in their robes, were buried under a pile of earth inside the mission, where they were found two weeks later by Governor Otermin on his retreat from Santa Fé. Strange to say the furnishings of the church had not been disturbed.

The present mission at San Felipe pueblo, near Thornton, New Mexico
Erected shortly after 1700

This pueblo suffered the same fate as the former Gipuy villages when a large part of it was washed away by a freshet; and about 1700 the present Santo Domingo was built a little farther east. One of the largest and finest missions in all New Mexico took the place of the former building; but it suffered the same fate as the others. The waters of the Rio Grande gradually washed nearer and nearer until in the spring flood of 1885 the foundation gave way, and in a short time the entire building had disappeared into this swirling desert river. It is interesting to note that Lieutenant Zebulon M. Pike, discoverer of Pike's Peak, Colorado, visited this church, while on his way to Chihuahua as a prisoner of the Spaniards.

The present edifice, with its adobe walled patio in front, was built shortly after the destruction of the old building. While it can lay no claim to antiquity the architecture is the most typical of the early New Mexico missions now found in the state. The natives take great pride in it, and before the annual fiesta, which occurs August 4, it is cleaned and whitewashed, and two large horses are painted by native artists on the front. The indians will not permit photographs to be taken of the building, and anyone attempting this must be careful that they are not detected.

Santo Domingo is easily reached by automobile over the main road from Santa Fé to Albuquerque, about midway between the two cities, or from Thornton station, on the Santa Fé railroad, which is just two and one-half miles from the pueblo.

SAN FELIPE MISSION [SAINT PHILIP] There have been three pueblos named San Felipe with a mission at each, the first dating back to 1605, although in 1598 San

Felipe and Santa Ana were placed in charge of Fray Juan de Rosas; but no churches were built at that time. The first San Felipe of the Spaniards, called Katishtya by the natives, was at the foot of Tamita mesa, where Coronado found them in 1540; and in 1591, when Castaño de Sosa passed through New Mexico the village was still at this location. It was he who first called it San Felipe, a name by which its people are still known. Oñate visited the pueblo in 1598 and a church was built seven years later by Fray Cristobal de Quiñones, who died there in 1607 or 1609, and was buried in the mission.

In 1680 the priest resided at the monastery of Santo Domingo; and the people of San Felipe joined those of Cochiti and Santo Domingo in the murder of the three padres at the latter pueblo. After the rebellion the church was destroyed, and in 1693 De Vargas found the inhabitants in a new location at the northern end of the summit of the Black mesa, west of the present San Felipe. In 1694 a church was built at the new village; but shortly after 1700 the inhabitants founded the present pueblo at the foot of the mesa. Part of the stone walls of the old mission of 1694 are still standing at the site of the village on the mesa above.

The present church was erected shortly after 1700, and was used until the Franciscans were expelled from New Mexico in 1823. On July 9, 1900, the fathers returned and took charge of this mission, which is now served by a priest from Peña Blanca, in connection with Santo Domingo and Cochiti.

San Felipe pueblo is located near Thornton station on the Santa Fé railroad, and may be reached from either Santa Fé or Albuquerque during the trip to

SANTA ANA MISSION, SANTA ANA PUEBLO, NEW MEXICO
Believed to have been erected shortly after 1694

Santo Domingo and Cochití. It is about three miles from Bernalillo. The annual fiesta is held on May 1.

SAN FRANCISCO MISSION AT SANDÍA [SAINT FRANCIS] Old Sandía, meaning "the watermelon" in Spanish, stood on the east side of the Rio Grande, at Alameda station, twelve miles north of Albuquerque. Coronado was the first European to visit this pueblo; and in 1598, when Oñate divided New Mexico into provinces this was one of the cities in Tiguex. The native name was Nafiat.

The mission of San Francisco was established there before 1614; for in that year the remains of Friar Lopez were buried in the new church at Sandía. It will be remembered that this padre was one of the three priests murdered in 1581 at the mission at old Puaray, the first in New Mexico; and in February, 1614, Estevan de Perea removed the body of Friar Lopez from Puaray to Sandía, where he was buried with great ceremony. There is an old tradition that when the funeral procession moved, the bones of the martyr performed many miracles, but the nature of them is not known.

After the Rebellion of 1680 Sandía was abandoned, and most of the inhabitants fled to the Hopi country in Arizona, where they built Payupki on the Middle mesa, the walls of which may still be traced. During his attempted reconquest in 1681, Governor Otermin burned the deserted Sandía. These people remained in Arizona until 1742 when Padres Delgado and Piño persuaded four hundred forty-one to return to the Rio Grande; but some afterwards went back to Tusayan, and in 1748, Father Juan Miguel Menchoro, who had labored among them for six years, brought three hundred fifty converts to New Mexico. The governor granted his request for land, and a new pueblo was founded.

A large adobe church was built by Father Menchoro in 1748 and consecrated to Nuestra Señora de los Dolores y San Antonio de Sandía (Our Lady of Sorrows and Saint Anthony of Sandía). This edifice was abandoned more than half a century ago, and a new one erected north of the town, amid the ruins of ancient Sandía; but the ruins of the old church still stand on the western edge of the village. Like all the early New Mexico missions the front was surrounded by a walled inclosure used as a burial ground, in which is an adobe mound, probably the base of the mission cross. The old monastery is now occupied by Mexicans.

The annual fiesta at Sandía takes place on June 13. This pueblo is located at Alameda station on the Santa Fé railroad, a short distance above Albuquerque, from which place it is easily reached by automobile.

SANTA ANA MISSION AT ALAMEDA. Two other missions named Santa Ana were established in New Mexico, but the only one in existence today is at Santa Ana pueblo, on the road from Albuquerque to Jemez Hot Springs. The other was at the former Piro village at Alamillo, twelve miles above Socorro. Prior to the Rebellion of 1680 a Tigua pueblo called Alameda, meaning "cottonwood grove," stood on the east bank of the Rio Grande, ten miles above the present Albuquerque; but owing to the changing course of the river the ruins are now a mile from its banks.

Little is known of the history of either this settlement or of the mission beyond the fact that about 1660 the pueblo had three hundred inhabitants, and a church was dedicated to Santa Ana. The mission was destroyed in 1680, and the next year the village was deserted. After the reconquest, the indians returned to Alameda, and the mission was reëstablished as a visita of Albuquerque; but its existence was short for there is no further record of it. The pueblo was permanently abandoned in a short time and is now one of the many ruins of that section, located near Alameda station on the Santa Fé railroad, midway between Bernalillo and Albuquerque, and near the main automobile road from Santa Fé.

VIII. From Albuquerque to Jemez

Albuquerque — San Felipe Church — Santa Ana Pueblo — Sia — The Jemez Missions, San José, San Diego, and San Juan.

ALBUQUERQUE. Albuquerque, the largest and most important city in the state, bears the distinction of being the third town founded by the Spaniards in New Mexico, or the fourth if we count the dead settlement of San Gabriel. As related elsewhere Santa Fé, founded by Oñate in 1605, was the first of the present towns; Santa Cruz, established by order of De Vargas in 1695, came second, while Albuquerque, by Governor Valdez in 1706, was third.

In 1703 De Vargas returned to New Mexico as governor and captain-general of the province; but while on an inspection trip he died April 14, 1704, at the place where Bernalillo now stands. In his will he directed that his remains be buried under the principal altar in the church at Santa Fé; but whether this was old San Miguel, or San Francisco is not known today. Some claim that it was the latter and that his remains are now in the cathedral, while others are just as positive that the bones of the conqueror of New Mexico rest under the ancient altar of San Miguel.

On March 10, 1705, Francisco Cuervo y Valdez arrived at Santa Fé, and served as governor until August, 1707. In 1706 Governor Valdez took thirty families from Santa Fé, to the site of Albuquerque, or Alburquerque as it was originally spelled, and founded "La Villa de San Francisco de Alburquerque," named in honor of the Duke of Alburquerque, viceroy of Mexico, or New Spain; but when Governor Valdez reported this the viceroy ordered the name changed to "La Villa de San Felipe de Alburquerque," in honor of the King of Spain at that time.

The first building in every Spanish town was a church, and so in 1706 San Felipe, which still stands in "Old Town," was erected. The name of San Felipe evidently comes from the change in the name of the town; but it is interesting to note that in October, 1776, when Fray Manuel Garcia took charge of the parish he called it San Francisco Xavier, under the belief that all his predecessors had made a mistake in the former name. It is a picturesque old church well worth a visit, but it was never an indian mission.

SANTA ANA PUEBLO [SAINT ANN] This must not be confused with either of the Santa Ana missions at ancient Alamillo pueblo near Socorro, or at Alameda near Bernalillo. Old Santa Ana mission was located at Tamayo, a Keresan village, the ruins of which still stand on the Black mesa of San Felipe, midway between the present Santa Ana and San Felipe pueblos. Oñate visited the village in 1598, and a mission was probably built soon afterwards, as Tamayo was one of the towns apportioned to Fray Juan de Rosas in that year. In 1680 the church and monastery were without a priest; and the inhabitants joined with the people of San Felipe and Santo Domingo in the massacre of the padres at the latter pueblo. Old Santa Ana was burned by Governor Pedro Reneros de Posada during his attempted reconquest in 1687, and the inhabitants fled far away; but in 1692, De Vargas induced them to return to their former locality, when the present Santa Ana was built.

The date of the erection of the present large church

is not known, but it was probably shortly after the reconquest. In 1782 this is mentioned as a visita of Sia mission.

Santa Ana is eight miles from the regular stage road from Albuquerque to Jemez Hot Springs, and fifteen miles beyond Sandía. The annual fiesta takes place in August.

NUESTRA SEÑORA DE LA ASUNCION AT SIA PUEBLO [OUR LADY OF THE ASCENSION MISSION] The exact date of the founding of this mission is unknown; but in 1598 Fray Alonzo de Lugo was placed in charge and a church was probably built shortly afterwards. North of the pueblo are the ruins of Kohasaya, while opposite is another ruin known as Kakanatzatia. The people of Sia claim that the village of today occupies the same site as when Coronado passed through the country.

Little is known of the early history of the mission. The people of Sia joined in the revolt of 1680, and the original church was probably destroyed at that time. When Governor Domingo de Cruzate attempted to reconquer New Mexico, he attacked Sia on August 1, 1689 and the bloodiest battle of the Pueblo rebellion was fought. About six hundred indians were killed and seventy captured and condemned to ten years in slavery. The people of Sia never forgot this terrible blow, and were friendly to the Spaniards from that time until the reconquest was completed by De Vargas in 1696. This resulted in much friction between them and the inhabitants of Jemez and Cochití, who were in constant revolt.

The mission was reëstablished by De Vargas on October 24, 1692, when the present church was built. By the side of the present large wooden cross in the plaza is a stub of wood, eighteen inches high, worn and weathered by the centuries, all that is left of the great cross erected by De Vargas so many long years ago; while the remnants of the old pavement laid by the conqueror at the same time can still be seen. In 1782 both Santa Ana and Jemez were visitas of Sia.

Sia pueblo is on the north bank of the Jemez river, seventeen miles northwest of Bernalillo and six miles from Santa Ana; and it can easily be reached by automobile from Albuquerque during the visit to Santa Ana and Jemez. The annual festival is held on August 15.

THE JEMEZ MISSIONS. Three missions were built among the Jemez, all at villages abandoned long ago and now in ruins in the vicinity of the present Jemez, a Keresan pueblo on the north bank of the Jemez river, twenty miles north of Bernalillo. This interesting journey may be made in one day over a good automobile road from Albuquerque to Jemez Hot Springs, but it is well worth a longer period.

The Jemez indians claim to have originated in the north, from which they migrated to the Guadalupe and San Diego rivers, tributaries of the Rio Jemez, where Captain Francisco de Barrio-Nuevo, of Coronado's expedition, found them in 1541 living in seven villages, which he named the province of Aguas Calientes. This has been identified as the Jemez Hot Springs region of today. Antonio de Espejo, the next explorer, reported the tribe living in seven villages; but in 1598 Oñate heard of eleven, although he only visited eight. After the establishment of the missions and the introduction of irrigation by the Spaniards, the Jemez were finally induced to consolidate in three pueblos, Gyusiwa, Astialakwa, and Patoqua, all now in ruins in the vicinity of Jemez Hot Springs. Each was the seat of a mission.

In 1622, Patoqua and Gyusiwa were abandoned on

account of raids by the Navajos, the greatest enemies of the Jemez, and the tribe was scattered; but five years later Fray Martin de Arvide gathered the various bands and resettled both villages. No mention is made of Astialakwa at this period, but it was probably not abandoned in 1622.

During the middle of the seventeenth century the Jemez made peace with their enemies, the Navajos, and the two tribes conspired to drive the Spaniards from the country; but the plot was discovered and twenty-nine of the former were hanged.

The Jemez took a prominent part in the Rebellion of 1680, shooting Fray Juan de Jesus Maria, the missionary at Gyusiwa, to death with arrows while at the altar of San Diego mission; but the priest at Astialakwa, with the Spanish alcalde and three soldiers escaped. When Governor Otermin came back the next year on his attempted reconquest, the Jemez fled into the mountains, but returned to their villages as soon as the Spaniards left the country. They fled again when Cruzate appeared with his army in 1689; and in 1692 De Vargas found them living in one large pueblo on the higher mesa; but he induced them to return to their former homes. They promised to aid him in his war against the other tribes, a pledge they not only failed to keep, but during 1693 and 1694 they were at war with the neighboring Keresan tribes at Santa Ana and Sia who remained true to their promise of allegiance to the Spaniards.

In July, 1694, De Vargas, with an army of one hundred twenty Spaniards and a small force of warriors from Santa Ana and Sia, marched against the Jemez in their mesa stronghold; and in the battle that followed the latter were driven from their pueblo with a loss of eighty-four killed. De Vargas followed this victory with an active campaign for a month, and when he went back to Santa Fé with three hundred sixty-one prisoners the Jemez hostility was broken for a short time.

They went back to Gyusiwa, but did not remain at peace long; for they took part in the revolt of 1696, and once more fled to their mesa stronghold, where they were joined by some Navajos, Zuñis, and Acomas. In June they were defeated with a loss of thirty by a small force of Spaniards and Sia warriors, after which they fled to the Navajo country where they remained several years before they returned and founded the present Jemez pueblo, called Walatoa by the natives.

SAN DIEGO DE JEMEZ MISSION [SAINT JAMES OF JEMEZ] The mission of San Diego de Jemez was founded early in the seventeenth century at Gyusiwa pueblo, at that time the principal Jemez village; and the ruins today show that this was the largest and most important of the Jemez missions. In 1598 the province of Jemez was assigned to Fray Alonzo de Lugo, who established his headquarters at Gyusiwa, and the church was undoubtedly started shortly afterward. A large mission and monastery were erected, but were probably not completed until 1617; hence that year has often been given as the date of erection. During the eight years prior to 1622, when Fray Zarate Salemeron was head of the New Mexico missions, he baptized over 6,000 converts among the Jemez.

As already related the pueblo was abandoned in 1622 on account of the constant Navajo raids; but in 1627 Fray Martin de Arvide gathered the scattered Jemez and resettled both Gyusiwa and Patoqua.

This tribe took a prominent part in the Rebellion of

RUINS OF SAN DIEGO DE JEMEZ MISSION
Founded in the seventeenth century at ancient Gyusiwa pueblo

1680, and while Fray Juan de Jesus Maria was holding services at the altar of San Diego mission, he was shot to death with arrows. After the defeat of the Jemez in 1694 an indian man and woman pointed out to De Vargas a spot near a kiva in the ruins of Gyusiwa as the grave of this padre murdered fourteen years before. De Vargas investigated and on August 8, unearthed a skeleton with an arrow still sticking in the shoulder. These bones he removed to Santa Fé and buried them in the parish church, probably San Francisco, on August 11, as those of Fray Juan de Jesus Maria.

The ruins of this church stand half a mile north of Jemez Hot Springs, and are among the most picturesque in all New Mexico. This was a massive building; with walls eight feet thick it has stood throughout the ages, and in its time it must have been a beautiful edifice.

SAN JOSÉ DE LOS JEMEZ MISSION [SAINT JOSEPH OF JEMEZ] The second Jemez mission was at old Patoqua pueblo, the ruins of which still stand on the mesa at the junction of Guadalupe and San Diego canyons, six miles north of the present Jemez. It must have been founded shortly after San Diego, for the church was standing completed in 1617. Patoqua was deserted in 1622, at the same time as Gyusiwa, on account of the hostility of the Navajos; but in 1627, when Fray Martin de Arvide gathered the scattered Jemez, it was resettled. It was permanently abandoned prior to 1680.

SAN JUAN DE LOS JEMEZ MISSION [SAINT JOHN OF JEMEZ] Little is known of the history of this mission, and its existence was evidently very short. About 1627, the same year that Padre Arvide gathered the scattered Jemez and resettled Gyusiwa and Patoqua, San Juan mission was founded at Astialakwa, the ruins of which are on the summit of the mesa at the junction of Guadalupe and San Diego canyons, six miles north of Jemez and in the vicinity of Patoqua. San Juan is sometimes mentioned as a visita of San José, but a priest was stationed at the former in 1680, and he escaped in company with the Spanish alcalde and three soldiers. It is certain that the mission was destroyed in the Rebellion and never rebuilt.

JEMEZ MISSION. After the present Jemez pueblo was founded in the early years of the eighteenth century, a mission was established; but it was evidently of little importance, for in 1782 it was made a visita of Sia. The old church, built over two centuries ago, is one of the interesting sights of a visit to this pueblo. The annual festival is held at Jemez on November 12.

IX. The Cities that died of Fear

Quarai – Tajique – Chililí – Abó – Grand Quivira, or Tabira.

Of all the mission ruins in the Southwest, the five pueblos of the Salinas Lake region in central New Mexico, known as "the cities that died of fear," hold the most romantic interest. They date far back into the dim past. Before the Rebellion of 1680 they were deserted, abandoned to the desert's whims, and for long centuries the massive ruins of these great churches have stood as monuments to the zeal of the Franciscan fathers of an almost unknown day. We have records of the discovery and some later history of the five ancient cities of the Salinas – Quarai, Tajique, Chililí, Abó, and Tabira, built by the Tigua and Piro tribes long before any European ever set foot in New Mexico. Missions were established at each of these settlements about 1629; but before the great rebellion broke out the inhabitants had fled before the terrible Apaches, never to return. And so these five once large pueblos, the ruins of which have attracted so much attention, have come down to us as "the cities that died of fear."

Why the ancient people ever selected this region for a home is just another mystery in a land of many mysteries; for they were constantly exposed to raids by the dreaded Apaches and Comanches. Eastward from the foot of the Cerro de los Manzano range is the Estancia valley, in the heart of which are the Salinas lakes ("the accursed lakes" of the ancient Pueblos), composed of a number of saline pools and marshes, whose bitter waters, unfit for man or beast, glisten invitingly under the desert sun. According to an old Pueblo tradition these lakes were once fresh, abounding in fish, but because a wicked witch once dwelt there the gods placed a curse upon them. This is "The Accursed Lake" legend told by Charles F. Lummis in his interesting book, *Pueblo Indian Folk Stories*. The Salt Lake, sacred to the ancients, was the home of the "salt mother" of the Pueblo indians of olden times.

A visit to the ruins of the five cities that died of fear and the missions built by the Franciscan fathers nearly three centuries ago, is one of the most interesting trips in New Mexico. They may be reached by rail to Mountainair, a town on the Belen Cut-off of the Santa Fé railroad, where there is a small hotel, and automobiles may be secured for the remainder of the journey. Eight miles north of Mountainair is Quarai; twelve miles farther we come to Tajique, and ten miles more brings us to Chililí. Starting from Mountainair again we find Abó twelve miles southwest, and at the foot of the Gallinas range, twenty-four miles south are the ruins of Tabira, better known as Gran Quivira.

QUARAI. MISSION OF THE IMMACULATE CONCEPTION. Eight miles northwest of Mountainair are the silent ruins of ancient Quarai, a Tigua pueblo that teemed with life when the first Spaniards came into the valley in 1598; and silhouetted against the turquoise blue of the New Mexico sky the jagged ruins of a christian church stand out long before the ancient city is reached. This mission was founded in 1629 under the name of Immaculate Conception by Fray Francisco de Acevedo, prominent in the early Franciscan work in New Mexico; and it was afterwards in charge of Fray Estevan de

Perea. Next came Fray Geronimo de la Llama, who died there in 1659 after many years work, and was buried by his faithful converts in his beloved church, which was his sepulchre for a hundred years. His bones were unearthed from the ruins on April 1, 1759, by Governor Del Valle and removed to Santa Fé, as related in a previous chapter.

According to an old tradition the people of Quarai made a temporary peace with the Apaches between 1664 and 1669, and plotted with them to drive the Spaniards from the valley; but the plan was discovered and the leaders executed. After this the Apaches renewed their raids with increased fury, and finally, in 1674 the people of Quarai were forced to flee to Tajique, twelves miles to the north.

This mission was built of the red sandstone peculiar to that section. History is indebted to Major James H. Carleton, of the American army, for the first description of the ruins of this great church. The following shows how it looked to him in 1853:

"These ruins appear to be similar to those of Abó, whether as to their antiquity, the skill in their construction, their state of preservation or the material of which they are built. The church at Quarra is not so long by thirty feet as that at Abó. We found one room here, probably a cloister attached to the church, which was in a good state of preservation. The beams that supported the roof were blackened by age. They were square and smooth and supported under each end by shorter pieces of wood, carved into regularly curved lines and scrolls. The earth upon the roof was sustained by small straight poles, well finished and laid in herringbone fashion upon the beams."

The total length of the church as measured by Honorable L. Bradford Prince is one hundred three feet; the width of the nave is twenty-seven feet, and the length of the transepts, forty-eight feet. The walls stand about twenty feet high, and are from four to five feet thick. The blocks of red sandstone used in the construction vary from one to four inches in thickness and are about a foot square.

Surrounding the church are the ruins of the dead city of Quarai, once inclosed by a wall for defense. Recent excavations have uncovered a round communal dwelling, similar to Tyuonyi in the Rito de los Frijoles. A spring in a grove nearby evidently furnished the pueblo with water.

SAN MIGUEL DE TAJIQUE MISSION. Twelve miles north of Quarai is ancient Tajique, the seat of the mission of San Miguel; but before reaching it the quaint old Spanish village of Manzano, nestled at the foot of Manzano peak, is well worth an hour. Two ancient apple orchards, believed to have been planted by the padres from either Quarai or Tajique, give the place its name of Manzano, meaning "apple tree."

The ruins of Tajique, a Tigua settlement much smaller than Quarai and not as important, stand on the north and west sides of the picturesque Mexican hamlet of the same name, on the south side of the Arroyo de Tajique, twenty miles north of Mountainair. The name is believed to be the Spanish form of Tushyityay, the original indian name. The mission of San Miguel was founded there about 1629, the same year as the Immaculate Conception at Quarai. Little is known of its history, but it is reasonable to suppose that it was built by Fray Francisco de Acevedo after he started the mission work at Quarai, and it was probably a visita of the latter.

THE CITIES THAT DIED OF FEAR 145

Tajique was one of the last of the cities that died of fear. At the beginning of 1674 it had only three hundred inhabitants; but in that year the people of Quarai fled before the Apache warriors, taking refuge with their kinsmen at Tajique and increasing the pueblo to nine hundred. They evidently believed that the combined strength of the two towns would hold the Apaches in check; but the red scourge of destruction swept down upon them with renewed fury and the next year they were driven out of their homeland forever. Drifting down the Rio Grande, they settled in the vicinity of El Paso, where their descendants may be found today.

NUESTRA SEÑORA DE NAVIDAD MISSION AT CHILILÍ [OUR LADY OF THE NATIVITY] Ten miles from Tajique and thirty north of Mountainair, in the very southeastern corner of Bernalillo county, are the ruins of Chililí, another of the Tigua cities that died of fear of the cruel Apaches. At the present time a Mexican hamlet of the same name, containing less than a hundred inhabitants, stands near the ruins, which may be reached by a thirty mile journey from Albuquerque over roads of uncertain condition in rainy weather; but when the sun is shining all roads in New Mexico are good.

Chililí was discovered by Don Juan de Oñate, or some members of his expedition, in 1598; and about 1630 Fray Alonzo Peinade, who took up mission work in New Mexico in 1608, erected the mission of Nuestra Señora de Navidad. After converting a number of the indians he died there and was buried in his church. Little more remains to be said of this mission. Adolph Bandelier tells us that the people of Chililí were driven out between 1669 and 1676 by the continual raids of the Apaches, and no attempt was ever made to resettle this pueblo. The inhabitants scattered, some going to the Tigua villages on the Rio Grande and others to the vicinity of El Paso.

SAN GREGORIO DE ABÓ MISSION [SAINT GREGORY] Returning to Mountainair we start on the southern journey to Abó and Tabira, or Gran Quivira, two of the most extensive and interesting mission and pueblo ruins in all New Mexico. The first is located twelves miles southwest of our starting point, where we find the ruins of the great church of San Gregorio at ancient Abó of the Piros. This is just twelve miles south of Abó station, on the Belen Cut-off of the Santa Fé railroad.

Abó was first visited by Europeans in June, 1598, when the brothers, Juan and Vicente Zaldivar, nephews and lieutenants of Don Juan de Oñate, led a small exploring party into the Salinas country, while the main expedition rested in the vicinity of modern Socorro. This is the same Juan Zaldivar who was killed a few months later at Acoma.

Abó was a large pueblo with a population of about two thousand; and in 1629 Fray Francisco de Acevedo, father of the missions of the cities that died of fear, founded San Gregorio de Abó. The size and importance of this city led Padre Acevedo to establish his headquarters there, and he erected a large church and monastery, the ruins of which are today among the largest in New Mexico. From this point he carried on his mission work among the Piros and Tiguas of the Salinas country, especially at the pueblos of Abó, Tabira, and Quarai, with Tenabó in the vicinity of Socorro as a visita, until his death at Abó on August 1, 1644. He was buried in the church.

The ruins of Abó are in a beautiful little valley in the foothills of the Manzanos, through which the diminutive Abó river winds its way. The valley has changed but little since the Piros were driven out by the Apaches two hundred fifty years ago. The hills are covered with trees, and here and there are the homes of settlers of a new nation born since the Piros lived there.

The massive, crumbling walls of the mission, built of red sandstone, stand on a little knoll in the valley, surrounded by the ruins of a once large pueblo. In 1853 Major James H. Carleton visited Abó and described the church as one hundred thirty-two feet long by thirty-two feet wide, with walls fully fifty feet high. Portions of the roof beams still in place at that time were charred and blackened, indicating that the building had been destroyed by fire, probably burned by the Apaches after the village was deserted.

The pueblo was in the form of a parallelogram, one thousand feet long by three hundred feet wide, laid out as a walled town, the outer walls of the houses forming a strong, continuous fortification with only one entrance. Some of the inhabitants are believed to have left as early as 1671; and by 1678 the entire city was deserted – abandoned to the Apache warriors and the whims of the desert.

GRAN QUIVIRA OR TABIRA. No other spot in the entire United States, with the exception of the Seven Cities of Cibola, can equal with romantic interest the name of Gran Quivira; and like the Seven Cities, it was only a myth invented by the Pueblos to lure Coronado away with the hope that the Spaniards would perish on the great plains.

When this conquistadore failed to find the reputed wealth of the Seven Cities of Cibola the natives told him of another city called Quivira, where gold was plentiful; and, guided by an indian known as the Turk, believed to have been a Pawnee, the expedition set out in the spring of 1541 in search of the end of this new rainbow. Becoming suspicious of the Turk, Coronado placed him in irons when the expedition reached the headwaters of the Rio Colorado in Texas. From this point the main force was sent back to New Mexico, but Coronado with thirty picked men continued north under the guidance of another indian named Ysopete. Reaching the Arkansas river in Kansas he followed it for many miles eastward, always hoping, but he never found Quivira, and he finally ordered the Turk strangled to death as punishment for his deception.

The Quivira myth was believed by the Spaniards for many years; and even down to the beginning of the past century efforts were made to find it. The name appeared on the early maps of the Southwest, shifting about from place to place wherever each new tale located it. It was soon changed to La Gran Quivira, and finally, after wandering about over the maps from the great plains to California, it settled on the long deserted Piro city of Tabira. Tales of gold buried to keep it from Coronado have lured many adventurers down to our own times to search for the hidden treasure of Gran Quivira; and to this day the charm of the mysterious hovers about the ruins.

Tabira was one of the largest of the Salinas pueblos; and in the midst of this silent, mysterious city that died of fear are the ruins of two great christian churches and a monastery, the largest in the entire Southwest. For years they defied all efforts to learn their story until Gran Quivira was identified as the forgotten Tabira, where, according to ancient Spanish chronicles, Fray Francisco de Acevedo founded the first mission in 1629; but it was not fully completed until about 1644, the year of his death. For some years after it was founded this mission was conducted as a visita of Abó; but its importance increased, and about 1660 the second church was started. Tabira was permanently abandoned between 1670 and 1675 on account of Apache raids, and the second building was never finished.

The walls of these enormous churches, standing thirty feet high, can be seen far across the plain long before the pueblo is reached. The oldest is about one hundred forty feet long, with walls six feet thick, constructed of dark blue limestone slabs peculiar to that locality. The stones used were not hewn or dressed in any way, but were laid in mortar just as they were gathered. The other building, sometimes referred to as the chapel, is one hundred eighteen feet long and thirty-two feet wide, with walls nearly four feet thick. This is all that is known today of the great mission of Tabira. After the inhabitants fled before the cruel Apache warriors they scattered, some going to the settlements in the vicinity of Socorro and Alamillo and others to El Paso, where their descendants may be found today.

X. From Albuquerque south to Socorro

The Isleta Missions, San Antonio and San Agustin – The legend of Padre Padilla's coffin – Nuestra Senora de Belen – San Luis Obispo de Sevilleta – Santa Ana – Nuestra Senora del Socorro – San Pancual – San Antonio de Senecu.

THE ISLETA MISSIONS. Old Isleta, situated in the Rio Grande valley twelve miles south of Albuquerque, is one of New Mexico's most historic spots. The village of today stands on the same site it occupied when Coronado came that way in 1540; and it was a stopping place for every other Spanish explorer and conquistadore who passed through New Mexico. Isleta, a Spanish word meaning "islet," was given to the pueblo because the spot where it stands was once a delta, or small island in the Rio Grande, but the changing course of that stream long ago made it part of the mainland. The native name is Shiewhibak, meaning "knife laid on the ground to play whib." Whib is a native foot race; and Charles F. Lummis suggests that the name comes from the knife-shaped ridge of lava upon which the village stands.

The people of Isleta did not take part in the Rebellion of 1680, when the pueblo had an estimated population of 2,000. The Spanish colonists in that vicinity took refuge there, and then set out for El Paso; and when Governor Otermin arrived August 27, a few days later, on his retreat from Santa Fé he found the pueblo completely deserted, the people having joined the rebels. During his attempted reconquest of New Mexico in 1681, Otermin surprised and captured the village without a battle, taking five hundred nineteen prisoners, who, with the exception of one hundred fifteen that afterwards escaped, were taken south by the Spaniards and settled at Isleta del Sur, on the Rio Grande below El Paso.

Isleta remained deserted until 1709 when Fray Juan de la Peña, head of the Franciscan mission work in New Mexico at that time, gathered scattered bands of fugitive indians that the military authorities had been unable to capture, and induced them to return to their pueblos. A large number of the wanderers with their families were assembled at old Isleta, when the present pueblo was founded.

An interesting story of the loyalty of the Isleta indians comes down to us from the Civil war days. The people of this village have always been noted for their thrift; and when the confederate forces invaded New Mexico in 1862, Ambrosio Abeytia, a native of Isleta and the wealthiest pueblo in the state, loaned the commander of the union troops $18,000 in species, taking only his receipt for the money. This was used for the maintenance of the federal forces and probably did much to save New Mexico for the union. But Abeytia's loan was forgotten after the war, and for twelve years he waited in vain. Finally he made a special trip to Washington, and laid the case before President Grant, who ordered it paid immediately.

SAN ANTONIO DE ISLETA MISSION [SAINT ANTHONY OF ISLETA] The first mission at Isleta, named in honor of San Antonio, was founded prior to 1629, the exact date not being definitely known. Many of the christian converts from Quarai, Tajique, Chililí, Abó, and Tabira settled at Isleta between 1675 and 1680, when those

Mission of San Agustin at Isleta pueblo before it was remodeled
This shows its original appearance; erected in 1709

cities died of fear. San Antonio church was burned after the retreat of the Spaniards to El Paso in 1680; and when Otermin returned on his attempted reconquest in 1681 he found that it had been turned into a sheep corral. Between that date and 1709, when Isleta was resettled it is probable that the mission was entirely destroyed.

SAN AGUSTIN DE ISLETA MISSION [SAINT AUSTIN DE ISLETA] When Isleta del Sur was established near El Paso by Governor Otermin with indians captured at Isleta in 1681, the name of the mission of San Antonio was transferred to the new village; and in 1709, when Isleta was resettled by Fray Juan de la Peña a new church was erected on the spot occupied by the first, and dedicated to San Agustin. This building is still standing after being in continuous use for over two hundred years; but the exterior has been remodeled by the recent addition of a new sloping roof, and sharp pointed steeples have replaced the former belfries. A balcony added to the front detracts from the mission appearance and gives the old church a modern finish entirely out of place with its surroundings. This is to be regretted, for the ancient edifice was certainly not improved by these changes. This building is one hundred ten feet long by twenty-seven feet wide, while the adobe walls are four feet thick.

Old San Agustin church has long been a landmark on the Santa Fé railroad, and an excellent view of it may be had from the overland trains as they stop for a few minutes at the junction. The annual fiesta takes place August 28.

THE LEGEND OF PADRE PADILLO'S COFFIN. Of all the weird stories of ancient New Mexico the legend of the rising of Padre Padilla's coffin in the church at Isleta is one of the strangest. Told from one generation to another for centuries, its origin has been lost in the unwritten archives of the past; but this uncanny story is firmly believed not only by the indians of Isleta but by many Mexican residents in that vicinity.

It will be remembered that when Coronado returned to old Mexico in the spring of 1542 the two padres, Fray Juan de Padilla and Luis de Escalona, announced their intentions of spending the remainder of their lives among the newly discovered tribes. Padre Padilla set out across the great plains in search of the famed Quivira which Coronado had failed to find. According to the old tradition he reached that mythical land, somewhere in the present state of Kansas, and was murdered by one of the plains tribes after he announced his intentions of going to another nation.

The old legend informs us that his body was carried back from Quivira to Isleta, and when the first church of San Antonio was erected he was buried under the floor, close to the altar, in a coffin hollowed out of a large cottonwood tree. Not only the indians but many Mexicans believe that the corpse came to the surface of the ground once a year in the long ago so that all might gaze upon the sainted padre. This story has survived from one generation to another down to the present time; and the people still believed that in some mysterious manner the coffin works its way up to the surface of the church floor. The assertion has often been made that the body is well preserved, mummified by the dry atmosphere and that the face is covered with long, black whiskers. Some people claim to have pieces of his robe, handed down in families for generations. It is a fact that some internal agitation, probably an undercurrent of water from the Rio Grande, does cause a disturbance of the surface of the ground each year at the spot where the priest's grave is supposed to be located. The people not only believe that the coffin comes up but that Padre Padilla rises, and, after taking a stroll about the pueblo, returns to his grave.

Historians have tried in vain to show that it is impossible for the remains of Padre Padilla to have been buried there, many long miles from the spot where he was killed and at a time when none of the New Mexico indians had been converted to christianity. There is no doubt that this is the grave of some priest. In an article written in 1895 Frank de Thoma claimed that the remains might be those of either Friar Ruiz, or one of his two companions who were murdered at old Puaray pueblo in 1581; or perhaps one of the martyrs of 1680; but nothing will shake the local belief that this is the grave of Padre Padilla.

NUESTRA SEÑORA DE BELEN MISSION [OUR LADY OF BELEN] On the west bank of the Rio Grande, in Valencia county, about twenty-five miles south of Isleta, was Belen, a settlement established by the Spaniards about 1766 as a refuge for Genizaros, or redeemed Pueblo indian captives purchased by the Spaniards from the predatory Apaches and Comanches. The mission of Nuestra Señora de Belen was established there, probably shortly after the village was founded. The settlement contained one hundred seven inhabitants in 1805, but this had increased to one hundred thirty-three in 1809, and during the past century it became Mexicanized. The ruins of the old mission may still be traced near the present town of Belen, on the Santa Fé railroad south of Albuquerque, and at the beginning of the Belen Cut-off.

SAN LUIS OBISPO DE SEVILLETA MISSION. Twenty

miles north of the present Socorro, on the east side of the Rio Grande, was the ancient Piro settlement of Sevilleta, meaning "Little Seville," named by the Spaniards on account of some fancied resemblance to that city. When Oñate passed up the Rio Grande valley in 1598 he called this pueblo Nueva Sevilla, or "New Seville;" but this was later changed to "Little Seville." Subsequently the Apaches drove the inhabitants out, and Sevilleta was deserted for several years. Between 1626 and 1630 the Franciscan fathers gathered the remnants of the tribe and resettled the place, at the same time establishing the mission of San Luis Obispo. The people did not take part in the revolt of 1680; but fled with Governor Otermin on the retreat down the Rio Grande; and Sevilleta was never again occupied. The next year Otermin found it completely deserted and in ruins.

SANTA ANA DE ALAMILLO MISSION. Early in the seventeenth century the Franciscans established a mission at Alamillo, a Piro pueblo on the Rio Grande, twelve miles north of the present Socorro. Little is known of its history, except that it was dedicated to Santa Ana. The inhabitants took no part in the Rebellion of 1680; and most of them joined the Spaniards on their retreat to El Paso. Those who remained were driven out by Governor Otermin and the village burned during his attempted reconquest in 1681. The site of this ancient settlement may be reached by automobile from Socorro, or from Alamillo station on the Santa Fé railroad; but there is little of interest.

NUESTRA SEÑORA DEL SOCORRO MISSION. In olden times the site of the present town of Socorro was occupied by a Piro village, given this name by Don Juan de Oñate in 1598 because of the friendly manner in which the Spaniards were received. The mission of Nuestra Señora del Socorro was established in 1626, and a church and monastery were erected. It continued in active operation until the pueblo was abandoned at the outbreak of the Rebellion of 1680, at which time this was a village of six hundred inhabitants, most of whom joined the Spaniards on their retreat to El Paso. They never returned to their former home, but settled on the Texas side of the Rio Grande where they built the pueblo of Socorro del Sur. No trace of the ancient village or the mission now remains. Socorro is on the main line of the Santa Fé railroad between Albuquerque and El Paso, and on the automobile highway to the south.

The first grapes in New Mexico were planted at Socorro by Padres Antonio de Arteaga and Garcia de Zuñiga, the founders of the mission.

SAN PASCUAL MISSION [HOLY EASTER] San Pascual was a small Piro village on the east bank of the Rio Grande, opposite the present San Antonio, thirteen miles south of Socorro. The mission of San Pascual was established there, probably about 1629, the year of the founding of San Antonio mission at Senecu, on the opposite side of the river. Practically nothing is known of its history, but the village was probably abandoned in 1675 at the time that Senecu was destroyed by the Apaches. The site may be reached from the present San Antonio, a station on the Santa Fé and also on the main automobile road to the south.

SAN ANTONIO DE SENECU MISSION [SAINT ANTHONY OF SENECU] Although some distance from the Salinas country, Senecu was another of the cities that died of fear; for many of the inhabitants were massacred and the town was destroyed in 1675 by raiding Apaches. This was a Piro pueblo on the west bank of the Rio Grande, thirteen miles south of Socorro, on the site of the present Mexican village of San Antonio, named for the old mission.

This mission of San Antonio was founded at Senecu in 1629 by two padres, Antonio de Arteaga and Garcia de Zuñiga; and a church and monastery were erected, the first on the lower Rio Grande. Fray Zuñiga died at El Paso in 1673, and his remains were carried back to Senecu and buried in his church.

The story of the fate of Senecu pueblo and San Antonio mission is one of the most tragic of the cities that died of fear. On January 23, 1675, the terrible Apaches suddenly swept out of the desert, surprising the inhabitants before they could raise a defending hand and massacring a large number of men, women and children. Alonzo Gil de Avila, the priest in charge, was among the killed. The pueblo was never again inhabited. The few survivors fled to Socorro, and finally drifted down to the Mexican side of the Rio Grande below El Paso, where they founded Senecu del Sur. San Antonio village, which occupies the site of the ancient pueblo, is on the main automobile road south of Socorro.

XI. From Albuquerque west to Zuñi

San José de Laguna – A curious lawsuit over a painting – San Estéban Rey de Acoma – Cebolleta.

SAN JOSÉ DE LAGUNA MISSION [SAINT JOSEPH OF THE LAGOON] Laguna, on the main line of the Santa Fé railroad, sixty-four miles west of Isleta and seventy-nine from Albuquerque, is one of the best known of the New Mexican pueblos, due to the fact that it is on the railroad and may be seen from the car windows. Formerly few trains stopped there and accommodations for the night were hard to secure; but this has been changed by the automobile, and as Laguna is on the main highway from the Pacific coast to the east it is receiving more attention. It is also the gateway to Acoma, twelve miles south. The name is Spanish, meaning "lagoon," taken from a large beaver pond located just west of the village in early times, but which disappeared long ago. The Keresan name of the pueblo is Kawaik. The Laguna people are of mixed origin, composed of four linguistic stocks. When they founded the settlement in July, 1699, the Spanish authorities made them a grant of 125,225 acres of land, mostly desert.

The mission was established and the church built in 1699; and in 1782 Acoma was made a visita. San José church, which is still in use after more than two centuries, is one of the picturesque sights of the pueblo.

One of the most famous lawsuits in the history of New Mexico, in which the Pueblo of Acoma was plaintiff and the Pueblo of Laguna was defendant, was fought through the courts in 1852 for possession of a picture of Saint Joseph, which was believed by the indians to possess miraculous powers. According to the legend this ancient painting was a gift from King Charles II of Spain to Fray Juan Ramirez, and it was taken by the padre to Acoma in 1629 when he founded that mission. The natives believe that Saint Joseph endowed this painting with miraculous powers, and throughout the centuries it has been held in great veneration by all the indians.

Through this picture Saint Joseph was appealed to on all occasions, during drought, pestilence or illness, or whenever an attack was expected from the Apaches or Navajos. The indian neophytes derived much comfort from the ancient painting, and the prosperity, peace, and health of Acoma were attributed to its powers. During all this prosperity at Acoma the neighboring pueblo of Laguna suffered from droughts and epidemics, washouts and floods, and calamities of all kinds.

In desperation the people of Laguna finally sent a delegation to Acoma and asked for the loan of the sacred painting. According to one story this was agreed to on condition that it would be returned in one month; but at the end of that period the people of Laguna refused to give it up. Another version is that the strange request was referred to the priests of both pueblos; and, believing that God would direct the result, Fray Mariano de Jesus Lopez, superior of the Franciscans, ordered that lots should be drawn after a season of prayer and penance in both villages.

The drawing decided that the picture should remain at Acoma, but while the people of that place were celebrating this victory some Laguna warriors stole the coveted painting from the mission. A bloody war would have followed had not Father Lopez persuaded the Acomas to allow the Lagunas to keep the picture for a short time on condition that they would return it promptly. The latter made many promises which they failed to keep, especially as prosperity came to their pueblo almost immediately. They believed that the sacred picture had brought this blessing to them, and they were afraid of a return of hard times if it should be taken back to Acoma. And so they kept it in spite of the advice of Father Lopez and the priest at Laguna. Fearful that the Acomas would steal it, a guard was placed over it day and night.

The years came and went until fifty had passed and still the sacred painting remained at Laguna; and during all that time the guard was never removed for a minute. At last the padre of the Acomas advised them to take the matter into court. They were loath to do this because they were fearful of the white man's ways; but they finally decided that there was no other solution short of war. A long, bitter fight through the courts followed; and the attorneys' fees kept both pueblos poor for years. The final decision was in favor of Acoma, the original owner.

A committee was appointed by the Acomas to bring the sacred painting back to its home after an absence of more than half a century; but they had only gone about half the distance to Laguna, when, miracles of miracles, they found the object of their veneration reposing under a tree. The Lagunas have never told how it got there, but the Acomas believe to this day that as soon as Saint Joseph heard of the court's decision he set out for home. The picture was taken back to Acoma, where it may still be seen hanging in its place in the ancient mission.

The old church at Laguna is still in use after more than two centuries, and is well worth a visit. The interior, with its indian decorations and antique paintings brought up across the deserts from old Mexico long years ago, is similar to other New Mexico missions of the Spanish period. The annual fiesta at Laguna, which takes place September 19, is one of the most interesting in the state.

SAN ESTÉBAN REY MISSION AT ACOMA [SAINT STEPHEN THE KING] Acoma, called "the sky city" because of its picturesque location on the summit of a mesa, guarded by perpendicular cliffs rising three hundred fifty feet out of the level plain, is one of those places of pleasant memory that we love to dwell upon during the years to come. High up on the great rock it lies, only reached by steep, winding trails cut in the solid rock of the cliffs, worn down by the tread of generations upon generations of moccasined feet, reminding you very much of the ancient ruin on the top of Inscription Rock, south of Gallup. Conquistadores, Franciscan fathers, Spanish soldiers, American troops and world tourists of a later generation have in their turn climbed that trail, some to give their life blood, since Acoma was first known by Europeans nearly four centuries ago.

Just when Acoma was built on this natural stronghold no man can say with any degree of certainty; for it was there in 1539 when Fray Marcos de Niza made his historic pilgrimage in search of the fabled Seven Cities of Cibola, and no indian tradition gives the slightest clue. It bears the distinction of being the oldest inhabited settlement in the entire United States.

The Acoma that you see today is the same that Captain Hernando de Alvarado, of Coronado's army, discovered in 1540, and called Acuco. Even then the tribe was warlike, and threatened to attack the Spaniards if they dared to cross a line marked in the sand. But the gallant Alvarado boldly entered the pueblo and gave its warriors to understand that he would meet force with force. In 1583, Antonio de Espejo, the next conquistadore who came that way, remarked upon the dizzy trail cut out of the solid rock of the cliff, and the cultivated land, where the tribe still farms at Acomita and Pueblito, fifteen miles away.

The people of Acoma were always warriors; and from that day in 1598 when Chief Zutucapan attempted to lure Don Juan de Oñate into a kiva so that he might kill him without interference, until the tribe finally submitted to Governor Pedro Rodriguez de Cubero a hundred years later, the history of the pueblo was written in blood. This was in the mission field assigned to Fray Andres Corchado in 1598, but on account of this hostility a church was not established there until thirty years later.

The trouble started on December 4, 1598, when Oñate's nephew, Captain Juan de Zaldivar, in command of thirty soldiers, stopped at Acoma while on his way to join his uncle at Zuñi, where the latter was preparing for his exploring expedition in search of the "Sea of the South." Never suspecting treachery, Captain Zaldivar climbed up the trail to Acoma with six troopers, leaving the main force camped at the foot of the rock. Three remained at the entrance of the pueblo and made their escape with the news of the battle.

Upon receiving the sad tidings Oñate gave up his expedition, hastening back to San Gabriel; and on January 21, 1599, Captain Vicente de Zaldivar, brother of Juan, arrived before Acoma with an avenging army of seventy. Early the next morning they assaulted the pueblo, and after a desperate battle of three days, in which six hundred indians were killed and the village partly burned, the Acomas surrendered. The loss of the Spaniards was not given, but it must have been heavy.

The first church at Acoma was built in 1629 by Fray Juan Ramirez, the first permanent missionary. In the Rebellion of 1680 Fray Lucas Maldonado, the priest in charge, was murdered, and Acoma was left to itself until De Vargas appeared in August, 1696. The great conquistadore was unable to capture the pueblo; but on July 6, 1699, the natives surrendered to Governor Cubero.

Some historians claim that the present church is the first one erected in 1629, with some additions made after the rebellion; but others contend that the original edifice was destroyed in 1680. Be that as it may, the present church, which was either built or remodeled in 1699, is one of the finest of all the ancient missions. It was selected as the model for both the New Mexico building at the Panama Pacific exposition held at San Diego, California, in 1915, and the state museum at Santa Fé.

This church, one hundred fifty feet long by forty feet wide, built of adobe, is a miracle of construction. The top of the great mesa upon which Acoma stands is absolutely barren of vegetation, soil, or dirt of any kind. There is nothing but the smooth native rock, and every ounce of material used in the mission was packed up that dizzy, winding trail by indian neophytes. The roof timbers, each forty feet long and a foot square, were carried on the backs of men from the San Mateo mountains twenty miles away.

The graveyard is a greater marvel than the church, and is probably the only one of its kind in the world.

On the top of that wind-swept, barren rock there was no spot for a burial ground. The Acoma converts wanted their dead with them in consecrated ground; and so they built a stone retaining wall nearly fifty feet high at the outer edge, and inclosing a square of two hundred feet. Then from the plain below they carried up enough earth on their backs, a sackful at a time, to make their sacred graveyard.

The trail to the village is called "El Camino del Padre," to this day, because of the story told that when Father Ramirez climbed it for the first time in 1629 he was greeted with a shower of arrows, but was saved by the sheltering cliff. It is also related that another padre was forced to leap over the edge of the cliff to escape from the warlike Acomas, who did not take kindly to his religion. His death seemed certain, but just before he jumped he opened an umbrella which acted as a parachute and carried him to safety.

Acoma is easily accessible from Laguna on the Santa Fé railroad and the transcontinental highway. This side trip of twelve miles takes you past the famous Katzimo, or Enchanted mesa, four hundred thirty feet high, which can only be ascended by the most perilous mountain climbing. The Acomas have a tradition that their ancestors once lived on the summit of Katzimo, but the trail was closed by a great storm, and the people tending their fields on the plain below were never able to reach their homes again. Those left on the rock starved to death.

The annual fiesta at Acoma takes place on the 1st of September.

CEBOLLETA. Cebolleta was one of the few missions established by the Franciscan fathers among the Navajos; and its existence was so short that it has almost been forgotten. This was a Navajo settlement, with a population of between four and five hundred, made by Padre Juan M. Menchero in 1746 in the very northeastern corner of Valencia county. Father Menchero had hopes of inducing the Navajos to abandon their roving, raiding life and settle down like the Pueblos. In 1749 the padre founded a mission there, but by the next year these desert nomads had grown tired of sedentary life, and Cebolleta was abandoned. A little Mexican hamlet of half a hundred people now occupies the site, which is about twenty miles north of Laguna, near Cebolleta mountain.

XII. The Seven Cities of Cibola

The Myth of the Golden Cities – Coronado's Expedition – Hawikuh, the first city – Kechipauan – Halona – Zuñi – Thunder Mountain – Inscription Rock.

THE MYTH OF THE GOLDEN CITIES. Of all the groundless tales that ever lured a treasure seeking adventurer into an unknown land, the story of the Seven Cities of Cibola, the pot of gold that tempted Coronado across a great desert wilderness, is one of the wildest fables in all history. Its origin will never be known. Shortly after the conquest of Mexico the Aztecs told the Spaniards of a land called Cibola, far to the north, where there were seven cities with streets paved with gold and houses set with precious jewels. Efforts were made to find it, Cortez himself leading one of the expeditions; and when Fray Marcos de Niza returned from his journey to New Mexico in 1539, reporting the discovery of Cibola with its seven cities of wondrous riches, all Mexico went mad with gold fever.

On Monday, February 23, 1540, Francisco Vasquez de Coronado, captain-general of the most picturesque and daring army that ever served under the Spanish flag, set out with his expedition from Compostela, on the west coast of Mexico, in search of the Seven Cities of Cibola. The number in this army varies according to the source of information. Mota Padilla gives it as two hundred sixty horsemen, seventy footmen and more than a thousand indians and indian servants, while Castañeda places the number of horsemen at three hundred.

Each rider was armed with a lance, sword and side arms, and most of them wore coats of mail and iron helmets, or vizored headpieces of tough bullhide. The footmen carried crossbows and arquebuses, swords and shields.

HAWIKUH, THE FIRST CITY. On July 7, the army reached Hawikuh, the ruins of which still stand fifteen miles southwest of the present Zuñi pueblo and near Ojo Caliente. Coronado believed that this was the first of the fabled Seven Cities and as such it has come down to us in history; but the author advances the theory in another chapter that the original Cibola of the old indian legend was land of the Hopis in northeastern Arizona. Hawikuh was the place where Estevan, the negro slave and guide of Fray Marcos de Niza, was killed by the natives in May, 1539.

This Estevan had been with Alvar Nuñez Cabeza de Vaca and his two companions, Alonzo del Castillo Maldonado and Andrés Dorantes, the only survivors of the Navarez expedition that was wrecked on the coast of Texas in September, 1528; and after nearly eight years wanderings across Texas, New Mexico, and Arizona they reached the Gulf of California. On account of his knowledge of the country, Estevan accompanied Fray Marcos de Niza in 1539. Pushing forward, the negro reached Hawikuh in advance of the padre and was murdered by the natives. After he learned of his guide's death, Fray Marcos kept on until he arrived within sight of Hawikuh; and the golden light of the setting sun, shining on the buildings far away on the horizon led him to believe they were covered with the precious metal coveted by all mankind.

When Coronado arrived before Hawikuh he was opposed by the Zuñi warriors, but after a severe battle on July 7, the Spaniards captured the village only to find that the indians had removed their women and children and the greater part of their belongings to the summit of Taaiyalone, now known as Thunder mountain; and the conquistadores learned that the first of the fabled Seven Cities supposed to be filled with gold and precious jewels were only ordinary pueblos. Coronado gave it the name of Granada.

From Hawikuh, Coronado sent an expedition under Don Pedro de Tovar to explore the country to the northwest, but he was commanded to return within a month. Tovar left on July 15, and discovered the Hopi villages in what was afterwards the province of Tusayan, in Arizona; and he brought back the first story of the Grand Canyon. The Hopis told him of a mighty river towards the west, inhabited by giant people; but as his time was limited to thirty days he returned to Hawikuh without further investigation.

On August 25, Coronado dispatched Don Garcia Lopez de Cardeñas with a party to verify these reports; and to him fell the honor of being the first European to gaze upon the wonders of the Grand Canyon. He was unable to find either a crossing or means of descending to the river, and so he returned with the news of the impassable barrier. Although Cardeñas was the discoverer of the Grand Canyon, El Tovar Hotel on the rim is named in honor of Pedro de Tovar, the man who first learned of its existence.

Francisco Sanchez Chamuscado, the next Spanish explorer, visited Cibola in 1580; and in 1583 Antonio de Espejo, who gave the tribe its name of Zuñi, found three Mexican indians who had accompanied Coronado, still living at Hawikuh.

In 1598 Don Juan de Oñate assigned the province of

Zuñi to Fray Andres Corchado; but active work was not started until the summer of 1629, when the first mission was established at Hawikuh by three Franciscan friars, Roque de Figueredo, Agustin de Cuellar, and Francisco de la Madre de Dios, members of the band of thirty religious men under Fray Estevan de Perea, as their custodian, who were sent to New Mexico by the Viceroy of New Spain, by order of the king. They reached Santa Fé on Easter Sunday of 1629, and Padre Perea succeeded Fray Alonzo de Benavides as mission custodian of New Mexico.

On June 23, 1629, these three priests, escorted by Governor Manuel de Silva Nieto with four hundred cavalry and ten wagons, left Santa Fé to establish missions in the land of Cibola. On the return journey Governor Nieto and his soldiers passed Inscription Rock on July 29, where they left a record in the inscription described in another part of this chapter. The Zuñis rebelled against the padres, and Nieto went back to Hawikuh, to settle the trouble as shown by another inscription dated August 9.

The three priests founded the mission of La Concepcion at Hawikuh, the principal Zuñi city, with Padre Roque de Figueredo in charge. No doubt the others helped him for a time, after which the missions at Halona and Kechipauan were established, all three priests assisting in the work at each pueblo.

A house bought from the natives at Hawikuh for the lodging of the three friars became the first mission; and in this small adobe building, erected by indians long before the coming of the padres, the first baptismal ceremony in western New Mexico was conducted on San Agustin's Day, August 28, 1629. They began the erection of La Concepcion mission at Hawikuh that same year, while work on the churches at Halona and Kechipauan was probably started at the same time or shortly afterwards. The fate of these three priests is not known, as they disappeared from Zuñi history before 1632.

The next priest at Hawikuh was Fray Francisco de Letrado, another member of Perea's band of thirty, who was first assigned to the Jumanos in the Salinas Lake region, east of the Rio Grande, where he labored for a time and then requested permission to go to the Zipias living to the westward. This was refused for some reason not now apparent, for Letrado is known to have been a fiery and zealous missionary; and Fray Martin de Arvide was sent in his stead, while Padre Letrado was ordered to Hawikuh. The Zipia is an unknown tribe today, but it may have been the Hopi, as they were the only other indians to the westward of Zuñi whom the Spaniards ever attempted to christianize.

Padre Letrado's work at Hawikuh was very short; for he was murdered shortly after his arrival. On Sunday, February 22, 1632, when the indians failed to attend mass he became impatient and went out to urge them to enter the church. He knew at once from their attitude that they intended to kill him; but he knelt down, holding a small crucifix in his hands, and remonstrated with them until he was shot to death with arrows. His corpse was scalped and carried away, and the scalp afterwards flaunted in their dances.

Five days after Padre Letrado's death, Fray Martin de Arvide, who had passed through Hawikuh on his way to the Zipia nation, was overtaken by five Zuñis and murdered. This indicates that Letrado was killed very shortly after his arrival, as they had both been assigned to their new stations at practically the same time.

Steps to avenge the murder of these missionaries were taken by Governor Francisco de la Mora Ceballos, who dispatched a few priests with a small force of soldiers under Tomás de Albizu, to Zuñi; and while they were encamped at Inscription Rock a soldier named Lujan carved this inscription: "They passed on the 23 of March of 1632 year to the avenging of the death of Father Letrado."

There has been considerable dispute as to whether Letrado was killed in 1630 or 1632. The Lujan inscription very plainly gives 1632; but it has been claimed that a month and a day was not sufficient time for the news to reach Santa Fé and for an avenging force to get as far as the rock. However, this is not impossible, and the best authorities now accept the year of 1632 as correct.

After the murder of Letrado and Arvide the Zuñis fled to their stronghold on Thunder mountain; and it is plainly evident that the Spanish force under Albizu was not strong enough to dislodge them; for no further record is found of the expedition. About 1635 the Zuñis ventured down and began to settle in the valley again; but mission work was not started among them until 1642.

Little is known of the history of La Concepcion mission from the time of Padre Letrado's death until 1670, when Fray Pedro de Avila y Ayala was stationed at Hawikuh and Fray Juan de Galdo at Halona.

On August 7, 1670, a band of Apache warriors (some authorities say Navajo) swept down upon Hawikuh, murdered Fray Ayala and many of the inhabitants, and then burned the church. According to the old story still told of that terrible raid, the priest's brains were beat out with a bell while he was clinging to a cross. His

Main Altar of La Concepcion mission at ancient Hawikuh

At the foot of this altar Fray Pedro de Avila y Ayala was slain by Apaches in the raid of August 7, 1670. Beneath the main altar beyond the steps, a skeleton was found in 1919

remains were recovered the next day by Fray Galdo, and buried at either Hawikuh or Halona. The pueblo was partly inhabited for a few years longer, but after the Rebellion of 1680 it was entirely deserted. Although it is generally believed that the church was never again occupied after the raid of 1670, Vetancurt states that La Concepcion was an active mission at the time of the great revolt, with a resident priest who escaped the massacre; but the building was burned.

Among the Zuñis an old tradition is still told of a priest who escaped death at the time of the rebellion by joining the tribe; and before he died he requested the indians to bury him in a christian church with his head touching the altar. The fact that when De Vargas induced the Zuñis to descend from their old stronghold on Thunder mountain in 1692, he found an altar in use with candles and vestments, gives some color to the story.

The ruins of the old Hawikuh mission stood for more than two centuries before they finally disappeared. Some authorities claim that about 1705 the roof timbers were removed for use in the roof of the church now standing in ruins at Zuñi pueblo; but this is hardly possible if La Concepcion was burned in 1670 and again in 1680. Some of the heavy timbers may have escaped the fire, but they would have been badly charred; and those in the present building at Zuñi show no evidence of fire. A section of the old wall standing in 1894 was removed by indians from Ojo Caliente who used the adobe bricks in the construction of houses.

For the next quarter of a century no trace of the historic mission was to be seen; but in 1919 the Hendricks-Hodge Hawikuh expedition, sent out by the Museum of the American Indian, New York City, in charge of Frederick W. Hodge, made some important discoveries in this ancient desert city where Coronado camped nearly four hundred years ago. The field work was under the immediate supervision of Mr. Hodge's assistant, Jesse L. Nusbaum, superintendent of Mesa Verde National Park, Colorado. Mr. Hodge very kindly furnished the author with a description of the work, and photographs of the mission after the excavation was completed.

Several feet of the walls of both the church and monastery were uncovered after having been buried under the drifting sands blown by the desert winds of more than two centuries. Scarcely a piece of wood used in the construction of these two buildings was found uncharred, showing that both had been destroyed by fire. This refutes the old story that the roof timbers in the present Zuñi mission were removed from Hawikuh in 1705; for as already stated no evidence of fire is to be found in the ruins of the old church at that pueblo. Before its destruction La Concepcion had evidently been stripped of its contents, probably in the Apache raid of 1670, or during the Rebellion of 1680 if it was occupied at that time; but a few Spanish objects were found such as iron fragments, crockery, a small wooden frame evidently for a picture, earthenware candlesticks of indian make, and similar objects.

The greatly decomposed skeleton of an adult male found beneath the adobe altar, with the skull towards the east as in the case of most of the late burials in the cemeteries at Hawikuh, again brings to mind the old Zuñi tale of the priest who escaped the massacre of 1680 by joining the tribe. Perhaps it is true after all; and the Zuñis may have been faithful to the trust he imposed upon them to bury him in a christian church.

On the other hand this grim skeleton may be the remains of Fray Pedro de Avila y Ayala, who was murdered in the Apache raid of 1670. Who knows? However, from the fact that the head was towards the east it is more reasonable to suppose that he was buried by indians, which gives an additional reason for believing the old Zuñi tradition of the priest who joined the tribe in 1680. It was customary to bury under the mission floors in olden times, and many skeletons were found in the church at Hawikuh; but only persons of importance were interred beneath the altars. And so we may assume that this was some priest from sunny Spain who found a sepulcher for his bones in the lonely New Mexico desert as a reward for his earthly labors.

KECHIPAUAN MISSION. Kechipauan, meaning "town of the spread-out grit," probably referring to the sandstone mesa, was another of the Seven Cities of Cibola, the ruins of which stand on a mesa east of Ojo Caliente and in the vicinity of Hawikuh, fifteen miles southwest of Zuñi. Little mention of it is found among the records of the early explorers, but Adolph Bandelier has identified it as the village called Canabi by Oñate in 1598.

A mission, the walls of which are still standing from eight to fourteen feet high, was founded there about 1629 by the first missionaries at Hawikuh and Halona; but historians have expressed the belief that the building was never completed, and nothing more is known of its history.

Unlike La Concepcion, the church at Kechipauan was constructed of stone with massive walls characteristic of the early Spanish missions of certain sections of New Mexico, such as Jemez and the Salinas Lake region. It was evidently built by the natives, for the walls were chinked with small stones as in all indian masonry. The stones at the corners and at the oblique openings for the doors and windows were laid with great care, showing considerable skill. A very unusual feature of the building is that all openings for the door and windows were splayed at an angle of about forty-five degrees. From the position of the beam holes on the interior it appears that the floor might have been raised above the ground with a small cellar beneath, another very unusual feature for in most missions the earth formed the floor. The inside is divided into six rooms, which the Zuñis claim were built as a means of defense against the Apaches after the church was abandoned; and in the south wall is a large stone upon which a rude mask has been carved. There is no record to tell us just how long this church was used, if it was ever completed, which now appears doubtful, as there were no wooden beams found about the place by any of the early investigators of the ruins of the village.

HALONA. A large mound of earth on the south side of the Zuñi river, opposite modern Zuñi, is all that is left of old Halona, another once popular city of ancient Cibola. It stood on both sides of this desert stream, and on a section of its ruins Zuñi pueblo was founded near the close of the seventeenth century; while buildings of the white race occupy part of the mound. According to F. H. Cushing, who spent many years among the Zuñis, the name Halona means "middle place of happy fortune," or "middle ant hill of the world." Mr. Cushing built one of the houses that stand on the mound, and in 1886 excavated a section of the ancient city.

Halona, discovered by Coronado in 1540, was visited by Chamuscado forty years later and by Espejo in 1583. In the fall of 1598 Don Juan de Oñate stopped there on his western journey in search of the "Sea of

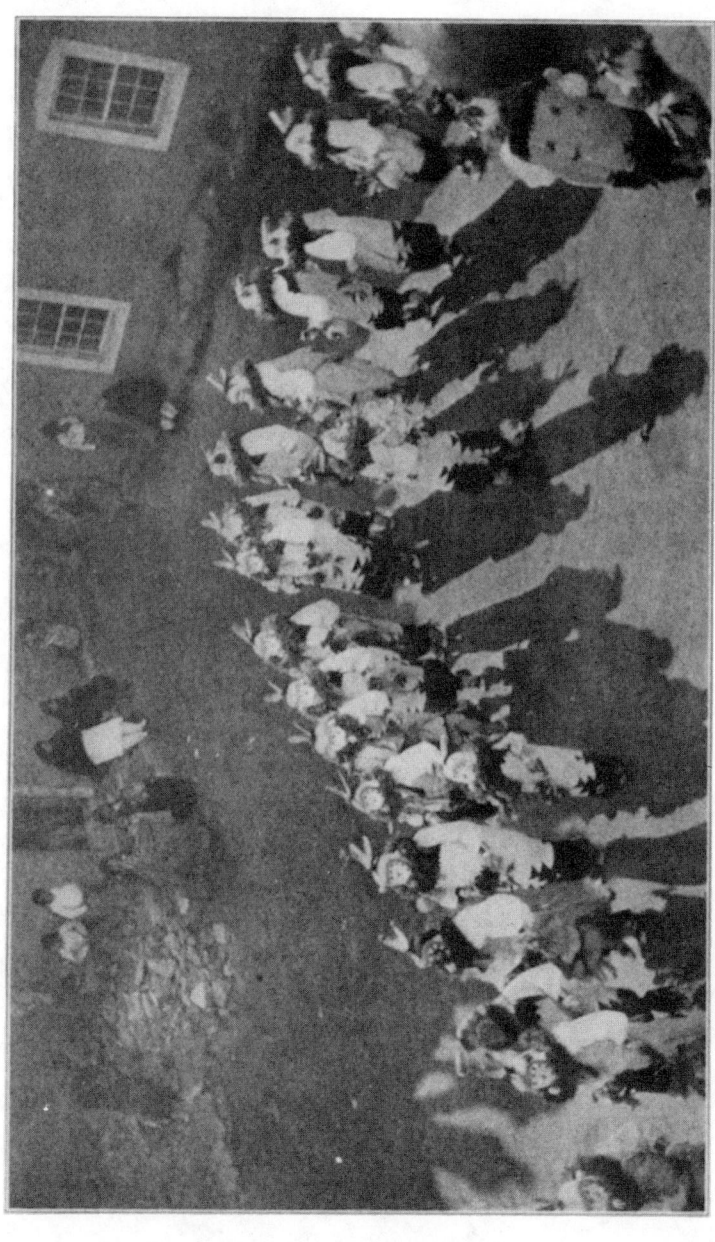

Canaque Dance, or Dance of the White Masks, at Zuñi pueblo, New Mexico

This dance is held once every four years. Photographs are forbidden and are only taken at great personal risk

the South," but turned back when he received the news of Captain Juan de Zaldivar's death at Acoma.

A mission was established in 1629 at the same time or shortly after that at Hawikuh; and on February 27, 1632, five days after the murder of Padre Letrado, as already related, Fray Martin de Arvide, was killed by five indians from Hawikuh, while on his way to the Zipia. Fearful of Spanish vengeance the natives of both pueblos fled to their stronghold on Thunder mountain, where they remained about three years.

The Halona mission was restored in 1643 and continued without interruption until the Rebellion of 1680. After the Navajo raid on Hawikuh on August 7, 1670, Fray Juan Galdo, the priest in charge of Halona, recovered and buried Padre Ayala's remains.

In 1680 the Zuñis occupied two pueblos in addition to Halona – Matsaki at the northwest base of Thunder mountain, and Kiakima, at the southwest base, both visitas of Halona mission. The tribe took part in the rebellion and after murdering their priest, Fray Juan de Val, on August 10, 1680, they burned the church at Halona and fled to their old stronghold on Thunder mountain, where they remained until after the reconquest. De Vargas passed through the Zuñi country on his way to the conquest of the Hopis in Arizona in 1692, as shown by the record he cut on Inscription rock, which may be seen to this day. On October 30, 1692, he arrived at Thunder mountain and received the peaceable submission of the tribe. Strange to say the Zuñis had preserved the sacred furnishings of the Halona church, which they delivered to De Vargas; and so ends the story of Halona mission, as the pueblo was never again occupied.

ZUÑI. After the arrival of De Vargas the Zuñis gathered at the site of Halona; but they found that it had fallen in ruins during the years they had spent on Thunder mountain, and so they built a new pueblo – modern Zuñi. In 1699 Zuñi mission was founded; but in 1703 the natives killed several Spanish soldiers who had mistreated them, and again fled to Thunder mountain. They were induced to return in 1705, and work on the church was resumed, it evidently not having been completed when the village was deserted two years before. It was without a roof, and so, according to most authorities the timbers were removed from the old mission still standing at Hawikuh, abandoned after the Navajo raid of 1670, but this is hardly possible in view of recent discoveries made by the Hendricks-Hodge expedition.

The Zuñis never took kindly to the white man's religion, and, with the exception of the Hopis, they were regarded by the Spaniards as the most warlike and difficult of all the Pueblo tribes to convert to christianity. After the completion of the Zuñi church in 1705 it was necessary to keep a garrison stationed there; and the mission maintained a precarious existence throughout the eighteenth century. The tribe was left entirely to itself after the Franciscans were expelled from New Mexico in 1823; and even after the American occupation no attention was paid to the Zuñis until the seventies when several unsuccessful attempts were made to christianize them. Of all the Pueblo indians in New Mexico this tribe has been affected the least by christian influence; and they still observe a great number of their ancient religious rites throughout the year, the most important of which is the Shallako, or ceremony of the winter solstice during the last days of November. Another important ceremony is the Canaque dance, held

RUINS OF THE ZUÑI MISSION AT ZUÑI PUEBLO, NEW MEXICO
Founded in 1699, it was completed in 1705

only once every four years, and this during the presidential year.

The most sacred shrine in all Zuñiland is Hep-ah-teen-ah, or the "Center of the Earth," a small hole in the ground covered by a pile of stones, just southwest of the pueblo. According to their legends, the Zuñi came upon the earth through this hole long, long ago. It is a sacred spot, jealously guarded to this day, and they frown upon visitors making a close inspection of the place.

Zuñi is still a village with a town crier, who goes through the streets each evening just before sunset announcing in a loud voice the events for the next day, and a priest of one of the clans makes a special announcement and offering each morning at sunrise. In case of sickness another takes his place. William Turner, who accompanied me on one of my visits to Zuñi, informed me that this man forgot his duty one morning, and the Zuñi held a special ceremony to atone to the sun for this neglect.

Attempts to christianize the Zuñis were given up by the catholics long ago. After the resident missionary was removed, a priest went to the pueblo occasionally at long intervals; but these visits finally ceased, and it has been many long years since regular services were held.

Today the ancient mission, built nearly two centuries and a quarter ago, stands in a state of picturesque ruin and dilapidation, slowly weathering away before the relentless desert elements. The large cross that stood before the entrance tumbled over long ago, and now lies under the balcony as though kicked out of the road. Many a year has passed since the graveyard in front, still inclosed by a crumbling adobe wall, was used; and human bones may be found scattered among the weeds.

Exposed to the desert sun and storms, this historic building is slowly but surely moldering away; and the interior presents a sad picture. The roof has fallen in these many years; but the great beams that were originally in the Hawikuh mission, built in 1629, are still in place, defying the elements to the last. Just over the doorway is the gallery built of squared timbers and supported by two pillars, with its earthen floor held in place by a framework of small timbers laid close together. When I last visited Zuñi on August 1, 1926, I was fortunate enough to find a small section of wood that showed by the marks that it had been cut with a stone ax. It might possibly have come from Hawikuh. The altar disappeared long ago; and the nave, where the indian neophytes once knelt while the padre held mass, is now overgrown with weeds and covered with rubbish.

Across the housetops of Zuñi, three miles to the east, the broad, flat summit of Thunder mountain looms up, sacred from time immemorial. Guarded by almost impregnable cliffs, it is little wonder the Zuñis fled there when threatened by the Spanish hosts. It is sacred to the tribe to this day; and in those cliffs are caves known to no white man, where secret ceremonies are still held.

INSCRIPTION ROCK [EL MORRO] The story of the Zuñi missions would not be complete without some mention of Inscription rock – El Morro of the early Spaniards, where every conquistadore and explorer who passed that way, even down to our own times, carved a record of his visit on the face of the cliff. It is forty-nine miles southeast of Gallup and thirty-five east of Zuñi, over roads that are good except in rainy weather. By starting early the round trip may be made by automobile in a day, with plenty of time to explore the rock and ruins on the summit; and if you wish to return by way of Zuñi you will still have two or three hours to spend at the pueblo; but twenty years ago it required three days for the round trip on horseback.

Inscription rock is now a National monument in charge of Evon Z. Vogt, custodian, who extends every courtesy to visitors. Twenty-seven ancient Spanish inscriptions have been found carved on the face of this great rock. The government has placed a fence around each one, and a little waterproof frame at the side contains a photograph of the original with the English translation below.

On one side of the rock is a little cove, where the traveler in ancient times was sure of wood and water. Long before the coming of the white man this had been a camping place for wandering bands of indians; and so when Coronado passed that way nearly four centuries ago he also built his campfires under its sheltering walls, but unfortunately he left no record of his journey. For centuries the smooth face of the cliff had attracted aboriginal artists, and hundreds of their interesting pictographs carved with stone chisels may be found on the solid rock. Then came the Spaniards, and apparently every conquistadore who marched through western New Mexico, from Don Juan de Oñate down through the centuries, left the record of his journey on the rock for all future generations to read. The inscriptions not only give the date and name of the leader, but the destination and object of each expedition; and they have been of great value to historians of later times.

The oldest authentic inscription that can be found today is that of Don Juan de Oñate, the first colonizer of New Mexico; but in the eighties both Adolph Bandelier and Frank H. Cushing discovered the names of the eight members of Chamuscado's expedition of 1580. However, they are among the lost inscriptions of El Morro; for no one since that time has been able to find them, although diligent search has been made. We know that they exist somewhere on the face of the great rock; for both Bandelier and Cushing were authentic and careful explorers.

The record left by Don Juan de Oñate on his second journey through western New Mexico, translated into English tells the world today; "Passed by here the governor Don Juan de Oñate to the discovery of the Sea of the South on the sixteenth of April the year 1606." It will be remembered that Oñate started on his first expedition to the discovery of the South Sea in 1598, but returned from Zuñi after receiving the news of Captain Juan de Zaldivar's murder at Acoma, December 4. He set out again in the fall of 1605, and on January 25, 1606, reached what he believed to be the "Sea of the South," but which we now know was the Gulf of California. This inscription was made on the return journey, as shown by the date.

With four hundred cavalry and ten wagons, Governor Manuel de Silva Nieto escorted the first missionaries to Hawikuh in 1629; and on his return he told the story of the expedition in the following inscription: "I am captain-general of the province of New Mexico for the King our Lord. He passed by here on return from the towns of Zuñi on the 29 of July of the year 1629 and he put them in peace on their petition, asking him his favor as vassals of his Majesty, and anew they gave their obedience all of which he did with clemency, zeal, and prudence as like such a most christian (not plain here) most extraordinary and gallant soldier of unending and praised memory."

The Zuñis evidently did not remain at peace very long; for twelve days later Governor Nieto again passed that way, going back to Hawikuh. From this it appears that the tribe rebelled against the priests shortly after Nieto left, and a messenger must have overtaken him before he reached Santa Fé. His second inscription telling the story of his return is the only one on the rock written in poetical form. It reads:

> Here (obliterated) governor
>   Don Francisco Manuel de Silva Nieto
> Whose indubitable arm and valor
>   Have overcome the impossible
> With the wagons of the King, our Lord,
>   A thing he alone put into effect
> Ninth of August Sixteen hundred and twenty-nine
>   That it might be heard, I pass on to Zuñi
>   And carried the faith.

That the Spaniards attempted to avenge the murder of Padre Letrado at Hawikuh is shown by the following inscription: "They passed on the 23rd of March of 1632 year to the avenging of the death of Father Letrado." This is signed by Lujan, a member of the Santa Fé garrison.

One of the finest and best preserved of the inscriptions is that left by General de Vargas, greatest of all the conquistadores. Cut in bold, legible Spanish, like the general himself, we read: "Here was the General Don Diego de Vargas who conquered for our Holy Faith and the Royal Crown all of the New Mexico at his own expense, year of 1692."

The Hopis did not take kindly to the Franciscan missionaries, and were ever rebellious against Spanish rule. In the revolt of 1680 the three priests in charge of the missions at Awatobi and Oraibi were murdered and all the churches destroyed; and from that day they were never again under Spanish domination, although several attempts were made to reconquer them. One of these expeditions is recorded on the rock by the inscription left by Governor Martinez in 1716: "Year of 1716 of 26 of August passed by here Don Feliz Martinez, Governor and Captain-general of this realm, to the reduction and conquest of Moqui (Hopi), and in his company the Reverend Friar Antonio Carmargo, Custodian and Ecclesiastical Judge."

This attempt failed, and Martinez was removed as governor.

The first visit of a catholic bishop to New Mexico is recorded by the following inscription, made when the Bishop of Durango passed the rock on his way to Zuñi: "Day 28 of September 1737 year arrived here the most illustrious Señor Doctor Don Martin de Elizacochea, Bishop of Durango, and day 29 passed on to Zuñi."

This is one of the last of the Spanish inscriptions; and, although there are others of interest, space will not permit of a detailed description. All were carved in the solid rock with knives and daggers. In most cases the work is well done, and the words may be read today almost as easily as when first cut.

An indian trader named Lewis, who camped there during his journeys to and from the Navajo country in the early years of the American occupation of New Mexico, was the first American to discover El Morro, and he guided Lieutenant J. H. Simpson to the rock in 1849, when it first became known to the American authorities. Like the conquistadores of old, Lieutenant Simpson left the record of his visit in the following inscription, still plainly visible: "Lt. J. H. Simpson, U. S. A., & R. H. Kern, artist, visited and copied these inscriptions, September 17, 18, 1849." R. H. Kern returned on August 29, 1851, as shown by another inscription.

The record of the passing of the first emigrant train through that section to California is found in the following inscription: "Isaac T. Holland, July 8, 1858, from Mo. First emigrant train." Other members of this party left their names, two of whom are "John Udell, aged 63, July 8, 1858, first emigrant," and "P. H. Williamson, July 8, 1858, Ohio."

As in the days of the conquistadores this became a noted camping place for our own soldiers after American occupation, and from the appearance of the rock every trooper who passed that way from the days of the old frontier down through the eighties and early nineties, left his name, date and command. There are hundreds of them.

If you have the endurance and a taste for mountain climbing you may add a little zest to your visit by scaling the cliffs of Inscription rock to the ancient ruins on the summit. The trail up the smooth, naked rock is hard but not dangerous; but be sure your heart is in good working order before you attempt it; for it will tax your strength to the utmost. However, you may add more than a little danger to your adventure by ascending the old trail of the prehistoric inhabitants of El Morro, which leads up the perpendicular face of the cliff. This ancient passage is more like a ladder, for in most places there are only holes cut for the hands and feet. On the summit are the ruins of a large pueblo; but the view of the surrounding country is sufficient reward for the hard climb; for it is one of the finest in all New Mexico, and a proper idea of the size and height of this immense rock cannot be obtained in any other way.

XIII. The Penitentes of New Mexico

As you travel over central and northern New Mexico, visiting the ancient missions and pueblos, you will see hundreds of wayside crosses, some large, many small, scattered over hill and vale and rocky gorge in that desert land. In some remote, almost inaccessible corner of the wilderness you may suddenly find one, as though an effort had been made to conceal it from the eye of man for all time; and far away on the summit of a hill you will see another clearly outlined against the evening sky, flooded in the golden light of the setting sun, just as another cross stood on Calvary at the close of another day long centuries ago. Then again you will find them at the side of the road, all with a little pile of stones around the base; and occasionally you will see one with a name and a date. All bore inscriptions once; but the desert sun and winter snows of the passing years soon weather them off. Each one tells a silent story of a bloody religious tragedy, of self-inflicted torture and suffering, the like of which no man has ever known since that other tragedy on Calvary long ago. Each one of those white crosses, bathed in the life-blood of some human being unable to survive the most fearful and agonizing suffering since the days of the Spanish Inquisition, marks the spot where his soul has found a refuge and rest from religious fanaticism.

It is impossible to believe that such things still exist in the United States at the present time unless you have been in the land of the Penitentes. Every visitor to

New Mexico has heard of them, more like a myth than grim reality, and when travelling through the Penitente country their moradas and wayside crosses are pointed out here and there; but very few travellers have ever witnessed the crucifixion with its Cristo, cross bearers, and whipping brothers, who beat their own naked backs with cactus whips until, not infrequently, their very life blood is spattered over the desert sands along the line of march.

These rites are held annually, in some sections several times a year; but the most important occur during the Lenten season, reaching a climax on Good Friday. This strange ceremony has been called the American passion play; but in religious frenzy it surpasses the famous Passion play of Oberammergau. That members of the cult are actually crucified even today in remote sections of the Penitente country is a well known fact in New Mexico.

The Penitente brothers, the official name of the sect, are found in Sandoval, San Miguel, Mora, Taos, Colfax, Rio Arriba, and Valencia counties, New Mexico, and in southern Colorado. The traveler from the east will see the first Penitente cross outlined against the blue sky on the summit of Starvation peak, a few miles west of Las Vegas on the old trail to Santa Fé. In a lonely arroyo twenty miles southwest of the capital is a morada with its accompanying cross high on a nearby hill; and as you go north from Santa Fé to Taos the wayside crosses and moradas increase in number.

Each community of Penitente brothers has a morada, or meeting house. This is built of adobe now, but some of the older ones in remote sections were of stone. These have nearly all disappeared. The old-time morada was without windows, the only opening being the one door-

A Penitente morada, or house of worship

way with a small cross on the roof above the entrance. These are slowly being replaced by the more modern buildings having one or two small windows, and some are without the cross, especially when near the road. The reason for this change is not generally known, but with the advent of the automobile and more tourists it is probable that the brotherhood does not wish the meeting places to attract attention. The morada and the church are two distinct buildings, the former being the meeting place of the Penitente brothers, while the latter is the house of general worship.

The brotherhood of each morada is governed by ten officers, known as Los Hermanos de Luz, or the Brothers of Light. The leader, called the Hermano Mayor, or Chief brother, is the ruler and his word is law. He not only guides the ceremonies, but settles all disputes among the Penitentes of his colony and frequently between the members and outsiders. The other officers are the Warden, Helper, Nurse, Teacher of the novices, Secretary, Pricker, One Who Prays, and Piper.

The principal ceremony takes place during Lent, but another is held on All Saints' Day. Self whipping is practiced during these periods as well as at funerals of members or their families. During the Lenten season the devotions flame to fever heat, culminating with the procession to the cross and the crucifixion on Good Friday.

One of the most weird sounds imaginable is the wild shriek of the Piper's reed flute. Carried on the night air to the farthest corners of the desert, it is the signal for the Penitente tortures to start; and it strikes terror to many a brave heart who hears the wail. Each night during Lent the brothers meet in the morada for prayer and instruction; and every Friday night until the last a procession of self-whippers marches from the meetinghouse to the Calvario cross at the end of the path.

The traveler who is hardy enough to brave the cold and terrors of the night is rewarded after a long wait with as strange a sight as mortal man ever witnessed. As the door of the morada opens the Piper comes forth, followed by five brothers clad only in white muslin trousers, each carrying a whip made of Spanish bayonet fibers with a knot of cholla cactus spines on the end. In the rear is the Hermano Mayor, while one or two others carry lanterns, and another guides the whippers.

With the Piper in the lead, the brothers form in line, singing a doleful chant which adds to the solemnity of the scene. Moving slowly, a step at a time as though in dread of the ordeal before them each of the whippers swings the terrible lash, first over one shoulder and then over the other, and with a swish and a dull thud it lands on the naked back, inflicting a terrible wound, each time cutting deep into the raw flesh. If one of the brothers should falter, or cringe before the torturous lash he is brought back to his self-inflicting punishment by the Guide who cuts into the quivering flesh with a blacksnake whip. When the cross is reached the five flagellants prostrate themselves before it as the others chant a hymn; and at its conclusion they all return to the morada.

Very few outsiders have ever witnessed the mysterious ceremonies in the morada; but those who have been permitted to enter its sacred portal tell a fearful tale of self-inflicted torture with the whip, and walking with bare feet on paths of cholla cactus.

On Ash Wednesday the "Christ" is selected by drawing lots; and during Lent the final preparations are made for the American Passion play. Good Friday is

PROCESSION OF THE PENITENTES TO THE CALVARIO CROSS FOR THE CRUCIFIXION ON GOOD FRIDAY

The only photograph of a Penitente procession known to be in existence

the greatest day of the year for the Penitentes. As the first light of the rising sun dawns over the Sangre de Cristo range to the east, the door of the morada opens and the Penitente brothers come forth for the last ceremony; for some of them it may be the last on earth. It is more than passing strange that these mountains which border the heart of Penitente land on the east should have been named Sangre de Cristo by the Spanish padres of old for this means in English the "blood of Christ."

The procession forms with the Piper at the head, followed by the Cristo staggering under the weight of a huge cross, and several others bearing lighter crosses. Slowly it moves towards the Calvario. In the rear are the whippers, naked to the waist and shivering with the cold; but this is soon forgotten in the agony of the self-inflicted tortures of the cactus whip. On each side are armed men who keep back the curious or any who might attempt to interfere, while kodak fiends are absolutely barred.

The weight of the cross borne by the Cristo is so great that he stumbles frequently and would fall prostrate more than once and probably receive serious injuries under his burden if some brother did not aid him. When the permanent cross at Calvario is reached a circle is formed with fourteen crosses; and around this the Penitentes march, stopping for a prayer at each cross, which represents one of the fourteen stations.

The time for the crucifixion has arrived but the Cristo does not show the least sign of fear as he watches the preparations. When all is ready he is stretched out on the cross he carried, and his arms and legs are bound so tight that the flesh turns blue. The cross is slowly raised with its human burden, and all is silent, except perhaps for the sobs of his mother or his wife. Surely no truer representation of the crucifixion of Our Lord was ever staged in all the world. His body slowly turns purple with cold and lack of circulation. At last the Chief Brother gives a signal, and the poor Cristo is taken down – unconscious, perhaps dead, and carried back to the morada.

If he lives, well and good; but if he does not survive the terrible ordeal he is buried secretly before the dawn of another day; and his boots or shoes, placed on the doorstep of his home, are the only word his relatives ever receive of his fate. It is simply a message that the unfortunate Cristo has gone on a long journey. The location of his grave is unknown to the family until a year later when one of those small wayside crosses so common in that section of New Mexico is erected over the sepulcher. It may be in some secluded spot; it may be at the side of the road; and at the foot of the cross each passing friend places a stone which soon becomes a pile known as the descanso.

Nor do the whippers always survive their fearful self-inflicted tortures; for it is not uncommon for one or more to die from exhaustion or infection brought on by their wounds and suffering. When this occurs they too are taken from the morada at midnight and buried secretly; and the next morning their relatives find their shoes outside of the door. I was told that when a Penitente dies from suffering caused by either crucifixion or whipping he is buried in an upright position in the grave, but I was unable to verify the statement from authoritative sources.

The last service of Lent takes place on the night of Good Friday. Just before darkness has fallen the weird notes of the Piper's flute pierce the night air – a summons to the people, and the entire Mexican population, men, women and children, turns out. A procession forms at the morada and marches to the little catholic church, where the service known among the Penitentes as tinieblas is held in utter darkness. The Penitente translation of this tinieblas service is "earthquake"; and they evidently look upon it as a culmination of the actual occurrence on Calvary after the crucifixion of Christ.

The Penitentes of the Southwest are descended from the Flagellantes that swept Europe in the Middle Ages. This sect appeared first in Italy in 1210, and with amazing rapidity the strange rites spread during the next fifty years until thousands of devotees were seen in processions throughout all Italy, carrying banners and crosses and lashing themselves with leather whips. The Flagellante movement grew with the passing centuries until it had spread throughout all southern Europe; but the date it was carried across the sea to the New World is not definitely known. However, it seems to be the general belief that the present sect is descended from the laymen's organization known as the Third Order of Saint Francis, and during the Spanish regime practically everyone of any consequence in New Mexico was a member. The expulsion of the Franciscans from New Mexico after the Mexican revolution left the Third Order without regular government, and the theory is that it drifted into the present Penitente organization.

However, the fact that the Penitentes existed before the revolution is shown by an ancient document in the cathedral of Saint Francis at Santa Fé. Under date of September 17, 1794, mention is made of the "Venerable Third Order of Penitente," which, it states, was founded in the two villages of Santa Fé and Santa Cruz, and "has been in existence since the earliest years of the Conquest."

People who have never been in the Penitente country believe that the sect is dying out, but this is not the case. In the region north of Santa Fé are many moradas where whipping processions take place every year, and a crucifixion is not infrequent. Alcalde is entirely a Penitente settlement, and they are so strong in the Taos and Abiquiu sections that they have a strong influence on politics. With the advent of the automobile tourist the decline has set in, and in a few years public performances will be rare. In former times only a few outsiders ever penetrated the Penitente country during the Lenten season; but now the automobile brings them in by the hundred. The condition at Alcalde in 1926 is only a fair example of what may be expected at every morada in a very short time. On account of being near to Santa Fé many machines were parked around the morada with headlights turned on the building the entire night preceding Good Friday. As a result the brothers remained within; and there was no procession to the cross at daybreak.

XIV. The Hopi Missions of Arizona

The Hopi Missions – San Bernardino de Awatobi – Cardenas discovers the Grand Canyon – Theory of the Hopi villages as the Seven Cities of Cibola – Destruction of Awatobi – San Francisco de Oraibi – Padre Garces discovers the Crossings of the Fathers – Escalante and Dominguez – Inscription House – Jacob Hamblin and the Mormons – Lee's Ferry – Garces' journey – San Bartolome de Shongopovi – San Buenaventura de Mishongnovi – Shipaulovi – Walpi or Kisakobi – Death of Padre Garces.

THE HOPI MISSIONS. Of the five missions founded in 1629 among the Hopis in Arizona all were destroyed in the Rebellion of 1680, and never again were these indians under Spanish rule. Several subsequent attempts to subjugate them resulted in failure; and when discovered by the Americans in the latter sixties the only signs left of the white man's religion were a few stone walls – ruins of ancient churches built by the Franciscan fathers nearly three centuries ago for the salvation of souls on the Painted Desert. Only the traditions of the black-robed priests they murdered long, long ago have been handed down from generation to generation.

The present Hopiland is the ancient Spanish province of Tusayan, which embraced the land of the Moquis. This name is erroneous but it persisted through the centuries until within the last twenty years when the persistent efforts of modern writers gradually changed it to Hopi, the native name of this tribe.

Although naturally friendly, the Hopis never took

kindly to any other religion than their own, and to this day they observe the world famous Snake and Flute ceremonies and many other native rites. Attempts made by Americans to convert them to a religion they do not understand have failed. Many years ago the Moravians founded a mission at old Oraibi, but it was never a success. Converts came slowly and did not remain true; and year after year, within sight of the steeple of this christian church, the Snake dance was held.

Sunshine, a Baptist mission at the foot of the Middle mesa, near Mishongnovi and Shipaulovi, the "twin cities of the desert," is another example of misguided efforts and failure. During a visit by the author to Hopiland in 1907, the missionary at Sunshine proudly exhibited the first Hopi baby ever born in christianity. This missionary was a very devout woman, but she hated everything pertaining to the Hopi religion, and refused to witness either the Snake or Flute dances, or, in fact, any other ceremony. Consequently all of the indians thoroughly hated and distrusted her, and the parents of this child were her only converts. To them she preached, and this baby was her sole reward for years of labor.

This was the attitude of all missionaries among the Hopis in those days. They did not understand the native point of view, and did not seem to want to. All Hopi rites were regarded as institutions of the devil; yet the missionaries failed to show these indians where christianity would be better than the religion they have known since the beginning of time. For years the indian authorities and congress have been swamped with petitions and pleas to stop the Snake dance by force; but no logical reason has ever been given for such an act. It would be a big mistake, just another great blunder in the indian problem. Several years ago this intolerance led the Hopis to request their agent to prohibit kodaks in the villages during the Snake dance. Cameras were permitted years ago, and on five different occasions the author was allowed to take photographs by the dozen without a word of protest; but the efforts to have the ceremony stopped had its influence on the head men who feared that these pictures would give the white people in the East a false impression of the dance, and Mr. Leo Crane, the Hopi agent, wisely issued the order prohibiting cameras in the villages at that time. Let the Snake dance go on. The time will come when it will die a natural death; for it is on the decline now. Missionaries, if you would christianize the Hopis take a lesson from the success of the catholic priests among the pueblos in New Mexico; study the Hopi religion and embrace it with christianity.

There are now eight pueblos in Hopiland: Walpi, Haño, and Sichomovi on the First, or East mesa; the twin cities of Mishongnovi and Shipaulovi, and Shongopovi on the Second, or Middle mesa, and old Oraibi and Hotevilla on the Third, or West mesa. Old Oraibi, which occupies the same site as when Tovar and Cardeñas visited the land in 1540, is now almost deserted and stands in ruins, although it was once, little more than twenty years ago, the largest village in Tusayan. After the upheaval in 1906 between the friendly and hostile elements the latter withdrew and founded Hotevilla to the northwest; and since then most of the families of old Oraibi have moved to the new pueblo.

The Snake dance, the greatest present day attraction of the Hopis, takes place in August; and during the even years it is held at Hotevilla, Shipaulovi, and Shongopovi, and in the odd years at Walpi and Mishongnovi. The automobiles have brought in so many visitors during the last fifteen years that the dance has become very much of a commercial proposition at Walpi and Hotevilla, where it is witnessed by thousands; but at the other villages it retains much of its old-time form and meaning. The Flute dance, an interesting ceremony which is visited by very few whites, alternates with the Snake dance, being held at Hotevilla, Shipaulovi and Shongopovi in the odd years, and at Walpi and Mishongnovi in the even years. These are both described in detail in another chapter.

The Hopi villages may be reached from either Gallup, Holbrook, Winslow, or Flagstaff on both the Santa Fé railroad and the transcontinental automobile highway. The distance from Gallup is about three hundred miles; from Holbrook to Walpi, ninety miles and to Oraibi, one hundred twenty; from Winslow to Oraibi, eighty miles and to Walpi, one hundred ten; from Flagstaff to Hotevilla is about one hundred five miles, with the other villages only a short distance farther.

SAN BERNARDINO DE AWATOBI. At old Awatobi, an ancient Hopi pueblo far out on the Painted Desert, are the ruins of San Bernardino mission, the first building erected by civilized man in Arizona. Only storm-ravaged, crumbling walls, surrounded by the ruined desert city of an ancient people, are left; but thereby hangs an intensely interesting tale of the days of the padres in the old Spanish Southwest. Awatobi, meaning the "high place of the bow," was an important Hopi city of ancient Arizona, but it was destroyed by fire and spear two centuries and a quarter ago. Today the site is marked by jagged walls protruding here and there from the desert sands, nine miles southeast of modern Walpi.

One of the original villages of the ancient Spanish province of Tusayan, Awatobi was first visited by Europeans when Don Pedro de Tovar, sent out by Coronado from Hawikuh, reached Hopiland in July or August, 1540. This expedition, the first white men in the present state of Arizona, led to the discovery of the Grand Canyon of the Colorado river; for the tales brought back by Tovar, telling of that great natural wonder, induced Coronado to send Don Lopez de Cardeñas on a tour of discovery into northeastern Arizona during August, September, and October, 1540. Cardeñas went direct to Awatobi and the other Hopi villages, where he secured guides, and then passed on to the discovery of the Grand Canyon.

It is interesting to note in this connection that at the time of the visits of Tovar and Cardeñas seven Hopi villages, the same number as in Cibola, were reported to Coronado; and the author believes that there is just the possibility that these may have been the "Seven Cities of Cibola," intended in the descriptions given by the indians to the early Spaniards. Fray Marcos de Niza passed through southern Arizona, and, had it not been that Estevan veered a little to the northeast in his general course, it is more than probable that the padre would have eventually reached modern Hopiland. In such an event the seven cities of the ancient Hopi would have been known today as the "Seven Cities of Cibola." It is a well known fact that the legend of seven cities with houses set with precious stones and covered with gold, originated in indian tales; and what is more probable than that the seven Hopi villages, surrounded by the Painted Desert, a land of many colors, was this mythical Cibola? Coronado took it for granted that Zuñi was Cibola because of Fray Marcos's description, but only five of those seven cities have been identified in the ruins of today.

When Don Pedro de Tovar was sent by Coronado to explore the province of Tusayan with a force of seventeen horsemen and one or two foot soldiers, he was accompanied by Fray Juan de Padilla. The reception of the first white men who visited Hopiland is an interesting item after the passing of nearly four centuries. The Spaniards reached Awatobi at night, and concealed themselves under the edge of the mesa, where they were discovered at daylight by some passing indians. The feelings of the Hopis when they saw this company of strange men, mounted on horses, an animal they had never seen before, we will never know; but they evidently did not regard the white men as gods, for they went out to meet them armed with bows and arrows, shields and war clubs. A line of sacred meal was drawn across the trail as notice that the village was closed to visitors. During the parley that took place at this meeting one of the Spaniards attempted to cross this sacred line and an indian struck his horse. This precipitated a clash, and in the fight that followed the Hopis were defeated; but no lives were lost, and the visitors were permitted to enter Awatobi. Doctor J. Walter Fewkes has identified the site of this battle as at Antelope spring, on the old Zuñi trail.

After the departure of Cardeñas following his discovery of the Grand Canyon, the Hopis saw no Spaniards for forty-three years; and the memory of their visits had almost become a tradition when Espejo, the next of the conquistadores, reached Awatobi in 1583.

He was well received, the people giving him presents of "hand towels with tassels," no doubt dance kilts made of cotton. Don Juan de Oñate, the next visitor, arrived at the Hopi villages in the spring of 1606; some say in 1598, but it must be remembered that he turned back from Zuñi in December, 1598, after receiving the news of the murder of Don Juan de Zaldivar at Acoma; and the record on Inscription rock shows that he passed there on his second expedition during which he discovered the "Sea of the South" on April 16, 1606, and undoubtedly made his first visit to Hopiland.

According to the best information the five Hopi missions were founded in 1629 by three priests, Francisco Porras, Andrés Gutierrez, and Cristobal de la Concepcion, who, with ten soldiers, arrived in ancient Tusayan on San Bernardino's day, and for this reason their first mission, which was established at Awatobi, was named in honor of this saint. While these missionaries were on their way to Arizona an apostate indian told the Hopis that the Spaniards would rob them, burn their pueblos, and devour their children. Even before that time some of the Hopis had believed that horses were man-eating animals. But in spite of these stories the padres were well received and made many converts during the first three or four years.

The old Spanish chronicles tell us that this success was due to Padre Porras, who performed a miracle by restoring the sight of the blind son of a chief. According to this old story a powerful chief brought his twelve-year-old son, who had been blind from birth, as a challenge to the padre and said: "If your God is as powerful as you say, ask him to give my son his eyesight."

After a prayer Father Porras made a paste of earth mixed with his own saliva, which he placed over the blind eyes, saying the one word, "Epheta," and the child instantly recovered his sight. The indians were so astonished at the miracle that a thousand of them were converted on the spot.

In his mission work, Padre Porras incurred the enmity of the native priests, and on June 28, 1633, they poisoned him while at Walpi. The fate of the other two priests who accompanied him to the Hopi villages in 1629 is unknown, but they were probably martyrs to those first efforts to carry the cross into the Painted Desert. The names of the missionaries stationed in Tusayan after the death of Porras are not known definitely; but in 1650 Fray José de Espeleta took charge of the work, and in 1674 José de Figueroa and Agustin de Santa Maria arrived in Hopiland. All three were murdered in 1680.

The great Pueblo Rebellion of 1680 spread to the far-off Hopi villages, and without the slightest warning they arose on August 10, killing four Franciscan fathers stationed in Tusayan. Padre Figueroa met death at Awatobi; and, according to an old Hopi legend, Espeleta and another priest were thrown over the cliffs at Oraibi. Some say that this was Padre Santa Maria, but the old records indicate that he was murdered at Walpi. Fray José de Truxillo was slain at San Bartolome mission at old Shongopovi; and thus the last of the permanent missions in Hopiland came to an end.

After the reconquest of New Mexico in 1692, De Vargas marched to Tusayan, and received the submission of the pueblos of Awatobi, Walpi, Mishongnovi, and Shongopovi; but he did not attempt to enter Oraibi on account of the hostile attitude of the natives. He found that Awatobi was protected by a wall around the town with an entrance so narrow that only one man could enter at a time.

It appears that the natives of Awatobi welcomed the Spaniards, and thus they incurred the undying hatred of the other villages. This friendly attitude, however, was not shared by Tapolo, chief of Awatobi, as will be seen.

After the reconquest the chief of Oraibi invited the Spaniards to send a priest to Hopiland, but whether he was sincere, in view of subsequent events, is very doubtful. This invitation was accepted by Fray Garaycoechea, who visited Tusayan in the spring of 1700, but only went as far as Awatobi, where he baptized seventy-three. He found that the church, destroyed in 1680, had been rebuilt, and that a majority of the inhabitants wanted the mission rehabilitated. The natives of the other villages were all hostile to the Spaniards and they especially hated the black-robed priests; and when Padre Garaycoechea's friends at Awatobi warned him not to proceed any farther he wisely decided to remain at that pueblo.

This brings us down to the great tragedy of the Painted Desert, the destruction of ancient Awatobi; a story of cruel desert warfare handed down from Hopi father to son these past two hundred years and more. After the Rebellion of 1680 peace and happiness reigned throughout Tusayan until Padre Garaycoechea's visit to Awatobi in 1700. According to the old legend this village became a Sodom and Gomorrah after the priest left. The men beat solitary workers in the fields, attacked women from other pueblos, and robbed hunters of their game.

There is no doubt but that the whole trouble grew

out of the friendship of the Awatobians for the Spanish priests and the christian religion. The Hopis of the other villages, and even Tapolo, chief of Awatobi, looked upon the christian converts as sorcerers and bad people who would bring evil upon the country. Finally, Tapolo plotted with Espeleta, chief of Oraibi, for the destruction of Awatobi; and one day a band of Oraibi warriors suddenly attacked the offenders, but were repulsed after a terrific battle in which many were killed on both sides. Alarm spread throughout all Hopiland, and the head men gathered at a great council of war held at Walpi. Tapolo declared that his people were christians, and the council, fearful that the hated "black robes" would return to the land and rebuild churches for these neophytes, decreed that the Awatobians must die. Fighting men were summoned from the other villages, and in the night a picturesque army of naked, gayly painted desert warriors descended upon the ill-fated pueblo, each man armed with bow and arrows, spear and war club, and carrying a torch and a bundle of greasewood.

The time was well chosen, for the inhabitants were attending a great religious ceremony in a large kiva (an underground room in the public plaza), and before the Awatobi warriors were aware of the presence of an enemy the invaders had captured the village. The ladder was withdrawn from the kivi, and the people were caught in a death trap. Arrows were shot into their midst, the bundles of greasewood and torches were thrown down upon them, and soon the room was a mass of flames. Great quantities of red peppers, gathered from the houses and thrown into the fire, added to the suffering of the doomed people, and the place became a hell from which none escaped.

RUINS OF SAN BERNARDINO MISSION AT OLD AWATOBI, ARIZONA
The oldest building in Arizona built by Europeans

The destruction of Awatobi was complete. No children were killed intentionally; but only the women who knew the tribal songs and ceremonies were spared, and two men of all the village escaped. One was saved by the Oraibi chieftain because he could grow peaches. The other knew the secret of raising good corn, and was taken captive to Mishongnovi. And to this day Oraibi is known as the "place of the peaches," and Mishongnovi is noted for its large corn crops.

This ends the history of Awatobi, for no attempt was ever made again to rebuild it, or.rehabilitate the Hopi missions. In 1895 when Doctor J. Walter Fewkes conducted extensive excavations at the ruins he discovered evidence of a great conflagration, and almost every object removed from the eastern section of the village was scorched. Many of the roof and floor beams had been burned and others charred, while all of the rooms were filled with ashes and the walls had been cracked by intense heat.

The church at Awatobi was the largest erected at the Hopi villages; and the few ruined walls which mark the site are the best preserved of any of the Tusayan missions. Much of the building has been buried beneath the shifting sands of the Painted Desert; and in his work Doctor Fewkes sank a trench ten feet deep, but failed to reach the floor. A quantity of glass, copper nails, an iron hook and a copper bell pivot were found in the excavations made at the foundation. Plenty of evidence of a massacre was discovered in the southeastern section of the pueblo, east of the mission, in the form of human bones and skulls. The skulls had been crushed or pierced with some sharp weapons, showing violent death. Pieces of the ancient mission bell were found in 1892 by Doctor Fewkes during his first visit to Awatobi. The ruins of the old bell towers, from fifteen to twenty feet high, which probably supported a balcony, form the best section of the historic building left standing today.

SAN FRANCISCO DE ORAIBI. A large flat rock and a pile of stones are pointed out at old Oraibi as the site of San Francisco mission, erected in 1629 by Fray Francisco Porras and his two companions, Andrés Gutierrez and Cristobal de la Concepcion. Oraibi, a native word meaning the "place of the rock," was the largest and most important of the Hopi pueblos when the first Spaniards went to Tusayan in 1540. At that time the population was reported at 14,000, but this was probably greatly exaggerated.

Little is known of the history of this mission. The people joined in the Rebellion of 1680, and after murdering their two priests, José de Espeleta and Agustin de Santa Maria, Hopi tradition tells us that they threw the bodies over the cliffs; and from that day to this no "black robe" has ever been stationed at Oraibi.

Oraibi is the only Hopi village that occupies the same site as it did in 1540, all of the others having been moved to higher locations after 1680. It kept its place as the largest pueblo down through the centuries until 1906, when the hostiles withdrew and built Hotevilla in September of that year. The story of the founding of this village is told in another chapter.

Although the Grand Canyon was discovered by Cardeñas from the eastern side nearly four centuries ago, 236 years elapsed before civilized man reached the western rim. On June 26, 1776, Padre Francisco Garcés, whose extensive travels throughout the Southwest between 1768 and 1776 have never been surpassed by any other explorer in North America, came upon the mighty gorge from the west, and crossed the river at the point afterwards famous as the "Crossing of the Fathers." Garcés was the first white man to cross the great chasm, for Cardeñas was unable to find a way from the rim to the river in 1540.

The point at which Padre Garcés crossed the Colorado river on June 26, 1776, was used by other priests who followed in his footsteps. Close upon his heels came two more Franciscan friars, Silvestre Velez de Escalante and Francisco Atanasio Dominguez, who crossed the Grand Canyon November 8, 1776, on the same trail followed by Garcés only a few months previous.

While stationed at Zuñi the year before this same Padre Escalante had crossed the desert to the Hopi pueblos and was the first of the hated "black robes" who had dared make this journey since Padre Garaycoechea's visit to Awatobi three-quarters of a century before. Escalante spent eight days of June, 1775, in Tusayan. He found the Hopis as antagonistic as ever against christianity, and in his report of the journey he advised that a presidio be established at their pueblos so that they could be converted by force of arms. No action of this kind, however, was ever taken by the Spanish authorities at Santa Fé.

In speaking of his journey of 1775, Padre Escalante tells us that there were seven Hopi pueblos with a population of 7,494. This gives some additional color to the author's theory that the Tusayan pueblos, surrounded by the terrible Painted Desert, were the original Seven Cities of Cibola. In Escalante's time two-thirds of this population was at Oraibi alone. While in Tusayan Escalante went west to the rim of the Grand Canyon of the Colorado, which he called the Rio Grande de los

Cosninas; but he returned without finding a crossing. Those old-time Spanish padres and conquistadores left little of the Southwest for the Americans of later generations to discover. During his sojourn in Tusayan, Padre Escalante conceived the idea of a northern route from Santa Fé to California by going around the head of the Grand Canyon. Of course he had no idea where this was; but, believing that it could be crossed farther to the north, he set out from Santa Fé on July 29, 1776, in company with Padre Dominguez and eight men, following the aboriginal trails that had been used by the natives for centuries.

This ancient route, now known as the old Spanish trail, goes from Santa Fé to Taos, from which place the padre explorers set out through the unknown. Travelling across northwestern New Mexico and the southern corner of Colorado into Utah, they went as far as Utah Lake, where they turned southwest down the Sevier river valley to the upper waters of the Virgin and on across southern Nevada and California to Los Angeles. On the return journey they followed almost in the footsteps of Padre Garcés, and thus we find them on November 8 at the crossing of the Grand Canyon discovered by the former just nineteen weeks before. Crossing the Colorado river at this point, Escalante reached the Hopi villages for the second time on November 16. He remained there until the twentieth and then started back to Santa Fé, where he arrived January 2, 1777.

It is interesting to note in this connection that in Navajo Canyon, one hundred fifty miles north of Flagstaff, where few white people have ever been, even to this day, is a cliff ruin known as Inscription House, so named from an almost illegible inscription, "Carlos Arnais 1661," carved on one of the walls. Who Carlos Arnais was or what he was doing in that section of Arizona one hundred fifteen years before Garcés, Escalante and Dominguez passed that way, we do not know today; but he was some adventurous Spaniard who wandered into that lonely corner of the world and probably left his bones to bleach on the desert sands with this inscription as his only requiem. Inscription House is an interesting ruin of forty-eight rooms twenty-five miles north of Red Lake and seven miles west of the trail to the famous Rainbow Natural Bridge.

The crossing of the Grand Canyon discovered by Padre Garcés in 1776 and used by Escalante and Dominguez is now known under the appropriate name of "El Vado de los Padres," or "The Crossing of the Fathers." Before the coming of the Spanish padres, this place had long been used by the Ute indians in their wanderings and it is sometimes referred to as the Ute Ford. Over three-quarters of a century later Jacob Hamblin, famous in the history of the Mormon church as the "Apostle to the Lamanites" because of his missionary work among the indians, was sent out by Brigham Young to find a passage across the Grand Canyon and to mark a trail for Mormon emigrants to the south. In November, 1858, he reached the Crossing of the Fathers, and for many years it was a noted landmark on the old Mormon trail from Great Salt Lake to the south. This ford is located exactly on the boundary line between Utah and Arizona.

It was hard to get wagons up and down the canyon at this point, and in 1860 Hamblin discovered a more practical route for wagons at the mouth of the Paria river, thirty-five miles southwest of the Crossing of the Fathers. The Colorado river is too deep to ford at this point, and it was 1864 before Hamblin succeeded in crossing on a raft; but it was not until early in 1872 that the first ferry was established. This was accomplished by John D. Lee, who was then hiding from the federal government on account of his part in the Mountain Meadows massacre on September 16, 1857, in what is now Washington county, Utah. He called it the Saint's Ferry, but from that day to this it has been known as Lee's Ferry, the name given on all the maps. This was the route ever afterwards followed by the Latter Day Saints in their journeys between Utah and the Mormon settlements in northern Arizona. While visiting one of his wives at Panguitch, Utah, Lee was captured November 8, 1874, by William Stokes, a deputy United States marshal, hiding under some straw in a log chicken coop. He was found guilty of murder in the first degree after a lengthy trial at Beaver City, Utah, during September, 1876; and on March 23, 1877, John D. Lee was executed before a firing squad at Mountain Meadows, Utah, the scene of the terrible massacre of just twenty years before in which one hundred twenty emigrants to California were murdered, presumably by indians.

Some twenty years ago Lee's Ferry was used extensively by Arizona sheepmen who purchased many sheep from the Mormons and drove them down over the old trail from Utah. In 1908 a railroad was projected from Salt Lake City down across Utah to Arizona, crossing the Colorado river at the old Mormon ferry; but after the survey was made the matter was dropped, probably because of the cost.

After this diversion we will return to Padre Garcés, the wandering missionary priest of the Southwest who made one of the longest and most important journeys on record. Leaving Tubac, Arizona, on October 21,

1775, by order of Don Antonio Maria Bucareli y Vrsua, viceroy of Mexico, or New Spain, he travelled across southern Arizona to the Colorado river; thence up that stream to Mohave, and west to San Gabriel mission, California. From there he came back through the Tulares to Mohave, from which place he went east to the Hopi villages; and to this intrepid Spanish priest we must give the honor of being the first white man to find a route across the Grand Canyon from rim to rim. Travelling eastward over the Painted Desert, he reached Oraibi July 2. The Hopis received him kindly, but refused to be baptized; and so he set out on his return journey July 4, 1776, going back to Mohave, then down the Colorado to Yuma, and up the Gila, finally reaching San Xavier del Bac mission on September 17, 1776. While it is in no way connected with this history, it is interesting to note that Padre Garcés was murdered by the Yuma indians at Concepcion mission, near Yuma during the massacre of July 17, 1781, when he and Padre Barraneche were beaten to death.

SAN BARTOLOME DE SHONGOPOVI. The old pueblo of Shongopovi, on the Middle mesa, meaning the "place of chumoa grass," is the site of the ancient Spanish mission of San Bartolomé, founded in 1629 by Padre Porras and his two companions. The original pueblo of Spanish times stood on a ridge of the foothills, near an ancient spring east of the present town, where the ruins of the old village have been identified. At this place the three missionaries of 1629 built a church, with San Buenaventura mission at Mishongnovi as a visita. In 1680 Fray José de Truxillo, the missionary in charge, was murdered, and the building destroyed; and the only trace of it today is found in the walls of a sheep corral, which formed one end of the church.

SAN BUENAVENTURA DE MISHONGNOVI. On two high eminences, or tables of the Middle mesa are the "twin cities of the Painted Desert," Mishongnovi and Shipaulovi, both built after the Rebellion of 1680. The original Mishongnovi of the Spanish period stood in the hills at the foot of the mesa and west of the present village, where the ruins have been discovered in recent times. This is the site of San Buenaventura, one of the missions of 1629, erected as a visita of San Bartolomé at old Shongopovi, three miles away; but the church was destroyed in 1680, and no trace of it remains.

Fear of Spanish vengeance led the people of Mishongnovi as well as those of Shongopovi to abandon their pueblos after the Rebellion of 1680, and move higher up on the mesa to sites that could be better defended. The name Mishongnovi means "at the place of the other which remains erect," referring to two large stone pillars. One has fallen, but the other still stands on a terrace below the present village, where many ceremonies are held.

Shipaulovi, meaning "mosquitoes," did not exist prior to 1680, but after the rebellion it was founded on its present picturesque location by a number of families from Shongopovi and Walpi. The original stock of the largest clan of this village originally came from Homolobi, one of the ancient Hopi homes now in ruins near Winslow, Arizona, which was abandoned on account of mosquitoes; and from this incident the present pueblo takes its name.

THE WALPI OR KISAKOBI MISSION. Old Walpi, or Kisakobi, was the site of another of the Hopi missions, but whether it was the last of the five to be erected we cannot say. About 1629, or shortly afterwards Padre Porras and his two companion priests built a church at this pueblo, then located on the northwest side of the west point of the east mesa, where the ruins have been identified by Doctor J. Walter Fewkes, of the Bureau of American Ethnology.

Kisakobi, meaning the "place of the ladder house," frequently referred to as old Walpi, was the second pueblo built by the Walpi people in Tusayan, the ruins of the first being located on a lower terrace among the foothills on the northwest side of the mesa. This village, called Kuchaptuvela, the "ash hill terrace," was the home of the Walpians when Tovar and Cardeñas passed through the land in 1540. Kisakobi, the second village, was built about 1629, the year the padres arrived in Tusayan. The name of the mission is not known definitely.

This is the site of the first tragedy of Hopiland. While visiting the church at old Walpi, Padre Porras, the father of the Hopi missions, was poisoned June 28, 1633, by the native priests, whose hatred he had incurred. Nothing more is known of the history of this mission until the Rebellion of 1680. Some accounts state that Fray Agustin de Santa Maria was killed there at that time, but the best authorities inform us that this priest was murdered at Oraibi. The church was destroyed in 1680, and all trace of the building has disappeared.

After the revolt of 1680 Kisakobi was abandoned because of the fear of Spanish vengeance and continual raids by the Navajos, Apaches, and Utes, and modern Walpi, the "place of the gap," was founded at its present location on top of the mesa. In olden times this was practically impregnable from attack by wandering war parties, or an avenging Spanish army.

Thus ended all attempts to christianize the Hopis

until Arizona came under the rule of the United States; but even to this day the efforts of missionaries have met with little better success. Ever since the coming of the first Spanish padres down through the centuries to the present time, these indians have opposed the white man's religion. Their Snake and Flute dances, and many other interesting religious ceremonies have given them comfort in adversity as well as prosperity. When their crops were almost burned out by the fierce sun devils, the gods of the underworld [2] have always answered the prayers of the Snake and Flute priests and sent rain. That was the answer these desert indians gave to the Spanish priests long ago; and that is the answer they give the missionaries today.

[2] The Hopi heaven is called the "underworld," and is below the earth, not above.

XV. The Southern Arizona Missions

The southern missions — Padre Eusebio Francisco Kino — San Gabriel de Guevavi, the first mission — The Pima Rebellion of 1751 — Lost Spanish mines — San José de Tumacacori — Pete Kitchen's famous pioneer road — San Xavier del Bac — San Ignacio de Sonoita — Jamac — Santa Gertrudes de Tubac — San José and San Agustin del Tucson — San Cayetano de Calabazas — San Luis de Bacuancos — Arivaca — San Francisco de Ati — San Serafin — The treasure of San Bernardino ranch.

THE SOUTHERN MISSIONS. Southern Arizona was the only section of the present Southwest included in the Jesuit mission field of Mexico; but the priests of that order were endowed with courage and zeal equal to the Franciscans who had charge of all New Mexico and northern Arizona. Although the Jesuits did not begin their work until after the Pueblo Rebellion of 1680 they constantly faced death from the fierce Apaches; and not for a single day in all their years of mission labor were these padres free from this menace. Many were the bloody raids, and many were the churches left in ruins. Like the Franciscans, the Jesuits had forever left their native land across the sea to carry the cross into the desert. Theirs was such a life of constant hardships that we cannot comprehend it today; and added to their privations was the ever present danger of a torturous death at the hands of the blood thirsty Apaches.

Old Arizona was a harsh, cruel land at best, barren and forbidding, where life was one continual fight against the desert and the Apache indians; but in defiance of both the desert and Apaches those brave Jesuit padres established their missions among the more peaceable Piman tribes. Although they conquered the desert, those priests of old never succeeded in converting the fierce Apache warriors, and the Spanish soldiers were unable to hold them in check. Year after year the missions were raided and the priests and their neophytes murdered; but in spite of all this, more came from the far southland of Mexico and even from Spain across the sea to offer themselves as martyrs on the Apache blood altar, vainly hoping to convert those desert warriors to the cross. The missions were abandoned long years ago, for the padres fought a hopeless battle; and, with the exception of San Xavier del Bac, they have all passed into the land of memories. Only a few crumbling adobe walls are left here and there to tell the heroic story of those tragic times.

Padre Eusebio Francisco Kino holds the same place in the Sonora and southern Arizona mission field that Padre Junipero Serra does to California; for the last twenty-four years of his life, from 1687 to 1711, were devoted to the salvation of the souls of the desert indians of what was then northern Mexico. During this period he established twenty-nine missions, with seventy-three visitas and baptized more than 48,000 neophytes. Eight of these missions were in what is now southern Arizona. With his headquarters at Nuestra Señora de los Dolores mission in Sonora, he wandered about from tribe to tribe; and during those years he made thirteen journeys into Arizona, exploring every corner of the southern part of the state, together with much of northern Sonora. His last visit to Arizona was in 1702. The remainder of his life was spent at Dolores

THE SOUTHERN ARIZONA MISSIONS 231

mission, where he was murdered by an indian on March 15, 1711, at the age of nearly sixty-seven years.

The dates of the founding of the southern Arizona missions and many other important incidents of that period were unknown for many years, but the discovery several years ago of Father Kino's lost journal, made by Doctor Herbert E. Bolton, of the University of California, has given us an accurate history of an important period in the Southwest. This great missionary was a Jesuit friar, who, while a professor in the University of Ingolstadt, Bavaria, promised to devote the remainder of his life to the converstion of the American indians if, through the intercession of Saint Francis Xavier, he should recover from a fever. True to his vow he went to Mexico in 1680, and began his lifework; and the finest of his missions that has come down to the present day he named San Xavier del Bac in honor of his patron saint.

On November 20, 1686, he left Mexico City for the unknown northland, arriving in upper Sonora, then known as Pimería Alta, in February, 1687. The Pimería Alta of Kino's time extended from the Altar river, in Sonora, to the Gila, part of which was included in the Gadsden purchase of 1853 and added to Arizona.

On March 13, 1687, Father Kino founded Nuestra Señora de los Dolores mission, which now stands in ruins on the Hacienda de Dolores in the valley of the San Miguel river, near Cupurpe, Sonora, about one hundred miles south of Tucson. This was his headquarters for the last twenty-four years of his life, and during this period he made over forty journeys through Sonora and southern Arizona, covering more than 20,000 miles. The walls of this historic mission have disappeared entirely and only the foundation can be found. The site is forty-eight miles from Magdalena, Sonora, over a very rough road.

Thirteen of these desert pilgrimages in search of souls for the cross were in what is now Arizona, and he was the first white man to visit many sections of the southern half of that state. In November, 1694, he discovered the great ruin at Casa Grande and held mass within those ancient walls, which centuries before had sheltered a race of people that has vanished from the face of the earth, leaving this as their only record. On February 5, 1702, Father Kino left Dolores mission on his last journey to Arizona. Reaching the mouth of the Gila on the twenty-eighth he travelled down to the Gulf of California, and then turned back to Sonoita mission, where he arrived March 22. Returning to Dolores mission this great missionary explorer spent the remainder of his life there, making short journeys through the surrounding country.

The Jesuits remained in control of the southern Arizona missions until ordered out of Spain and its possessions by King Carlos III in 1767, when the Franciscan fathers were placed in charge. The latter remained until they were expelled from Mexico in 1824.

SAN GABRIEL DE GUEVAVI. The first mission in what is now southern Arizona was San Gabriel de Guevavi, founded by Father Kino between 1687 and 1691. While the latter date is more generally accepted, the Right Reverend A. B. Salpointe, Roman Catholic bishop of Arizona, has raised a slight doubt by the statement in his *Soldiers of the Cross* that it was in 1690; but this is clearly a mistake, no doubt arising from the date of Padre Salvatierra's arrival at Dolores mission. However, the Right Reverend Thomas O'Gorman declares that Guevavi was built in 1687; but he fails to give his authority.

As already related Kino's first mission in Sonora was Nuestra Señora de los Dolores, founded March 13, 1687. He next established San Ignacio at Caborca, then San José de Himeris, and finally Nuestra Señora de los Remedios, all in modern Sonora, in the year 1687. Dolores is not far from the present Arizona line, and it is possible that in some of his wanderings he went as far north as Guevavi, but this is only conjecture.

Until the discovery of Father Kino's journal it was generally believed that Guevavi was not founded until 1720, nine years after his death; but this ancient manuscript gives the best evidence in establishing the date as in 1691. In December, 1690, Padre Juan Maria de Salvatierra [3] was appointed superior and visitador of the missions of Sinaloa and Sonora. He went immediately to Nuestra Señora de los Dolores, where he and Kino made plans for spiritual conquests throughout Pimería Alta and as far as California. They set out on their first journey and while at an indian village called Tucubabia, on the Altar river, in northern Sonora, a a delegation of Sobaipuris visited them with a request that they send a priest to their country. This tribe, now extinct, lived along the Santa Cruz river in Kino's time, and the padres returned with the messengers to their village at Guevavi, where they established San Gabriel mission. This was Kino's first entrance into modern Arizona, and it was early in 1691. That he and Salvatierra established a mission at Guevavi at that time there can be no doubt; for we find that he made this a

---

[3] The Life and Explorations of Salvatierra has recently been published by the Arthur H. Clark Company.

stopping place during his entradas, or journeys into Arizona during the next eleven years

In 1701 Padre Juan de San Martin took charge of Guevavi with San Cayetano de Calabazas and San Luis de Bacuancos as visitas. Just how long he remained is not certain, but after Kino's death in 1711 no Spaniard is known to have set foot in Arizona for twenty years, and the missions were abandoned until 1731, when Fray Juan Baptista Grasshoffer took charge of San Gabriel de Guevavi, and Fray Felipe Segesser was sent to San Xavier del Bac. Padre Grasshoffer died at Guevavi at a date unknown, and the next missionary of whom there is a record was Fray José Carucho.

The southern Arizona missions were not in existence during the great Pueblo revolt of 1680, but the Pima rebellion of 1751 almost wiped them from the face of the earth. Like the New Mexico insurrection, this was the work of one man, Luis, an indian from Saric, Sonora, whom the Spaniards had named as "Captain-general of the Pimas of the Mountains." Using this appointment to his advantage he secretly worked the Piman tribes into open rebellion; and, joined by many Papagos and Seris, they arose on November 21, 1751, driving the Spaniards from southern Arizona. Padres Francisco Xavier Saeta, Enrique Ruen, and Tomas Tello, stationed at Sonoita, Arizona, and Caborca, Sonora, and about one hundred Spaniards were murdered. Both Guevavi and San Xavier del Bac were plundered, but the priests escaped to Suamca, Sonora.

During the half century prior to the outbreak the Spaniards had discovered many mines in both southern Arizona and Sonora, which they operated with indian labor. This and not the padres was the principal cause of the rebellion; for the Jesuits took no part in the search for gold, and the natives did not take kindly to hard labor. After the revolt many of the shafts were filled, and all trace of the hated mines destroyed as far as possible.

From that day to this every section of the Southwest has had its legend of a lost Spanish mine, the romance of which has led many men of later generations to brave the desert thirst and the Apache warriors; for man will follow the lure of gold, even to his death, and stories of those lost mines have led men into the mountains and deserts year after year, many of them never to return. Some of those old Spanish mines have been found and worked again, but many exist only in myths. A few were really rich; and it has been proven that some were only "pockets" which the Spaniards worked out, while the ore found in others is of such a low grade that it does not pay the expenses of mining today; but it was nearly all profit for the Spaniards, for the labor was done by indians at little expense.

The old Montezuma mine, rediscovered as the Black Jack, twelve miles north of Vulture, Maricopa county, was one of the filled-in shafts that proved to be very rich. A lost mine which has baffled the best gold hunters of the Southwest is the Iron Door mine, made famous in recent years by Harold Bell Wright's stirring romance, *The Mine With The Iron Door*. The old legend tells us that it is in the Santa Catalina mountains, north of Tucson.

When the discovery of "color" in the Cañada del Oro, the Canyon of Gold of the old Spaniards, led to a rush into the Santa Catalinas in the early nineties, the old story of this lost mine was revived, and many prospectors made a determined effort to find it. The Cañada del Ora is a wild, rugged gulch in the western end of the range not far from Oracle from which it is reached over a rough trail; and somewhere in its rockbound slopes, the old story of the conquistadores says, is the Iron Door mine.

The author first heard the story of this lost mine from Frank Webber, an old Arizona prospector, who, with two companions, spent ten years searching for the end of this Spanish rainbow. After they had hunted for several years they began to doubt its existence. One of this trio who could read and write Spanish went to Mexico City, where he found in the ancient records of mines that had been worked for the crown of Spain, this entry: "The Iron Door mine; located on the south slope of the Santa Cataline mountains facing Tucson." That was all; not a word that would give them a clue to the location. But it proved that there really had been an Iron Door mine. The south slope of the Santa Catalinas covers a large area, and it was a big undertaking for three men to find a lost mine with no better description. But with the determination of the old-time prospector they continued the search for several years longer.

Once when they found an old shaft about eighty feet deep, with an ancient windlass rotten with age, still in place, and much broken pottery scattered about, they believed that they had discovered the long lost Iron Door mine at last. But the report of the samples of ore which they received from the assayer showed it to be of such low grade that they could not make wages mining it. This had either been a pocket, or had been worked because the labor cost the Spaniards little or nothing.

When I asked Webber if he was sure that this was

not really the Iron Door mine, he replied; "I've often thought of that, and the more I think of it the more I believe that it might have been the old Spanish mine."

Since then the south slope of the Santa Catalinas has been combed by hundreds of prospectors. No canyon, gulch, or cave escaped them; but to this day the Iron Door mine is still one of the secrets that the Catalinas guard jealously. Mr. Wright's novel has revived interest in the old story, and a company was organized in Tucson in 1924 for the purpose of searching for the Iron Door mine – a project that old-timers who prospected in the years of the gold rush to the Cañada del Oro are watching with interest.

The Painted Desert has its lost Spanish mine in the Padre, supposed to be located somewhere on the barren waste of northeastern Arizona; but unfortunately for this story no gold was ever found by the Spaniards in that section.

The story of the lost Taiopa is the most romantic of all mines worked for the crown of Spain before the Pima rebellion. Located somewhere in Sonora, it is supposed to be fabulously rich. According to the old tale told by prospectors for the last hundred years, there was a mission near this mine, but the indians so loved the padres that they not only warned them of the revolt but escorted them to safety. Before leaving, the fathers told their neophytes that they would return some day, and as a guide they must always keep a fire burning in the mouth of the shaft so that the padres could find their way. The fathers never came back, although their converts waited patiently year after year, and as one generation succeeded another it became a tradition of the tribe that some day the black robes would return; and so the faithful indians have never allowed this fire to die in all the years that have passed since the beloved padres left.

Unfortunately for the truth of this romantic legend, the priests were never known to take any part in mining operations. Theirs was the business of saving souls, and they left to others the search for early riches; but the story was universally believed by the old-time prospectors, and every gold hunter, both Mexican and American, who has ranged the hills and deserts of Sonora for more than a century has kept a careful watch for the light of the fire that never dies, the beacon to the lost Taiopa and fabulous riches.

The old records in both Mexico City and Madrid have been searched, but no mention of such a mine has ever been found. This has led many to doubt its existence. On the other hand some bands of the Pimas in Sonora claim to know its location; but, contrary to the general belief, indian tales of lost mines and hidden riches are not always trustworthy, as for example the myths of the Seven Cities of Cibola and Gran Quivira that lured Coronado into New Mexico.

The existence of the famous Taiopa might well be doubted but for the fact that for many years the Pimas of Sonora occasionally sold small quantities of very rich ore at some of the mining camps, and all efforts to either follow them to the source of supply or bribe them failed. Indians are very superstitious, and they believed that the one who revealed the secret would drop dead. Not for many years has any of this ore been brought in, and it is possible that those who knew its location are dead.

The story of how a woman was once permitted to look upon the Taiopa is still told by old-time prospectors in the Southwest. Some thirty years ago a Pima chief was nursed back to health by a Mexican woman, and after he returned to his village he frequently sent her pieces of ore very rich in free gold. She was convinced that this came from the Taiopa, and she finally persuaded the chief to show her the place. With two indian women as her guides she was taken secretly at night through rugged canyons and over high mountains until on the fourth night they arrived at the mouth of a shaft, and in the moonlight she could plainly see an old arrastra and ore dump. But she was hurried away by the squaws after she had gathered a few samples of the ore, and the next evening they arrived at the village. The Mexican woman was completely baffled, for she had no idea of the route either going or returning; and the secret of the lost Taiopa is still safe from the white man.

After this diversion on lost Spanish mines we will now return to the history of Guevavi. The missionaries returned to Arizona in 1752, and the presidio of Tubac was established to guard them from hostile raids; but a resident priest was not stationed at Guevavi until 1754. In 1763 this mission was in charge of Fray Ignacio Pfefferkorn, who was replaced the next year by Fray Jimeno, and in 1767, just prior to the expulsion of the Jesuits, Fray Pedro Rafael Diaz was in charge.

By the decree of King Carlos III in 1767, the Jesuits were expelled from Spanish dominions, and compelled to abandon more than one hundred missions they had founded in the New World. The mission field was turned over to the Franciscans; and in March, 1768, fourteen priests were sent to Sonora from the Franciscan college of Santa Cruz at Queretaro, Mexico.

The Arizona missions were placed in charge of Padre Francisco Garcés, with headquarters at San Xavier del Bac. This is the priest who discovered the Crossing of the Fathers in the Grand Canyon, and afterwards founded the modern city of Tucson.

The name of Guevavi was changed to Los Santos Angeles de Guevavi. Fray Juan Cristobomo Gil de Bernave, the first Franciscan missionary, remained until he was appointed president of the missions in 1772, when he removed his headquarters to Carrizal, Sonora, where he was killed by Apaches the next year.

The decline had set in, and Guevavi maintained a precarious existence under Franciscan rule. The indians refused to work, and paid little attention to the priests, beyond attending mass. The place was exposed to the raiding Apaches, who swept down upon its defenseless inhabitants on several occasions; and finally, in 1784, it was permanently abandoned.

Today a few crumbling adobe walls amid the desert cacti and sage brush mark the site of this church, the first building erected by Europeans in southern Arizona. All trace of the indian village that once surrounded the mission has vanished completely; and until recent years the location of Father Kino's first mission was forgotten, known only to wandering cowboys and indians. The spot is on the west bank of the Santa Cruz river, in Santa Cruz county, below the ancient settlement of Tubac, and nine miles northeast of Nogales on the Mexican border.

SAN JOSÉ DE TUMACACORI. On the lonely desert, two miles south of the historic little village of Tubac, the first Spanish settlement in southern Arizona, is the picturesque ruin of San José de Tumacacori, once the most beautiful church in all northern Mexico. This

RUINS OF SAN GABRIEL DE GUEVAVI MISSION IN SOUTHERN ARIZONA
From a rare old photograph in the possession of the author

was another of Father Kino's missions, founded by him about 1692, as a visita of Guevavi. Tumacacori, the "curved peak," was a settlement of the Sobaipuri, a tribe of Piman stock now long extinct, which was reduced by Apaches raids until the handful that remained was absorbed by the Papagos.

The present great church which stands in ruins was erected prior to San Xavier del Bac, according to Professor Byron Cummins, of the University of Arizona, and Henry O. Jaastad, a prominent architect, who have found that certain faults of construction in this building were avoided in the church of San Xavier. This fact goes to show that Tumacacori was built first. Like all the early missions the original building was probably a single room, which was later enlarged.

Surrounded by a beautiful garden and fields cultivated by the indians where enough grain, vegetables and fruit were raised to support the padres and the little settlement of neophytes, Tumacacori was a beautiful spot in the days of the mission's greatest glory. The raiding Apaches frequently swept down upon them, and finally, in 1752, a military presidio was established at Tubac; but it was little protection from those fierce desert warriors that this handful of Spanish soldiers could give to either the padres or their converts.

The Apaches were natural warriors, "tigers of the desert" they have been called, and for two centuries, down through the years of the Spanish period until long after the Americans came they kept life from being monotonous for the settlers of southern Arizona.

Tumacacori was a point on the main line of travel from Tucson to Sonora, and in 1854 a bold Kentuckian named Pete Kitchen built a ranch which he named

Petrero, near where Nogales now stands on the Mexican border. He successfully defied the Apaches for more than a quarter of a century; but one by one he buried all of his neighbors and comrades, and he saw his own son shot down within sight of his ranch fort.

Down the Santa Cruz valley from Tucson past Tubac and Tumacacori to his ranch and beyond into Sonora, he laid out a road which today is the main line of travel to the south. It soon became bathed in the blood of Arizona's pioneers, and in the picturesque language of the old frontier it was known as "Pete Kitchen's road from Tucson, Tubac and Tumacacori Tuhell," especially the latter locality. This aptly describes the condition of affairs in southern Arizona during two centuries of Spanish and American occupation, before the Apaches were finally conquered.

Tumacacori was raided twice by these fierce desert warriors, and left in ruins; but the padres returned undaunted and started all over again. Taking advantage of the intense midday heat when everyone was lazily sheltered from the fierce rays of the desert sun, the Apaches suddenly swept down upon the mission one day in 1769. There was practically no defense. The church was soon a mass of flames, and everything combustible was quickly consumed, leaving only the blackened adobe walls. Thus it stood in ruins for several years; and the neophytes drifted away until in 1772 only thirty-nine were left.

Little is known of its history from that time until Guevavi was abandoned in 1784, when Tumacacori was made an independent mission instead of a visita. The church was almost rebuilt. Adobe houses for the indians and a wall for protection were erected, and the mission prospered for more than a third of a century.

Ruins of San José de Tumacacori mission in southern Arizona
Founded by Father Kino about 1692

The end came one night between 1820 and 1824, the date is uncertain, when the Apaches suddenly appeared out of the desert night. All was confusion in an instant. The thatched-roofed buildings were quickly fired with lighted arrows, and in a few hours Tumacacori was a blackened ruin in the desert waste. No attempt was ever made to rehabilitate it; and today it stands just as the Apaches left it that tragic night over a century ago.

Many legends of the days of the padres hover around this somber ruin. One ancient, weather-beaten, dried up Mexican, who looks old enough to remember back to those times, will tell you that before the Jesuit fathers left they buried a large amount of gold secured from the surrounding mines. In later years treasure hunters have honeycombed the desert with trenches and holes, but nothing was ever found. And according to the tale of another desert wrinkled descendant of the conquistadoers, the padres built an underground passage from the mission to be used as a refuge in case of attack; but no trace of it has ever been found.

This battered ruin, standing silent and alone amid the desert wastes, under the blazing Arizona sun, is a monument to the zeal and heroism of the Spanish priests of an heroic age, who for their religion flirted with death every day in that desolate land. This is the largest and most picturesque ruin left in the United States today. Its battle-scarred walls, ruined belfry and great circular dome beneath which was once the altar, stand out in bold relief for miles across the desert, against a pictorial setting of sage and cacti, framed with the eternal blue of the Arizona sky. This historic spot on the main highway to Mexico is easily reached by automobile from Tucson, fifty miles away to the north.

SAN XAVIER DEL BAC. San Xavier del Bac, on the Papago indian reservation, nine miles south of Tucson, is the only one of the Arizona missions, either north or south, which stands today just as it appeared in the years of its greatest glory. This survivor of the days of the padres in that desert land is the best preserved, the finest and most interesting of all the Spanish missions left in North America. California with all its splendor has nothing that can equal it, and the missions of New Mexico are dwarfed in comparison.

Surrounded by a picturesque Papago indian village of adobe huts and grass wickiups, the white domes and towers of San Xavier rise above the mesquite and sage to guide the desert-weary traveller just as in the days of the Jesuit and Franciscan fathers. But there is a big difference in the surroundings. Father Kino's old journal tells us that this indian settlement was the garden spot of the desert, where such trees as fig, quince, orange, peach, pomegranate, and apple, and vegetables and farm products introduced by the Spaniards, grew abundantly. These have all disappeared, and the desert has gone back to mesquite, sage and cacti.

From the day San Xavier was founded by Father Kino in April or May, 1700, until the Jesuits were expelled from Spain and its possessions in 1767, this was the most prosperous mission in the Southwest. Padre Francisco Gonzales was the first resident priest; but for twenty years following Father Kino's death in 1711 San Xavier was abandoned, and no white man set foot in Arizona until the mission was rehabilitated in 1731 or 1732, with Fray Felipe Segesser in charge. The fathers came and went without interruption until the Pima rebellion in 1751, when the church was plundered and once more left to the desert's whims, Fray Fran-

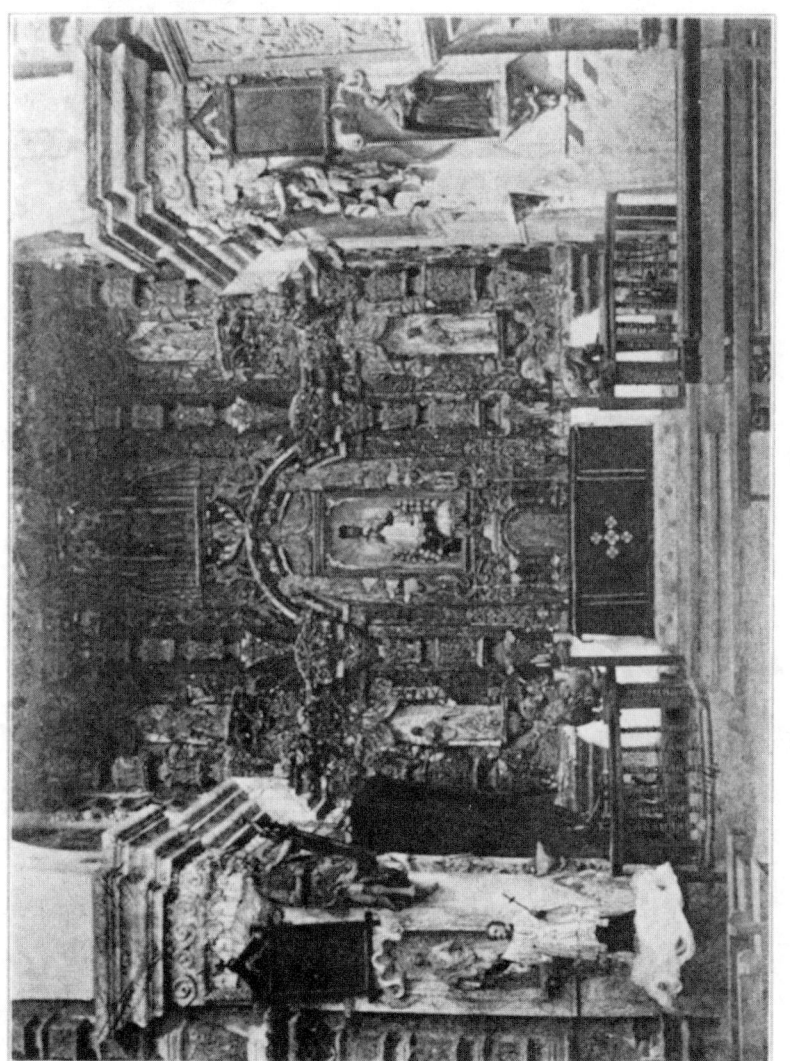

The Interior of San Xavier del Bac Mission
Erected between 1783 and 1797

cisco Paver, the priest in charge, escaping to Suamca, Sonora. The padres returned in 1752, but the mission maintained only a precarious existence during the remaining years of the Jesuit regime; and twice before 1767 San Xavier was raided by Apaches.

In June, 1768, Fray Francisco Garcés, the first Franciscan, took charge, and San Xavier entered a new era. This is the same Padre Garcés already mentioned as the explorer, and with him as companion to San Xavier went Fray José del Rio. Before the end of 1768 the mission was destroyed by Apaches while Padre Garcés lay sick at Guevavi. These raids continued at intervals until 1772, when with a population of 270 surrounding the mission, a firmer stand was made against the hostiles. During that period the church was large but poorly supplied with furniture and vestments.

Padre Garcés was the most beloved of all the priests during all the years of mission work in southern Arizona. Armed with only his faith in God he wandered from tribe to tribe, winning the love and devotion of the indians, who referred to him affectionately as their "old man," although he was young in years. He devoted his life to this work until his death in 1781, as already related.

The decline of San Xavier set in about 1810; and when the Franciscans were ordered out of Mexico in 1824, following a change in the government, the mission was left to the mercy of the Apaches and the desert elements; and many a long year passed before a priest came that way again. That the building was not entirely destroyed is due to the love and care of the Papagos, who did not forget the teachings of the padres.

The foundation of the present edifice, which is the most beautiful and best preserved of all Spanish missions in North America, was laid by the Jesuits before their expulsion; but the actual construction of the building was started in 1783 by Padre Battasar Cavillo, and completed in 1797 by Padre Narcisco Gutierres, the latter date still being legible above the main portal. Both preached the gospel of love to the Papagos at San Xavier for many a year, and when death halted their earthly labors they were buried in the church which stands as a monument to their heroism.

The expulsion of the Franciscans from Mexico marked the end of the Arizona missions. As soon as the fathers left San Xavier the sacred articles of the altar and the furnishings were secreted by the Papagos, and for more than a quarter of a century the beautiful church was deserted except when some wandering band of Mexican or American outlaws passing that way, sought shelter from the desert storms, or the sun's burning midday heat. That the buildings were not entirely destroyed is due to the love and care of the faithful Papago neophytes, who patiently waited year after year for the return of a priest; but it was 1859 before the padre came back to them. Then they hastily returned the furnishings and the long silent mission bells pealed a joyous welcome; and even though the father came out from Tucson to hold services only once every two weeks thereafter this was enough to hold those indians true to the faith.

Only one tower of the church was ever completed. A romantic story of the past tells us that when the other was half finished a priest fell and was killed; and no work was ever done on it again.

The restoration of San Xavier began in 1906, and was carried out under the direction of Bishop Granjon.

The brick wall which had surrounded the church in ancient times was rebuilt, the buildings were all restored to their original condition, and today this mission is the most beautiful in all North America. Only the bullet-scarred doorway tells the grim story of long ago. It is easily reached by automobile over a good road from Tucson nine miles away.

SAN IGNACIO DE SONOITA. Sonoita, a Sobaipuri rancheria on the Santa Cruz river, north of the present town of Nogales, was first visited by Father Kino in the fall of 1698 when he gave it the name of San Marcelo; and thereafter it was a regular stopping place for this wandering missionary during his journeys to and from Arizona until his last visit in 1702. Just when the mission was established is not known definitely, but it was undoubtedly during one of Father Kino's early visits. The name was later changed from San Marcelo given it by Kino, to San Ignacio.

This mission was always a visita of Guevavi. The date of the erection of the church is unknown, nor is there any description of the building; and little is actually known of its history. Padre Enrique Ruen was murdered at Sonoita on November 21, 1751, a martyr of the Pima rebellion, and the place was deserted until the return of the fathers to Arizona. The mission was permanently abandoned in 1784 at the same time as Guevavi, and today the church has completely vanished.

Like Tucson, Tumacacori, Tubac and Tuhell, Sonoita was a station on Pete Kitchen's famous road already mentioned. In July, 1861, when the removal of American troops from frontier forts left the Arizona border defenseless, the Apaches swept down the Santa Cruz valley, murdering many settlers in the vicinity of

Sonoita; and until this red scourge was forever wiped out a quarter of a century later many whites were killed and scalped in the region of the old mission.

JAMAC. A visita of San Gabriel de Guevavi mission was established in 1732 at Jamac, another Sobaipuri rancheria; but its existence was very short, and little mention is found of it in the old records. The exact location is unknown, for both the mission and the village disappeared long ago, and no trace of either remains today. It was somewhere in Santa Cruz county, in the vicinity of Guevavi, near the Mexican border.

SANTA GERTRUDES DE TUBAC. With the return of the Jesuits to southern Arizona in 1752, a Spanish presidio, garrisoned by fifty soldiers for the protection of the missions, was established at a place called Tubac, meaning "adobe house," thirty miles south of Tucson. This was the first Spanish settlement in Arizona, and in 1754 it had a population of four hundred eleven, which had increased to five hundred ten years later when Captain Juan B. Anza commanded the garrison. A church called Santa Gertrudes was established at the new settlement for the benefit of the soldiers as well as for the indians living in that vicinity.

When Padre Garcés founded the present city of Tucson in 1772 the garrison was ordered removed from Tubac to the new pueblo, but this did not actually take place until 1776. The few settlers then left at the old village were exposed to Apache raids, and it would have been completely deserted had they not been prohibited from leaving the locality by a government order; and in 1784 the town was garrisoned by a company of Pima allies.

The mission declined rapidly after the removal of the presidio, but it was revived slightly in 1824 when a

Mexican garrison was stationed at Tubac. After these soldiers were removed a few years later the mission was permanently abandoned; and in 1851, when troops were once more quartered at Tubac to protect the frontier from Apaches, the old church was in ruins.

Much interesting history centers around this ancient Spanish settlement, now marked by a few adobe houses and mud walls. After the withdrawal of the Mexican troops in 1854 the town was completely deserted; but it was rehabilitated in 1856 by Colonel Charles D. Posten, head of the old Arizona Mining Company which opened the old Spanish mines in the Santa Rita mountains with modern machinery, and the town soon became the center of extensive operations. Good houses were built, farming was started on a large scale, and during those years preceding the Civil war Tubac had every prospect of becoming the most important settlement in all Arizona, even surpassing Tucson.

The Arizonian, the first newspaper in the territory, was published at Tubac during those early years by Colonel Ed. Cross on the first printing press ever brought into Arizona. This press was shipped around the Horn and transported overland from California; and later it was used by the *Tombstone Nugget*, published at Tombstone, Arizona, in the latter seventies. It is now in possession of the Pioneer Historical Society in Tucson.

The story of the abandonment and destruction of Tubac is typical of the Apache reign of terror. The outbreak of the Civil war spelled disaster for this town buried in the heart of a lawless, cruel land, for in July, 1861, the government ordered all federal garrisons in Arizona to the seat of the war in the East. The dust of the departing troops had scarcely disappeared over the horizon when two hundred Apaches appeared out of the desert, bent on murder and pillage, and besieged Tubac; but a messenger for help got through to Tucson, and a rescue party led by Granville H. Oury arrived just in time to save the handful of Americans from massacre.

Almost immediately on the heels of the Apaches came a band of seventy-five Mexican bandits to plunder the settlement; but they were repulsed and fell back to Tumacacori which they burned. Realizing that it would only invite death to remain, the Americans deserted Tubac, seeking refuge in Tucson. Today the ruins of this boom town of the old Southwest are half buried under the shifting sands of the Arizona desert, a grim relic of the bloody years of long ago. The remnants of this ghost city stand on the west bank of the Santa Cruz river, thirty miles south of Tucson, on the main highway to Mexico, which follows the route of Pete Kitchen's famous pioneer road.

SAN JOSÉ AND SAN AGUSTIN DEL TUCSON. The "Ancient and Honorable Pueblo of Tucson," now the largest city in Arizona, owes its beginning to a mission established at an indian village in the desert; but contrary to the popular report its history as a Spanish settlement does not date far back into the sixteenth century as many would have you believe. Although Father Kino stopped on March 6, 1699, at an indian village near the site of the present city and gave it the saint's name of San Agustin Oiaur, no Spanish settlement was located there until Padre Garcés's mission of 1772.

The name Tucson is of Papago origin, derived from "Styook-zone," meaning, the village at the foot of the black hill, which stood in Father Kino's time at the

THE SOUTHERN ARIZONA MISSIONS 257

base of the Sentinel peak, the "black hill" of olden times.

A visita of San Xavier del Bac, known as San Cosme del Tucson, was established after 1700; but it was abandoned with the other missions after Kino's death in 1711, and the village was without a priest for many long years. After the restoration of peace in 1752 another visita was established, but it was of little importance until 1763 when the church of San José del Tucson was erected for the accommodation of three hundred thirty-one indians living there. That was during the last years of Jesuit control, and the building fell into ruins after their departure; but in 1772 Padre Garcés came from San Xavier and built a pueblo, a new church and a house for the priest. In 1776 the presidio was removed from Tubac, and the new settlement, which was destined to become the most important in southern Arizona, was christened San Agustin del Pueblito del Tucson.

Old drawings show that the church of San José, or San Agustin as it was later known, was a beautiful building, two stories in height, with deeply set doorways and plain decorations on the exterior of the first floor, and large, imposing arches on the second. The ruins, now reduced to little more than a mound of earth, still stand near the Santa Cruz river.

Tucson's history was written in blood from the earliest times; for the Apaches were cursed with the bloodlust, and they indulged in the game of man hunting, first as a pastime and then as a business. They wanted war, and they did not care who they fought. First it was the surrounding tribes; then the Spaniards and Mexicans, and finally the Americans. Before the coming of the Spaniards they tried to destroy the village of more peaceable Papagos "at the foot of the black hill"; and in order to protect both the Spanish settlers and his indian neophytes from these human tigers Padre Garcés enclosed the entire pueblo in 1772 by a high adobe wall, which gives the city the distinction of being the only walled town ever in the United States.

This wall was built in the form of a square, and is described as about five feet higher than the low roofs of the houses which stood against it. It was improved from time to time until the town was well fortified and capable of resisting the most desperate indian attack. Mounted in a circular tower, or bastion, at each corner were two small cannon, described by a writer of the period as "more dangerous to the garrison than to the enemy." Only one gate gave entrance to the fort when first built, but another was added later. The first stood at the junction of the present Alameda and Main streets, where some of the original wall was afterwards used in buildings in that locality.

For nearly three-quarters of a century this adobe wall protected the town from the Apache indians, that ever present source of death that stalked through old Arizona. Part of the ancient fortress stood until the Americans came, and as late as the fifties it was used to repel an Apache raid. One side extended west along what is now Pennington street to the court house; thence up the old Calle Real of Spanish days (now Main street) to Washington, and along that thoroughfare for some distance until it turned south to Pennington.

The name of the old Jesuit mission of San José was changed by the Franciscans to San Agustin shortly after Padre Garcés founded the settlement of Tucson;

but the old records do not show just when this took place. The old church of San Agustin was abandoned before the American occupation, and when the First United States Dragoons raised the Stars and Strips on March 10, 1856, after that section of Sonora became a part of Arizona by reason of the Gadsden purchase, the ancient mission was only a mass of crumbling ruins.

SAN CAYETANO DE CALABAZAS. Another mission on Pete Kitchen's pioneer road was San Cayetano de Calabazas, located on the Santa Cruz river south of Tubac. Some say that it was founded by Father Kino in 1694 as a visita of Guevavi; but this is doubtful, although a mission was established there at a very early date, for Calabazas, Spanish for calabashes, was a Papago indian village near the beginning of the eighteenth century. In 1760 there were one hundred sixteen neophytes, but these had dwindled away to sixty-four in 1772. According to the old records there was originally no church, or house for the padre, and it is probable that services were held by a priest from Guevavi. After the latter was abandoned in 1784 Calabazas was a visita of Tubac until both a church and residence for the priest were erected in 1791, after which it was changed from a visita to an independent mission.

The history of old Calabazas, one of Arizona's "dead cities" of a past generation, teems with romance. Gold was discovered by the Spaniards at an early date, for we find that in 1777 mines were worked in that vicinity; and during the same year one Señor Ortiz applied for a grant for the great ranch owned in later years by Don Manuel Gandara, governor of Sonora in the latter forties.

The Gandara property was one of the most famous of the old Spanish ranches in the entire Southwest in the eighteen thirties and forties; and from his great adobe mansion, surrounded by an army of peons and vaqueros, Don Manuel ruled like a feudal baron of old while his cattle grazed on a thousand hills, until a change in political fortunes forced him to flee from Mexico to California.

When the lord of Calabazas was appointed governor of Sonora he established a military post near his ranch as an added protection against the Apaches; but the garrison was removed about the time of the Mexican war. The presidio buildings were of stone and in such good condition that the old post was occupied during 1856 and part of 1857, after the Gadsden purchase, by four companies of the First United States Dragoons, commanded by Major Stein. During the Civil war Fort Mason was established a short distance south of Calabazas, nearer the Mexican border, and garrisoned by California volunteers.

Some time after the Mexican war Don Gandara abandoned Calabazas ranch, for Bartlett found the buildings in ruins and the place deserted when he visited the spot in July, 1852. During the early sixties James Pennington, a noted Arizona pioneer after whom Pennington street in Tucson was named, took up his residence in the deserted buildings in defiance of the raiding Apaches, declaring in the picturesque language of the frontier that he had as much right there as the infernal indians and he would live there in spite of all the devils out of hell. But it is very doubtful if he referred to his aboriginal neighbors as "infernal." Those old-time Arizonians generally described the Apaches with stronger adjectives. And "in spite of all the devils out of hell," meaning the Apache indians in frontier parlance, Pennington and his family of five hardy sons and daughters held Calabazas with their rifles; but after several years of fruitless work he gave up the struggle, and in 1869 he and a son were killed by Apaches near Crittenden.

When the Southern Pacific railroad was built south to the Mexican border Calabazas enjoyed a short boom, and its promoters had great hopes for the future. A townsite was laid out and Arizona's "coming city" was advertised far and wide by an elaborate pamphlet circulated among prospective purchasers of lots. This was a real work of art with an illustration of a wonderful city in the desert, with large business blocks, on the banks of a mighty river where steamers lay at anchor. This stream was shown as flowing south into the Gulf of California. In reality mesquite thickets and cacti stood where the artist had pictured the imposing buildings; and the river is the Santa Cruz, a small desert stream flowing north instead of south, with scarcely enough water to float a canoe. Needless to say the Calabazas boom was very short lived; and the place today is marked by the crumbling walls of the old mission and the Gandara ranch buildings rear Calabazas station on the Southern Pacific railroad.

SAN LUIS DE BACUANCOS. On October 26, 1699, Father Kino visited a Pima rancheria known as Bacuancos, located on the Santa Cruz river near the present Mexican boundary. According to the old Spanish records it was in Pimería Alta seven leagues south of Guevavi, which would place its site over the line in Mexico. In 1701 when Padre Juan de San Martin took charge of Guevavi both San Cayetano de Calabazas and San Luis de Bacuancos are mentioned as his visitas. It probably ceased to exist after Kino's death in 1711, when all of the Arizona missions were abandoned for a period of twenty years.

ARIVACA. This was a Pima village west of Guevavi, but its location is not known definitely. It was a visita of Guevavi at a very early date, but little mention is found of it in the early records, and it was evidently of little importance. It remained a visita of Guevavi until 1751, when it was the camping place of the rebellious Pimas; but after the revolt the village was permanently abandoned.

SAN FRANCISCO DE ATI. This was a Pima village visited and given this saint's name by Kino in October, 1699. It was located west of the Santa Cruz river, but no mention is found of a mission there until one was established in 1756 by Padre Ignacio Pfefferkorn. It was evidently of little importance, and was probably abandoned when the Jesuits were ordered out of Mexico.

SAN SERAFIN. A Pima rancheria northwest of San Xavier del Bac was visited by Kino in 1699 and named San Serafin. Little is known of its history, as the old Spanish records only mention it occasionally under such names as San Serafin, San Serapin Actum, and San Serafino del Napcub, all apparently the same place. The last record found is by Padre Garcés, who called it San Serafino de Napcub. It was evidently always a visita, probably of San Xavier del Bac.

THE TREASURE OF SAN BERNARDINO RANCH. On the international boundary line eighteen miles east of Douglas, Cochise county, Arizona, is San Bernardino ranch, famous in the history of the old Arizona cattle range. This property, baronial in its extent with its 73,240 acres, most of which are in Mexico, was originally a land grant made by the Mexican government in 1822 to one Ignacio Perez. It passed through various hands until 1884, when it was purchased by John Slaughter, Cochise county's famous gun-fighting sheriff from 1887 to 1890, who cleaned up the outlaws in the Tombstone country.

After he retired as a peace officer Slaughter made this his home ranch from 1890 until his death on February 15, 1922; and for nearly a third of a century it was one of the most famous cattle ranches in the entire Southwest, one of the kind you read about but seldom see. The house is a long one-story adobe structure of the Spanish type, with enough buildings scattered about to make a small town, and surrounded by a number of giant cottonwoods in an otherwise treeless country. The international boundary line passes through the large stable just back of the house.

This ranch takes its name from the ruins of an old mission located just across the line in Mexico and about a mile from the Slaughter house. Its history is obscured in the past, and the author has been able to learn but very little; for the old records and journals mention it so seldom that the information is of little value. In fact, the only definite statement is found in Padre Garcés's *Diary*, edited by Doctor Elliott Coues. This tells us that the old Spanish highway from Chihuahua to the north passes through San Bernardino, almost in the extreme southeastern corner of Arizona. No mention is made of a mission at this point, but from the fact that the present San Bernardino ranch is located in the extreme corner of southeastern Arizona it is more than probable that this is the point mentioned by Coues, especially when local tradition says that this was a mission, and the appearance of the ruins bear this out.

One evening some twenty years ago two Mexicans with pack burros camped at the ruins of the old mission. They were seen by the people at the ranch, but no particular attention was paid to them as Mexican travellers were not infrequent in that vicinity. The next morning they were gone; but inside of the mission was a deep excavation, revealing a concrete vault that had been covered with a cement slab. The cavity was empty, and the secret of its contents remains a mystery to this day. The Mexicans were never seen again; and the fact that they had dug only in this one spot gives rise to the belief that they had a chart, or some directions. Those who know the story firmly believe that this vault contained some treasure buried by the padres before the mission was abandoned, probably just before they fled from the raiding Apaches long ago. If anything of value was discovered by the two Mexicans it is the only treasure ever known to have been found at any of the missions, although diligent search has often been made at many of the old churches.

XVI. The Dance for Rain at Cochití

"And so in Cochití that day
  They slowly put the sun away;
And they made a cloud and they made it break,
  And they made it rain for the children's sake;
And they never stopped the song or the drum,
  Pounding for the rain to come."
— WITTER BYNNER

The deep booming roll of an indian drum borne on the desert wind, followed by the sharp crack of a rifle every few minutes, told us that we were nearing the ancient Pueblo of Cochití where the dance for rain was to be held that day. We left Santa Fé early in the morning, and after driving some thirty miles, down the famous La Bajada hill, terror of all level country motorists, and up the winding Rio Grande, we experienced our first thrill of what proved to be a long remembered day, when we heard the wild boom of that indian drum. There is no other sound in all the world like it. Mournful as the wail of a lost soul, it carries a weirdly appealing note of protest against the encroachments of a civilization that has no room for a dying race.

It was July 14, the date of the annual fiesta to San Buenaventura, the patron saint of Cochití; but mixed with the christianity of an alien people is the ancient ceremony of the dance for rain, or the green corn dance as some call it, held by the Turquoise and Calabash societies — a survival of the Pueblo religion practiced before the coming of the conquistadores.

Fiesta day in an indian pueblo, always the big event

of the year, is an experience never to be forgotten in these prosaic days when the old frontier has vanished forever. Visitors go from all the neighboring villages, and Mexicans from the surrounding territory join in the festivities, while Americans from far and near come in their big automobiles.

As we drew nearer to the village the noise increased; and we could see figures dressed in all the gaudy attire of the indian – buckskins, beaded and fringed, blankets, silver belts, and turquoise necklaces, while the spire of a christian mission towered above the one-story adobe buildings of the town. The drum boomed out its solemn note and the rifle cracked at regular intervals, while the shriek of modern jazz from a three-piece Mexican orchestra that played unceasingly all day long on a small dance platform back of the church added a festival air to the occasion. Mexican *señoritas* and *caballeros* from far up and down the Rio Grande had gathered there, not to attend the morning mass then in progress, nor the dance for rain in the afternoon, but to hold a *baile* all of their own; and they danced all day long to the screeching music of that orchestra, not even stopping for lunch. Gathered around the platform was one of those picturesque crowds typical of New Mexico – indians, Mexicans, and Americans all dressed in the garb of the fast-fading frontier.

Pop, watermelons, ice-cream cones, and candy dispensed from hastily erected eating stands gave the scene a civilized touch. Even the "hot dog" vendor was there, and his wares seemed as popular as at an eastern fair.

The pavilion, shaded from the fierce desert sun by a canvas tarpaulin, was filled with dancers, most of whom were Mexicans. All day long that orchestra fiddled out dance music, and, mixed at intervals during the afternoon with the boom of the indian drum and the weird native chant of the green corn dancers in the village plaza, a strange musical combination, only possible in an indian pueblo, was produced. Certainly no one who was at Cochití that day could say that the modern jazz of the white man's civilization was even equal to the dance music of a pagan religion handed down by word of mouth from one generation to another since the beginning of time.

Soon after our arrival we went to the ancient Spanish mission of San Buenaventura, meaning Saint Good Fortune, where an elaborate mass was being held by a priest from Peña Blanca as a prelude to the ancient dance to the gods of rain that afternoon. These indians are all good Roman Catholics. No other denomination holds as strong an appeal to the indian mind, and no other missionaries have ever understood the aborigines of the Southwest like those Spanish priests of old. Converted by the daring padres who, with the conquistadores, defied the desert long years ago, the Cochití people have handed down through the generations this new religion, mixed with the ancient rites of their own gods. The priests of today have kept up the traditions established by the padres; and where protestant missionaries have failed with the indians, the catholics have succeeded. The secret of this success is simple. The padres were not intolerant, protestant reports to the contrary notwithstanding. They did not interfere with the native religious rites cherished through long centuries before the coming of the white man; and after more than three hundred years they have succeeded in welding the two together into a catholic religion peculiar to the Pueblos of New Mexico.

In a group of indian men standing on the outside of the church door was one holding a Winchester carbine, apparently on guard, and another beside a large drum stood ready to send its booming voice out over the desert. Through the open door we could plainly hear the chant of the priest in the mass service, and as his voice ceased and the indian choir started to sing, the drum sent its wild roll out on the desert winds. The man with the gun fired several shots into the air, which we afterwards learned were to scare evil spirits away.

"Are white people allowed to go in?" we asked an indian at the door.

"Certainly," he replied politely in perfect English.

As we entered the portal of this ancient edifice built by De Vargas in 1694, we were greeted by a strange scene. Standing under the balcony, which is always found over the doorway on the inside of all the old Spanish missions in New Mexico, was a mixed group of white people and indians; and the latter politely made way for us so that we could see the service. A dim, ghostly light struggling in through the dust and grime left by the passing years on a few small windows high up in the walls, lighted the interior with a soft glow that added to the weird charm of the occasion.

There are no seats in an indian mission, and kneeling on the dirt floor, the men on one side and the women on the other, were the neophytes of Cochití. Hanging along the walls were the sacred pictures representing the stations of the Cross; and the old tin candlesticks, brought up from Chihuahua before the American occupation, were still in use. At the far end of the building we saw an altar, resplendent with all the christian ornamentations that appeal to the indian mind. The large painting of San Buenaventura was in the center of the wall above, while the Nativity, the Transfiguration, the Last Supper, and three scenes of the Crucifixion, all very ancient, cracked with age and covered with the dust of years, formed the reredos.

In front of the altar was the priest from the Mexican settlement of Peña Blanca holding mass for San Buenaventura, and at each side were two indian altar boys who joined in the chant at the proper time; while from the loft above us came the voices of the indian choir. It was one of those scenes which civilized man is only privileged to witness on special occasions; and as we gazed at the priest and his indian converts who knelt with bowed heads, a feeling of reverence came over us for those Spanish priests of old who had voluntarily accepted the hardships of that desert land nearly three centuries ago, that they might add a few converts to the Cross. We realized that their martyrdom and sacrifices had not been in vain; for this was their monument.

I was armed with a letter of introduction to Marcial Quintana, the governor of Cochití, asking as a special favor his permission for me to photograph the dance. He readily gave his consent to take snaps about the village and of the indians; but the dance — that was another matter and I would have to obtain authority from the members of the Turquoise and Calabash societies. He promised to do what he could for me.

When the Turquoise people retired to rest after their first ceremony in the plaza that afternoon, a messenger summoned me to a council; and I followed him to the meeting place of the clan in the shade of the old mission. One other white man was present, a photographer from the museum at Santa Fé, who also wished to take pictures of the dance. An indian council where matters of importance are to be discussed is always opened with a smoke. In olden times the pipe of peace was passed around from mouth to mouth; but customs have changed somewhat since De Vargas's day, and the cigarette has taken the place of the old red peace pipe, and any white men present are expected to furnish the smokes. I was well aware of what would be expected of me in an indian pueblo, and I went to Cochiti that day armed with many packages of cigarettes, which I immediately passed around, and after all had indulged in a smoke the council began.

This was a strange council held there within the shadow of the ancient mission built over two hundred thirty years before, to decide whether the white man should be permitted to take photographs of the dance for rain. About thirty indians were present, and, attired in all their dance paraphernalia of fox skins, kilts, red velvet shirts and cotton trousers, some leaning against the old wall, others squatted on the ground, those men of old Cochiti made a picture that will never be forgotten; while from the plaza came the deep toned boom of an indian drum and the weird chant of the Calabash people.

Governor Marcial was as good as his promise, and I could see that he was strongly in favor of granting the coveted permission; but the others were divided on the subject. Finally we were asked why we wanted pictures of their dance, and each of us had to make a speech, giving our reasons. The museum photographer wanted to preserve them so that when the dance would be held no more the people of future generations would know what it was like. I told how I wanted to take them back east so that people who had never seen an indian except in a show would understand them better. We were both very eloquent, and they listened patiently, although only a few could understand English; but after we were through Marcial translated our speeches for the benefit of those who could not. Another long discussion followed; but the final decision was against us and the permission was absolutely refused.

Disappointed but not beaten, I went to the plaza and during the remainder of the ceremony I surreptitiously made several exposures with excellent results. As far as I know these were the only photographs taken that day of the dance for rain.

I will now go back to the beginning of the dance. About two o'clock the members of the Turquoise clan climbed up the ladder through a hole in the roof of their council chamber, known as an estufa or kiva, and marched in single file to the church. After chanting for a few minutes the dancers formed in a double line composed of eighteen men, the same number of women, and eighteen small boys and girls, and marched into the plaza. Behind them was a man with a large drum leading a group of thirteen male singers dressed in velvet and printed calico shirts with white cotton trousers and moccasins. They were ornamented with hand made silver belts and long necklaces of turquoise and shell beads. Some wore buckskin leggings, and all had the silk headband universally worn by most tribes in the Southwest. In the rear of the procession was the bearer of the Turquoise standard, a long pole decorated with feathers, which he waved to represent falling rain.

The eighteen male dancers were dressed in white kilts with gray fox skins hanging behind and belts of sleigh bells around their waists; while the upper part of their nude bodies and legs were painted a turquoise color. A gourd rattle which they shook at intervals was carried in one hand and in the other was a bundle of pine twigs and a small branch, which they waved. On their feet were moccasins with woven garters at the knees. The women wore black skirts of native weave with long red belts wound around their waists, and on their heads were the high headdresses known as tablas, carved out of a board and painted in blue and red.

Two koshares, or delight makers, capered at the side of the dancers, trying to make sport of every little incident that occurred. We would call them clowns, but their primitive efforts to make amusement were pathetic, although enough to bring a laugh from the indians. These koshares were entirely naked except for a "G" string and a headband; and their bodies were painted white with a few black stripes around them. In the center of the plaza was a large pool of water and when one of the koshares ran into this, splashing around until he washed off the paint, a roar of laughter arose from the crowd. They continued their antics during the entire ceremony, occasionally going among the spectators to play their jokes.

At one end of the plaza was a large booth of Navajo blankets built to shelter the sacred statue of San Buenaventura which had been carried from the church after the mass that morning. At the end of half an hour the members of the Turquoise clan slowly marched to this place, and each in turn reverently kissed the robe of their beloved saint which they have worshipped for generations.

This ended the first part of the dance for rain; but

THE DANCE FOR RAIN AT COCHITÍ

This ancient tribal dance takes place in the public plaza, in the shadow of the christian church of another race

the boom of a drum was heard again and into the plaza marched the Calabash people, all dressed the same as the Turquoise clan except that the naked bodies of the men were not painted. Around the pond they danced, their performance being similar to the preceding one; and then they too paid their respects to the statue of San Buenaventura. Then the Turquoise people came again, each clan alternating with the dance until sundown.

Among the spectators of this pagan dance held within the shadow of the ancient mission were several sisters of mercy from Santa Fé and the catholic priest from Peña Blanca; and I wondered how many protestant missionaries would have done the same.

As we hurried along the Rio Grande and over the hills to Santa Fé that evening, great black clouds, split by vivid flashes of lightning, boomed up over the Jemez mountains to the west and rolled out across the valley, drenching the desert land in a terrific downpour. And who can say that the dance for rain at Cochití that day was not a success?

XVII. The Land of the Snake Dance

The last old-time Snake Dance at Oraibi – The founding of Hotevilla – Lost on the Little Colorado – The Mishongnovi Snake Dance of 1907 – The Oraibi Flute Dance of 1907 – A visit to Hotevilla – The Mishongnovi Flute Dance of 1908 – The Oraibi Snake Dance of 1908.

THE LAST OLD-TIME SNAKE DANCE AT ORAIBI. Buried in the heart of the Painted Desert of Arizona, a land that still holds many mysteries concealed in its little known corners, is the ancient Spanish province of Tusayan, where the last of the picturesque old West made its final stand against a civilization that has little room for the romantic past. And in that land of yesterday is the home of the Hopi, a tribe of indians that has been fighting the white man's ways for nearly four hundred years; but strange as it may seem they are the most peaceable of all our indians, and since the Spaniards were driven out in 1680 they have never been engaged in open warfare against the whites. They love their own ways better than anything civilization has to offer, and they preserved until recent times the strange beliefs of their fathers almost as pure as when Coronado's conquistadores first found them in 1540. The nature of their country has been their protection; for the white man cared little for this desert. All they ask is to be left alone to live their lives in their own way; but the traveller in their land is always welcomed, for hospitality to the stranger is part of the Hopi religion.

Nearly half a century ago they attracted world wide attention when Captain John G. Bourke, of the United States Army, returned from Hopiland with an account of their Snake dance, the strangest religious ceremony in all the world. During the next thirty years a few white people braved the desert's hardships, and visited the annual performance; but it was a hard journey in those times and two days at least were required, with good fortune, to cover the distance to the villages, while a week was generally consumed on the round trip. It meant all the hardships of camping on the desert, alkali water, poor food and little of it, and travelling very light.

Some of the more fastidious made the journey in wagons, taking a camp outfit and a full line of supplies; but this required more time and was expensive; and so the trip to the Snake Dance never became a popular excursion. But to the cowboys and stockmen of the old Arizona range it was a lark, just a vacation; for the hardships of the Painted Desert held little terror for them. In those days the author was riding range for the old C O Bar outfit in the San Francisco mountain country, and such a journey was all in the day's work to the cowboy of yesteryear. We simply caught up saddle horses from the *remuda*, tied a slicker, an extra blanket, a gallon canteen full of water, a coffee pot and tincups, and a small frying pan and canvas bucket onto our saddles, and stuffed some crackers, bacon and rice into our saddle bags, and we were ready for a hundred miles of desert. This was enough to last until we could replenish our scanty larder at some trading post on the Little Colorado river, or at Fred Volz's stores at the Fields and Oraibi. It was in this way that the author made his trips to Hopiland, travelling as light as possible with just one saddle horse and no pack outfit.

On account of the few white visitors in those times the Snake dance was influenced but little by contact with civilization. A religious ceremony it was in the beginning and as such it remained for many years. The automobile has done more to rapidly change the old-time West than any other factor; for in a little more than ten years it has invaded the most remote corner, and frontier institutions have practically disappeared. A journey across the desert that required three days for us to make on horseback twenty years ago is now covered in as many hours by a motor car; but the visitor to Hopiland today misses much of both the journey and Snake dance that we enjoyed when northern Arizona was the last frontier. The automobile traveller can never know the thrills of riding on horseback mile after mile, hour after hour, across the burning sands under the blazing desert sun; nor can he know the feeling produced by the Snake dance when it was purely a religious ceremony, and he was one of ten or fifteen white persons present.

Now at least fifty motor cars cross the desert to the Snake dance for every white visitor who attended in the old days. This has had its influence on the performers, especially at Walpi and Hotevilla, where the ceremony is now nothing more than a show. The old-time priests are nearly all gone, and the younger generation love to play to the grandstand. Before many years it will have ceased altogether.

Visitors to the Snake dance today may leave Flagstaff, Winslow, Holbrook, or even the Grand Canyon, the nearest railroad towns, the morning of the public performance and be back again late that night, although two days are usually taken for the round trip. They have seen a few half naked, gayly painted indians dance around the plaza with wriggling rattlesnakes dangling from their mouths, and they are satisfied. They have seen Navajos from the surrounding desert and Hopis from the other pueblos, resplendent in native jewelry of silver and turquoise, and they are convinced that they have seen the last of the old West, not realizing that it was an attraction staged for their benefit and the money they bring.

The Snake dance alternates with the Flute ceremony, each being held once in two years at each pueblo. During the odd years (1927, 1929, etc.) the Snake dance occurs at Walpi and Mishongnovi, and the Flute dance at Shipaulovi, Shongopovi, and Hotevilla; while in the even years such as 1928, 1930, etc., the Snake dance takes place at Hotevilla, Shipaulovi, and Shongopovi, and the Flute dance at Walpi and Mishongnovi. No Snake ceremony was held at Hotevilla prior to 1908, as that pueblo was not founded until the fall of 1906, and the dance took place at old Oraibi, which is now almost deserted and in ruins.

The last of the old-time Snake dances ever held at ancient Oraibi was in 1906, the first year the author visited Hopiland. The Snake ritual had been held at that village since long before that October day in 1492 when Columbus sighted the first land in the western world; for old Oraibi was the only one of the Hopi pueblos occupying the same site as in the days when Tovar and Cardeñas, first of the conquistadores, marched across the unknown deserts from ancient Hawikuh of the Zuñis.

I had ridden the cattle ranges of northern Arizona

for several years prior to 1906, but had never attended a Snake dance, as I was generally at some far distant point at that time. In August, 1906, while returning from Mexico I heard that the Snake dance had been postponed until September on account of factional differences at Oraibi, and so I decided to go. At Flagstaff, Arizona, I learned that it would take place on September 5, and after spending several days with some cowboy friends I set out on horseback from Canyon Diablo with Fred Volz, the indian trader at that point and an old acquaintance. Mr. Volz, who has been dead these many years, was one of the pioneer indian traders of northern Arizona, and for more than a quarter of a century he conducted trading posts at Canyon Diablo, the Fields, halfway to Hopiland, and at old Oraibi. His store at Canyon Diablo was burned several years ago, and nothing but ruined stone walls are left to mark the site of one of the best known indian trading posts of old Arizona.

In those days Canyon Diablo, sixty-five miles from Oraibi, was the nearest railroad point; and we covered the distance in two days, arriving on the evening of September 4. As we approached Oraibi we passed an occasional cornfield in the bottom of the wash, guarded from wandering burros by a half naked indian; for there are no fences in Hopiland. Hopi farming generally consists of planting the seed and then waiting for nature to do the rest; but fortunately not many weeds grow on the desert, for the corn is cultivated very little. After the planting, the Hopi farmer erects a brush wickiup where he will retire from the fierce rays of the Arizona sun and watch his crop grow, and incidentally guard it from predatory burros.

When one of these little animals is caught in a cornfield his ears are cropped to show that he is a thief; and most of the burros in Hopiland have very small ears.

The government agent at Keam's Canyon once told me that the Hopis have about 1,500 acres of desert land in crops each year, and 1,000 acres of peaches. The average corn crop is about 25,000 bushels annually. After harvest the corn is dried on the housetops, and then stored for winter use. They are very frugal and each year lay one-third away for that traditional rainy day, or I should say dry day in Hopiland. This is only used when a prolonged drought causes a failure of the crops.

This corn is the typical indian maize, the same as was grown by the ancient cliff dwellers long centuries ago. It is planted in hills several feet apart, and grows about three or four feet high. Through long years of adapting itself to the desert the leaves are very long and bend over until they touch the ground. In this way the roots are shaded from the burning sun, and what little moisture the ground contains is conserved. I once sent some of the seed back east. My father planted it in his garden, and in one season with abundant rainfall it abandoned its desert characteristics by growing nearly seven feet high.

At the foot of the mesa about a mile from old Oraibi in those days were a number of buildings used for the government school, postoffice, residences for the school teachers and other government employes, and a trading store, together with a few indian families who had adopted the ways of civilization. The trading store where we stopped had been established by Mr. Volz many years before, but a few months previous to our visit he had sold out to Mr. Antonio Armijo. Every white visitor was there that night, but there were only a few. One outfit had come from Gallup, New Mexico, and another from Winslow; but there were not over fifty all told, the greatest number by far that I ever saw at a Snake dance.

The next morning we arose early and climbed to the edge of the mesa before dawn; for at sunrise of the day of the dance the Snake race is held, and already the cliffs were covered by a great throng of indians, with an occasional white visitor here and there. It was one of those scenes which have now passed into the history of the old Southwest. The first light of approaching day was just appearing across the desert far to the east, and all eyes were turned expectantly towards the plain, for the contestants would start at sunrise from a point several miles away and run to the village. After what seemed an endless period the sun suddenly shot up above the rim of the desert, and a great shout went up from many throats; for this was the signal for the race to start. Presently a long line of swiftly moving figures, so far away that they looked like ants, could be distinguished out on the plain. Rapidly they drew nearer and nearer until they disappeared among the sand hills at the foot of the mesa; but they reappeared here and there as the trail wound over the top of some hill. The spectators went wild with excitement as the racers approached, and they shouted words of encouragement to their favorites. Finally the first man, closely followed by several others, came in sight at the foot of the steep path up the mesa. This was the supreme test, for endurance now counted more than speed; but the first man held his place and soon arrived at the top, the others struggling up in a few minutes.

Immediately after the race came the scramble for

the green corn, which was a general fight for corn stalks between the boys and girls. The boys started to run with the corn and were pursued by the girls, the latter trying to capture the stalks, the boys running and dodging to keep beyond their reach. The contest did not last long, but it was very spirited and caused much amusement for the spectators. The participants were all between the ages of sixteen and twenty-five; but those I saw at Mishongnovi the next year were only children. The corn fight was the last ceremony until the public Snake dance late in the afternoon.

The Snake dance, which is a religious ceremony to the great plumed water serpent and the gods of the underworld to send rain to save the Hopi crops, was first observed so far back in the dim, half-forgotten past that even the oldest men, the legendary historians of the tribe, have no definite record of the beginning. All they know is a legend of the weird, impossible adventures of the original Snake youth long ago, but they give this as the beginning of the Snake dance; and, like many another religious myth, it was probably the dream of some Hopi youth dead centuries before Coronado started in search of the Seven Cities of Cibola.

The Snake legend tells how this ancestral Snake youth made a voyage in a rude boat down the great river to the ocean. This was evidently the Colorado, for that is the largest stream in the Hopi world. When the young man reached the sea he landed on an island where he met the Spider Woman, who became his counselor and guide through the underworld – the Hopi heaven. The story of that journey, which rivals Dante's *Inferno*, tells how the Snake youth encountered many dangerous serpents and beasts, but his guardian, the Spider Woman, gave him medicine, or charms, with which to pacify them. After many adventures and narrow escapes from death he came to the land of the Snake people, who initiated him into their clan, teaching him the secrets of the wonderful ceremony that would please the gods of the underworld so much that they would send rain to save the Hopi crops and this is supposed to be the rites now performed during the nine days prior to the public dance.

When the youth was ready to return to his own land he was given the dance paraphernalia of the Snake people, and a Snake maiden was sent with him as his wife. And so the Snake youth and the Snake maiden returned to his home on the mesas of what is now the Painted Desert; but it was then a beautiful land of green grass, flowers, and trees. They were welcomed by his people who had given him up as lost. Later the Snake maiden gave birth to a number of rattlesnakes. These were welcomed by the tribe, but when they bit the Hopi children who attempted to play with them, the people became so enraged that they drove the young snakes and their mother from the village.

A terrible drought then fell upon the land. The crops were scorched and the springs dried up; and that was the beginning of the Painted Desert of today. The people were greatly alarmed when they saw their beautiful country being burned into such a terrible, arid land, and they sent for the Snake youth, who was considered very wise. He told them that the gods of the underworld were very angry because they had driven the Snake people away, and he advised them to bring them back; but before the Hopis departed on this mission he taught them the songs and prayers that would please the gods, after which he sent them down into the valleys to gather all the snakes they could find.

The next four days were spent in searching towards the four points of the compass. The snakes were taken to a kiva in the village, and during the next three days they washed them and offered songs and prayers of repentance to the gods. On the evening of the ninth day, just as the sun was setting behind the distant mountains, the young men of the village danced in the plaza with the snakes, and then released them far out on the desert to carry the prayers of the Hopi people to the gods of the underworld.

The Hopis believe that the members of the Snake clan who hold the dance are descended from this Snake youth and maiden, and when they die their spirits turn into serpents. As a result snakes are never killed in Hopiland; for if you kill one you destroy some departed member of the clan.

The public Snake dance is the climax of an elaborate nine-day ceremony, the beginning of which is announced by the village crier on a morning early in August just as the first rays of the rising sun appear over the rim of the great desert. In a loud voice he informs the Hopi world that in nine more suns the nine-days Snake ceremony will begin. The voice is heard no more, but from every quarter the village dogs send forth a wail of protest against this early disturbance. True to the announcement, on the ninth day following, the Snake and Antelope people repair to their respective kivas, an underground room in the village plaza in which all secret rites are held.

The first day is spent by the Snake priests in making preparations for the snake hunt, and the next four in gathering serpents from the four points of the compass; first to the north, then to the west, then the south, and finally to the east. All species from the deadly sidewind-

THE DANCE PLAZA AT ORAIBI, ARIZONA, DURING THE GREAT SNAKE DANCE OF THE HOPIS IN 1906
The last of the old-time Snake dances ever held at Oraibi

er and the big desert diamond-backed rattler to the harmless racer and bull snake, are captured and carried to the Snake kiva, where they are put through the washing and purification rites during the sixth and seventh days. On the evening of the eighth day the Antelope, or Corn dance is held as a preliminary of the Snake dance, and the next evening the final performance takes place.

Two societies, the Snake and Antelope, take part in the Snake ceremonies, but only the Snake men dance with the serpents. The people of the Snake clan claim direct descent from the ancestral Snake youth and Snake maiden; and membership in the Snake fraternity is limited to males born in this clan, the line of descent being through the mother. Thus a youth whose mother was a Snake woman is eligible for membership; but his children are not unless he marries a Snake woman. A girl whose mother was a Snake woman is also a Snake woman, and her male children are eligible. All Snake men do not join the Snake society, but each year one or two boys are generally initiated and taught the rites of the order from childhood.

After the Snake race ended that morning at Oraibi in 1906 we spent the remainder of the day exploring the village. All day long bands of indians, both Navajos and Hopis, came in from the other villages and the farthest corners of the then unexplored Painted Desert, to witness the great Snake dance; and as the afternoon advanced the spectators gathered in the dance plaza where the kisi had been erected. This kisi is a booth constructed of green cottonwood boughs, just large enough to conceal the man who passes the snakes out to the dancers. There must have been fully two thousand indians and not more than fifty white people gathered there in old Oraibi that day to witness the strangest religious ceremony in all the world. The buildings covered with spectators in their native costume, the high mesa and the desert that stretched away to the horizon like the traditional rim of the world of Hopi legends made a memory picture that will never be forgotten.

Late that afternoon as we were waiting amid such strange surroundings, an indian with a blanket draped over his shoulders came from the Snake kiva carrying a large buckskin bag filled with serpents, and entered the kisi. A flutter of excitment passed over the spectators, for this was a sign that the dance would soon begin.

The sun was far down in the western sky, and a few minutes later a priest in full dance regalia climbed from the Antelope kiva, quickly followed by nine others. Slowly they formed in line and marched single file to the center of the plaza where they made four ceremonial circuits, each man stamping violently on a board over a hole in front of the kisi as a signal to the gods that the Hopis were dancing. After this was completed they lined up with their backs to the kisi.

Dressed in all the barbaric finery of the southwestern indian, they presented a picturesque appearance. Down the chest and back from each shoulder were two zigzag lines representing lightning. Both arms from the wrists to the elbows, and the legs from the knees down were solid white. Their chins were black with white stripes across the mouth. Eagle feathers were plaited in the hair, and each man wore a white kilt of native weave that almost reached his knees. Around their waists were white sashes, with long ends beautifully embroidered in black, red and green, and several coils of shell and turquoise beads encircled their necks. A tortoise shell rattle covered with sheep and goat hoofs, which was fastened to each knee, gave a dull, clanking sound when the wearer walked. The attire was completed with embroidered anklets and a fox skin hanging from the waist in the rear, while each man carried a painted gourd rattle with which he kept time for the chant during the performance.

All eyes now turned eagerly towards the Snake kiva as the chief priest of that society, dressed in full dance costume, climbed through the hole in the roof, followed by sixteen others who marched in single file to the center of the plaza. Their entrance was more animated than that of the Antelope men, and after the four ceremonial circuits, made in a more spirited manner, they lined up facing the Antelopes.

The Snake men were dressed in short blue kilts decorated with white zigzag lines forming a figure representing the great plumed water serpent. At their knees were the tortoise shell rattles, and each priest held a snake whip made with two long eagle feathers fastened to the end of a short stick. Their faces were painted coal black, but their foreheads, forearms and legs below the knees were white, with splotches of the same color on their breasts and back. Their moccasins were red, and a bunch of eagle feathers was fastened in the hair. The attire was completed with hammered silver bracelets and necklaces, and a fox skin hanging down behind.

At one end of the line of Antelope priests was one with white skin and tow-colored hair — a full-blooded Hopi albino, a number of whom are to be found in this tribe. And strange as it may seem, this man with the pinkish-white skin was one of the most radical of the hostiles.

When the Snake men lined up before the kisi they

locked arms, and started to sway their bodies from right to left, keeping time with the snake whips and the Antelope priests with their rattles, as they sang a traditional song of the Snake clan in a low, dismal chant. At the end of a quarter of an hour a Snake man entered the kisi, the remainder breaking up into groups of three, consisting of a carrier, a gatherer, and a hugger. The first group paused for a moment before the kisi, and the carrier and hugger stooped down. This was the climax of the entire performance, and every eye was riveted on the weird scene, for the carrier held a squirming rattlesnake in his mouth when the two priests arose. The hugger took his place immediately behind, with his left hand on the carrier's left shoulder and his right, containing the snake whip over the other shoulder ready to guard the dancer's face from the deadly reptile; but this was not necessary for a rattlesnake cannot strike unless coiled. As each group passed the kisi a snake was handed out and in a few minutes all were slowly dancing around the circle, each carrier with a wriggling rattlesnake dangling from his mouth. It was supported by his hands, but firmly gripped between his teeth and about a foot back of the venomous head, which moved before the dancer's face in a most threatening manner. Some of those snakes were big ones, their tails almost touching the ground, while others were the deadly little sidewinder. I have heard people claim to have seen priests bitten; but, although I have witnessed several dances, I never saw an indian struck.

After circling the plaza several times, a dancer would lay his snake on the ground and secure another. Sometimes the released reptile would coil, ready to strike, but when the gatherer waved his snake whip over it, it would uncoil immediately and try to escape

The Last Old-time Snake Dance of the Hopi Indians ever held at Oraibi, Arizona, 1906

by darting towards the spectators. This always produced a flutter of excitement; but the snake never got far, for the gatherer would immediately swoop down and seize it with a rapidity that was marvelous. These men were expert and fearless, and they never had to grab twice.

As the dance progressed the number of snakes in the hands of the gatherers increased, and I saw one carrying five rattlers. One big fellow that he held near the tail was coiled several times around his naked arm. As I watched closely, the deadly reptile drew its head back several inches and then darted quickly at the arm as if trying to strike; but its mouth never opened and I am confident that it did not bite. At any rate the indian did not pay the slightest attention to it, and the big snake remained coiled around his arm until the end of the dance.

This was the performance we had travelled over many miles of sun-scorched desert to that little known corner of the old West to see; and as I gazed at the amazing spectacle of deadly, writhing rattlesnakes and weirdly picturesque dancers and spectators, it was hard to realize that I was still in America, only a few miles from a great transcontinental railway. It was one of those strange, wild scenes, common in the far West in the old days, but which have one by one vanished before the onward march of civilization until this, the strangest of them all, was the only one left on the last frontier. And now it, too, has passed into the land of yesteryear, for that was the last of the old-time Snake dances ever held at Oraibi.

The last scene of this strange desert drama was the most thrilling and dangerous of all. After the last snake was carried around the circle the chanting ceased and the Snake men gathered in a group at one side, the gatherers in front with their hands full of the deadly reptiles. The chief priest of the Snake society stepped forward and made a large circle of sacred cornmeal on the ground, with six radiating lines from the center to the circumference, representing the six Hopi directions – east, west, north, south, up to the sun, moon and stars, and down to the underworld.

The gatherers stepped forward and threw the snakes within the sacred circle; for an instant the chief priest said a prayer over the writhing, deadly pile, and then as he gave a signal every Snake man leaped forward, plunging his hands fearlessly into the loathsome mass, trying to seize as many snakes as possible. A scrimmage on the one-yard line never surpassed that fight, where the only rules of the game were to get a snake by fair means or foul. The man who failed was disgraced, and some strange tugs-of-war took place when two priests emerged holding the same serpent. As soon as a man got away with one or more snakes he ran down the trail and far out onto the desert, where he released them to carry the prayers of the Hopi people to the gods of the underworld for rain.

This was not the last act of that strange desert drama. When the dancers returned they went to the roof of the Snake kiva and drank large quantities of an emetic, served to them by a Snake woman. Vomiting was produced by sticking a finger down the throat, and in a short time all were hanging over the edge of the cliff like seasick travellers on board ship. This is a purification process and has nothing to do with an antidote for snake poison.

The question naturally arises as to the means employed by these indians to counteract the snake venom when bitten. The secret is very simple. A rattlesnake cannot strike unless it is coiled, and a Hopi always makes it uncoil before attempting to handle it. They must have an antidote, however, for no Hopi was ever known to die from snake bite; but for many years it was unknown to the whites. Reverend H. R. Voth, a former missionary at Oraibi, claims to have discovered the remedy, which was guarded so jealously by the Snake clan. According to information imparted to him by an Oraibi Snake priest it is made from two herbs that grow on the desert, specimens of which he had identified by botanists as *suaeda torreyana* and *linum rigidum*.

Doctor J. J. Thornber, dean of the College of Agriculture of the University of Arizona, Tucson, informed the author that *suaeda torreyana* is a shrub growing from three to six feet tall, found in central and southern Arizona, where it is commonly known as ink-weed, burro-weed, and sometimes as pickle-weed. As it grows in alkali soils it contains a very large per cent of salts, and is grazed to some extent by stock. Frequently the leaves turn black after a heavy frost in the late fall, hence the name ink-weed.

Linum rigidum, commonly known as wild-flax, belongs to the flax family and is distributed generally over Arizona. This is a small plant, growing from six to twelve inches high, and is found in arid places, grass lands and foothills. It has a large yellow flower during the late spring or early summer. Doctor Thornber states that neither of these plants have any medical properties that he is aware of. Mr. S. F. Blake, botanist of the United States Department of Agriculture, has also informed the author that neither of these plants contain any properties known to be of value in the treatment of snake bite. This looks as if the Oraibi

Snake priest had misinformed the Reverend Mr. Voth in order to guard the secret from the knowledge of the white race.

This was the last of the old-time Snake dances ever held at Oraibi, for it has vanished before the onward march of the white man's civilization; and those who saw that ceremony were fortunate, for it was the best that had been held in years. Such a picturesque crowd as was gathered in old Oraibi that day will never be seen again under similar circumstances in all the Southwest. It too has passed with the Oraibi Snake dance into the history of the old West.

THE FOUNDING OF HOTEVILLA. The story of the founding of Hotevilla is known to very few people outside of the Hopi country; but it is one of the most interesting tales of modern Arizona. For many years there were two factions at old Oraibi known as the hostiles and the friendlies. The former merely wished to be left alone to live their old indian life in their own way; to perpetuate the ancient religion and customs of their fathers, and they wanted nothing from the white man. The friendlies were just the opposite; for they were willing to take all the help they could get from the great father at Washington, and send their children to the government school.

About 1896 a small band of Hopis emigrated from Shongopovi on the Middle mesa, where the inhabitants all belong to the conservative element, and joined the hostiles at Oraibi. This caused further irritation between the two factions; and the feeling increased from year to year until matters came to a head in the summer of 1906. This feud was the cause of the delay of the Snake dance that year, as the usual date is from August

15 to August 30; and this led to the final break and downfall of old Oraibi, greatest of Hopi pueblos.

The trouble apparently quieted down after the dance, and more friendly relations between the two factions seemed to have been established; but this was all on the surface, for on September 7, Ta-wa-quap-te-wa, chief of the friendlies, learned of a plot among the hostiles from Shongopovi to assassinate him. Determined to drive these trouble makers from the village, Ta-wa-quap-te-wa secretly gathered and armed his most trusted men, but in some manner the plan leaked out and the hostiles prepared for battle. Bloodshed would have undoubtedly followed if the government employees living at the school at the foot of the mesa had not learned of the trouble. Led by the field matron, who was very popular with both sides, they went to the village and demanded that all lay down their arms. The indians agreed to this, but Ta-wa-quap-te-wa was still determined to drive the Shongopovi intruders out of the pueblo, together with any of their Oraibi friends who espoused their cause.

He started in by going first to the house of Yu-ke-o-ma, chief of the hostiles. A lively struggle followed, but the friendlies were victorious and ejected the hostiles by physical force. Each building that sheltered the trouble makers was then cleaned in a similar manner, and Ta-wa-quap-te-wa's forces took possession of the village.

Yu-ke-o-ma informed his followers that this was all according to a prophecy that one faction must leave the mesa forever, and that this would be decided by the side that could push the other across an established line. A council of war was held and both sides agreed to abide by the result of this contest, the defeated ones to leave the village forever. This was according to the ancient law of the tribe for the settlement of disputes; but never within the memory of the oldest men had it been necessary to resort to it.

A line was drawn across the main plaza where the Snake dance had taken place only a few days before, and then began a desperate struggle, the like of which no white man had ever seen before in Hopiland – the world-old struggle between civilization and a patriotic little band of indians fighting to perpetuate the religion of their ancestors. The friendlies won, and the hostiles, true to their agreement, gathered up their possessions and moved to a location five miles west of Oraibi, where they founded a new village which they christened Hotevilla.

In the meantime a swift runner had been sent to Fort Wingate, New Mexico, for help, and two companies of cavalry hurried to Oraibi to restore order. An effort was made to induce the hostiles to return, but Yu-ke-o-ma refused unless the head of his rival, Ta-wa-quap-te-wa, was delivered to him. Instead of receiving Ta-wa-quap-te-wa's head as a present, for the officer in command did not consider this the proper thing, Yu-ke-o-ma and his lieutenant, Ta-wa-hong-ni-wa, were banished from the reservation, and twenty-seven other members of the hostile band were arrested and sentenced to various terms of imprisonment, their chief offense being their love of religious liberty. The children of Hotevilla were captured by the soldiers and taken to the school at Keams Canyon.

THE MISHONGNOVI SNAKE DANCE OF 1907. A year later I was back on the Arizona cattle range, and when the C O Bar branding wagon arrived at Flagstaff on

August 10, I learned that the Snake dance would take place at Walpi on the fifteenth and at Mishongnovi on the eighteenth; and, as all of my comrades with the outfit were going on a big horse roundup, which always has more attractions for cowboys than indian dances, I decided to make the journey myself. The next day I met an artist named Louis Akin, who had once lived at Oraibi, and was anxious to go to the dance, but he had no horse. This was the beginning of a warm friendship between us which lasted until Louis'death at Flagstaff on January 2, 1913. Akin is one of the best known of that group of early artists of the picturesque old South west, and his paintings of the Grand Canyon and of life in Hopiland are today recognized as among the best. At the time of his death he was engaged in securing material for the mural decorations in the Southwest room of the American Museum of Natural History.

I secured an extra horse from the outfit, and on August 12 we left Flagstaff, travelling very light with only a small frying pan, coffee pot, aluminum stew pan, and canvas bucket between us, and a tin cup, aluminum plate, spoons, and a gallon canteen full of water each in addition to an extra blanket and slicker, for it does rain on the Arizona desert in August; while I had a kodak and plenty of film strapped on my saddle. Our food consisted of a little rice and two cans of tomatoes, for we expected to reach Tolchaco mission on the Little Colorado river that night.

This mission had just been established a year or two before, and we were not familiar with the route. We travelled the main road to Tuba City, which runs through the pine forests east of the San Francisco peaks; past Sunset mountain, an extinct volcano burned to a sunset red by the fires of long ago, and then across the largest lava beds in the world. But we missed the point where the trail to Tolchaco turned off, for it was little used at that time, and very dim, and when we discovered our mistake late that afternoon we were far out on the plains of the White mesa.

I had worked through that section at different times, hunting stray cattle, and after we emerged from the pine woods I knew by the many familiar landmarks that we were off our course. We had gone too far to turn back that night, and I headed for the nearest water; but darkness came on before we reached it and we made a dry camp, wiping out our horses' mouths with our handkerchiefs soaked in a little of our precious water. I have camped hundreds of times on the desert and in the mountains, under some strange conditions and scenes, but that night is one of those memories that the passing years have not dimmed; and I can still see Louis cooking a little rice over a flickering blaze, while I watched the horses graze, for we did not dare take the chance of hobbling them.

We were awake before sunrise the next morning, and in the first light of the new day I recognized a high mesa about a mile away with the ruins of an ancient citadel on the summit, known among the cowboys as the Aztec fort. The steep, almost perpendicular sides of this table mountain make it an ideal site for defense. The surrounding country can be seen for many miles; and at the base of the slope is a natural reservoir in the bottom of a large volcanic blowout. We needed water for the horses, but only a little mud remained in the bottom.

This region, which contains a great number of ancient ruins scattered over a wide area, is about ten miles west of Black Falls on the Little Colorado river, and some forty miles from Flagstaff. I had visited these ruins three years before while hunting stray cattle with a cowboy comrade; and Akin and I decided to pay them another visit as we could not reach Walpi in time for the dance. How many centuries ago they were inhabited no man knows; but Doctor J. Walter Fewkes, of the Bureau of American Ethnology, who had conducted extensive explorations there several years before identified them as ancient Wukoki of Hopi traditions, built by the Snake clan during its migration from the north in prehistoric times. Doctor Fewkes's investigations led him to the conclusion that these people are descended from the ancient cliff dwellers.

On a large, flat rock in the center of a small canyon at Glore Spring, which we reached about ten o'clock, is a square tower, three stories high, the only specimen of this type of aboriginal architecture in Arizona. Like a castle of medieval times it stood out sharp and clear against the sky line; and it was easy to picture it as the stronghold of some Hopi chieftain long ago. On another rock nearby are the ruins of what was once a large pueblo very much like the Hopi villages of today; and the many pieces of broken pottery and metates for grinding meal that are scattered about indicate that the village was inhabited for a long period. A short distance away is the graveyard where many skeletons were unearthed by Benjamin Doney, the first man to explore the ruins, and latter by Doctor Fewkes. In one of the graves Mr. Doney found a little copper bell with strange symbols on the sides, resembling Chinese characters; but its history remains a mystery. This Benjamin Doney was the father of my cowboy comrade who had first taken me there.

These ruins were discovered about forty years ago by a sheepman named Glore, who used many of the metates scattered about together with stones from the buildings in constructing a corral for his sheep. This fence of metates was still in place when I first visited the spot. An ancient reservoir, built to catch the water from the canyon during the rainy season, and a small spring were the main sources of supply for this pueblo; and we found a little of the precious fluid. In one room that had been excavated we saw one of the few stone chimneys and fireplaces that have been discovered in the ancient ruins of Arizona.

It is so easy to drift back into the past when you are in that land of long ago; and we, who had seen the descendants of the ancient inhabitants of this pueblo, living today in similar villages, fell to dreaming. No sign of the white man's civilization was there to mar the picture; and those crumbling walls that had been ruins for hundreds, perhaps thousands of years before the first Europeans came into the country, sprang into life with the ghosts of long ago, and we could see a line of half naked Snake priests dancing in the canyon with rattlesnakes in their mouths, just as their descendants would be dancing in a few days at far-off Walpi and Mishongnovi. Indeed, the scene was probably little different from what we really witnessed five days later. But water was scarce and our commissary was low; and so we left that land of the past centuries to its ghosts and headed for that other land in the north, across many miles of desert trails, where this same race of people lived just as their fathers did so long ago in old Wukoki.

Late that afternoon we reached the Little Colorado where we were sure of a supply of water such as it was.

This river is a typical desert stream, fed by a country almost as large as the state of Pennsylvania; and a heavy rain a hundred miles away one day will fill it from bank to bank for almost a week. The water is heavy with fine sand which gives it a reddish brown color; and our horses refused to drink it, but we were not so particular; for, in the language of the Arizona cowboy, it was wet. We finally managed to find a clear pool along the bank that had stood for several days, and our animals consented to take a drink. Some of the most rugged bad lands in the Southwest are found from Grand Falls to the point where Cameron Bridge now spans the Little Colorado Canyon; and through that country we struggled, reaching Grand Falls about noon of the second day.

Half buried under the drifting sands of the Painted Desert a short distance above the falls we came to the ruins of Wolfe's Store, an old-time indian trading post of the old West, that had been abandoned some years before. The stone walls of the store building, constructed like a fort, were all we found left of this once famous outpost of the old frontier in Arizona; and it has no doubt disappeared completely during the years that have passed since then. Painted above the door in faded letters we read, "Wolfe's Trading Post," the only mark of identification left.

A few miles more brought us to Tolchaco mission on the banks of the Little Colorado, where David Ward kept an indian trading store; but I understand that both the store and the mission have been abandoned these many years. After a short rest we secured a fresh supply of provisions, forded the river and pushed on to the Fields, fourteen miles farther north, where we camped for the night.

This was another of the old-time indian trading posts of Arizona, but it too was in ruins at that time, having been abandoned the year before. As already related this store was established by Fred Volz, and was a noted trading post in the days when Arizona was the last frontier. Mr. Volz always gave the indians a big feast on Thanksgiving and Christmas. Navajos and Hopis came for many miles, and after the guests had gorged themselves beyond the capacity of a white man they would engage in native sports such as horse and foot racing and chicken-pulls. In this pastime a chicken was buried with only its head sticking out of the ground; and the contestants would ride past at full speed, trying to pull the unfortunate fowl out by reaching down and seizing the head as they swept by.

This was not my first visit to the Fields; for I had been there just a few months before the old post was abandoned and knew it in the last days of its passing glory. We found the place changed very little. The buildings still stood in a cottonwood grove which Mr. Volz had guarded carefully for they were the only trees for many miles; but when I stopped there again the next year I found that many changes had taken place. The grove had been chopped down by the Navajos for hogan poles, and all that was left of this once famous trading post were the four adobe walls and dirt roof of the store building; but even this has been completely wiped away by the passing years — a sad ending to those who had known the Fields in former days.

From the Fields the trail leads north directly across the Painted Desert to the Hopi villages. The next evening we reached Mishongnovi, the largest town on the Middle mesa, where the next Snake dance would be held, and camped at Toreva, the Flute Spring which gushes out of the great cliffs that guarded the pueblo from enemies in ancient times. Mishongnovi and Shipaulovi, known as the "twin cities of the Painted Desert," stand opposite each other on two high eminences on top of the mesa, only a short distance apart.

Practically all white visitors, even at the present time, attend the Snake dance at Walpi and Hotevilla, and that one day is all they ever see of Hopiland; but that has been the salvation of the old indian life and religion of the pueblos of the Middle mesa, where the presence of strangers has had little influence on the ceremonies.

The central plaza of each village where all public ceremonies are held, presents a strange, picturesque appearance at all times. Naked children, men in calico trousers and shirts, or only a breech cloth around the loins; maidens with their hair done up in the large squash blossom whorls, matrons carrying babies slung on their backs in shawls, women water carriers, dogs, chickens, and burros make a picture that is never forgotten; and you can spend days wandering about the streets, always finding something new.

On the evening of the eighth day of the Snake ceremony we witnessed the Antelope dance. This was somewhat similar to the Snake dance the following afternoon except that after the preliminary chant an Antelope priest, holding a bundle of green corn and melon vines in his mouth and accompanied by a Snake man, danced between the two rows of performers. It was short and only one pair took part.

The Snake race is always one of the big events in Hopiland, and before daylight the next morning we were groping our way through the semi-darkness up the steep mesa trail. It was a hard climb, and dawn was just breaking when we reached the top; but the indians were already there, and we found a picturesque gathering of half a thousand Hopis on the very edge of the mesa, huddled together in the chill morning wind that swept in from the desert, all eyes turned towards the east, waiting for the first rays of the sun, the signal for the runners to start. The ghost-like figures wrapped in gayly colored blankets, were distorted by the semi-darkness of the early morning, as they stood out like statues outlined against the gray sky on the very edge of the high cliff.

Only four white men were present, two cowboys having joined us the day before, and we looked strangely out of place amid that throng of indians born and bred on the Painted Desert since the beginning of time. Such gatherings, once so common in the days when Arizona was the last frontier, will live long in the memories of those fortunate enough to have witnessed them.

At one side a crowd of naked boys stood shivering in the cold air, their little bodies decorated with circles of white pigment which gave them the appearance of being dressed in convict suits. Each held several stalks of corn, ready for the green corn scramble that would take place at the end of the race; and waiting nearby was a group of little girls, who would soon wrestle with the boys for possession of the corn. This scramble was different from that which I had witnessed at Oraibi the year previous, for the participants were all much younger, being between the ages of five and ten years.

Did you ever see the sun rise on the desert? Only one other work of the great Master can equal it – the desert bathed in the wonderful light of the full moon.

That land was forgotten when water was portioned out to the rest of the world, but it is rich in some of nature's most beautiful gifts. As we watched, a great ball of fire suddenly shot up over the rim of the world, and the desert was flooded in a golden glow that brought out all the wonderful colors of buttes and mesas, toned with a softness that is lacking in the harsh glare of midday. That was the Painted Desert at its best.

A shout went up from the spectators, for this was the starting signal of the Snake race; but the distance was too great to distinguish the runners. Finally the faint tinkling of a bell was borne up to us on the still morning air, and a mighty shout went up from the spectators as they excitedly pointed to the runners just visible far out on the desert like a long line of swiftly moving ants. We watched until they disappeared among the sand hills and rocks that surrounded the mesa. The sound of the bell grew louder and louder; and then a half naked figure suddenly appeared around a huge boulder far below us and rushed swiftly up the steep trail to the village. Close behind him others came into view until a dozen scantily clad figures were strung out along the winding path. The spectators became more excited, shouting words of encouragement to various runners until the first staggered over the top, clad only in a shirt and moccasins. He was almost exhausted by the mighty strain, but he hastened to the Snake kiva nearby for his prize.

This was a scene well worth witnessing, and one which I had missed at Oraibi, for the kiva there is some distance from the edge of the mesa. Slowly a Snake priest, naked except for a breech cloth, known in the picturesque language of the Southwest as a "G" string, climbed up the ladder from the underground chamber and handed the winner a few prayer sticks, or bahos, which he eagerly seized, and hastened away, greatly pleased with his reward for a hard day's work. Later he would deposit these in his cornfield to bring the blessing of the Hopi gods upon his crops.

The other racers slowly appeared, for there was no longer need for haste, and sat down to rest. Their dress or rather the lack of it would have shocked a civilized community, but it did not seem out of place in that indian village on the Painted Desert, where "G" strings and shirt tails were the height of fashion.

Before the last runner had staggered up the trail, the scramble for the green corn stalks was raging fiercely between the boys and girls; for as soon as the winner of the Snake race appeared, the boys started to run across the mesa, waving their corn stalks defiantly at the girls. This affair was not as spirited as the one at Oraibi, for the boys were all much younger, and the girls soon captured the corn.

The last ceremony of the morning was as interesting as it was weird. A group of half naked Snake men stood on the edge of the mesa awaiting the arrival of the runners, and as the last one staggered up the trail and sat down to rest, a priest "shot" his "lightning frame" towards the heavens and then twirled his "bull roarer," producing an uncanny roaring sound. After each had gone through this performance they descended into their kiva; and the public ceremonies were over until the Snake dance in the afternoon.

The lightning frame, which looks very much like one of those old-fashioned folding hat racks we used to see on the kitchen wall of every farm house, is uncoiled or "shot" in representation of lightning. The

THE HOPI SNAKE DANCE AT MISHONGNOVI, ARIZONA, IN 1907

Even today the pueblos of the Middle mesa are seldom visited by white people during the ceremony

bull roarer is a flat, oval-shaped stick tied to the end of a short rope, and when twirled it produces a sound intended to resemble thunder.

The Snake dance is a big event to the people of the Painted Desert, and all day little bands of indians drifted in from the surrounding country, until by mid-afternoon fully a thousand were gathered on the housetops and walls surrounding the plaza, which is much smaller than at Oraibi. Three other white people came in during the afternoon, making seven who witnessed the dance at Mishongnovi so long ago. The spectators could not see the priests as they climbed from their kivas, for the floor of the plaza is the solid rock of the mesa covered with only a few inches of earth, and the ceremonial chambers were on the edge of the village out of sight of the public square.

When the sun had almost reached the far-off San Francisco peaks, plainly visible across a hundred miles of desert, an indian carrying a large buckskin bag filled with snakes entered the kisi; and a few minutes later an Antelope priest dug a hole in front of the booth, covering it with a board. In front of the kisi was the shrine of Buhoki, owned by the Water House clan which is represented in the Antelope society at Mishongnovi. This is a small permanent structure built of stone about two feet high and covered with a large slab, and is only seen at this village.

Presently we heard the stamping and shuffling of feet, accompanied by the clanking of rattles, and a few seconds later eleven Antelope priests in full dance regalia, marched single file into the plaza. Four times they went around the square, each man stamping violently on the board as a signal to the gods that the Hopis were dancing; and then they lined up with their backs to the kisi, while one knelt for a moment before the shrine of Buhoki to deposit a prayer stick as an offering from the Water House clan. They were dressed similar to the Antelopes I had seen at Oraibi the year before.

Then the sound of rattles and the quick tread of marching feet were heard again, and the next instant fourteen Snake men strode into the plaza, all dressed and painted in the same manner as those at Oraibi, except that their kilts were red instead of blue. Rapidly and in a more spirited manner than the Antelopes, they made the four ceremonial circuits, each man stamping on the board, and then they lined up facing the kisi. At one end of the row of Snake men was a boy impersonating a warrior by wearing a cotton mesh skullcap which represents the ancient war bonnet of the Hopis. Mishongnovi is the only village where this feature and the offering at the shrine of Buhoki are seen.

When the chanting ceased a Snake man entered the kisi and the dance started. This was similar in all respects to that seen at Oraibi, except that the carriers held the snakes between their teeth without using their hands; and the performers were not influenced in the least by the presence of white people, for there were only seven of us, almost lost amid that great throng of picturesquely garbed indians. As the strange rite progressed the dancers worked themselves into a religious fervor, the weird incantation of the Antelope priests, keeping time with their rattles, adding to the uncanniness of the scene. Occasionally there was a break in the chant and the dancers stopped immediately, but this was only for a few seconds. The last scenes were more spirited than at Oraibi; and as the sun disappear-

THE HOPI FLUTE DANCE AT ORAIBI, ARIZONA, IN 1907
The ceremony of the Cakwalenya, or Blue Flute society in the village plaza

ed behind the far distant San Francisco peaks the last Snake priest climbed up the trail from his mission of returning the reptiles to their desert home to carry the Hopi prayers for rain to the great plumed water serpent.

THE ORAIBI FLUTE DANCE OF 1907. The next morning, August 19, we went to Oraibi to see the Flute dance that would take place late that afternoon. This is another interesting ceremony for rain; and, as in the Snake dance, two societies take part, the Cakwalenya, or Blue Flute, and the Macilenya, or Drab Flute. Its origin is unknown, but the Flute clans are believed to have come from the south. For the first time in the history of Oraibi only the Blue Flutes took part in the ceremony of 1907, as the Drab Flute people had gone to Hotevilla with the hostiles.

By the time we reached Oraibi early in the afternoon the clan had gone to the Flute spring at the foot of the mesa and about half a mile from the village, where we saw the priests dressing and preparing for the ceremony as we climbed down the trail; but when I attempted to take photographs I found, much to my surprise, that they resented this intrusion. During two years' experience at Snake dances no objections had been made to a kodak; nor did I ever again have this experience among the Hopis, although the next year I entered the house of the chief of the Blue Flute Society at Mishongnovi when their secret ceremonies were in progress, and photographed the altar. However, I stood by my guns, or rather kodak, and in spite of orders from the chief priest, who was also the ruler of Oraibi, I secured a number of good pictures.

There were eighteen performers in addition to the three Flute children. Twelve were dressed in white kilts with long sashes embroidered at the ends in red, green and black, while eagle feathers were braided in their hair, and necklaces of silver and turquoise beads hung around their necks. On the back of each was a sun emblem, or shield, an important symbol to the sun god, painted in the Hopi colors of yellow, green, red, white, and black, on buckskin stretched over a hoop with a border of eagle feathers and dyed horsehair entirely around the rim. This symbol is also used in the Soyal held during the last days of December. During the entire ceremony each man played a primitive reed flute, which produced a weird sound hardly music but with some melody. The chief priest wore nothing but a blanket around his shoulders.

The colors of the sun emblem have a symbolic meaning, and represent the entire Hopi universe; yellow for the north, the west in green, the south in red, the east, white, and the heavens in black. The asperger was attired in a kilt around his loins.

Instead of singing traditional songs at the spring as in most other ceremonies, the Flute men played their strange tunes for almost an hour, and then marched to the village plaza, where the Flute procession was formed with the chief priest in the lead. Three Flute children were flanked on each side by six flute players, and behind them came the asperger, while the bearer of the sacred Flute standard brought up the rear. The chief made the rain cloud symbol on the ground with sacred meal, the children cast small offerings upon it, and the Flute men played their strange music, while the asperger chanted and dipped a small brush resembling a whisk broom into a bowl he carried and threw water to the four cardinal points, then up to the heavens and down to the underworld. This performance was continued at intervals as the clan slowly crossed the plaza to the kisi, where the procession paused for a few minutes and then marched to the house of the chief priest where the offerings of the Flute children were left at the altar.

A VISIT TO HOTEVILLA. The next day we decided to visit the new village of Hotevilla, where Akin had several friends among the hostiles; but before starting we purchased some groceries at the trading store, for we heard that these people were in destitute circumstances. A hostile at the post volunteered to guide us. Near the village a number of children were playing, but the instant they saw us they scampered through the sage brush like scared rabbits, crying "bahana, bahana," (white man). They were afraid we were soldiers coming to take them back to the school which had closed for the summer; and even after our guide had assured them that we came as friends they gazed at us with fear in their eyes as we rode into Hotevilla. Most of the hostiles welcomed us, but a few held aloof, even refusing our presents of coffee and canned corn and peaches. We soon found some of Louis' old friends who greeted us with open arms, and when we left we did not carry back a single thing we had taken with us.

Hotevilla at that time consisted of a few stone houses, and a large number of brush wickiups, pleasant enough in summer but a poor shelter from the long desert winter. The courage of those indians won our admiration; for they were in such destitute circumstances that we did not see how they could last. Their crops had been burned out, and many of their sheep had died from scab; but they absolutely refused to return to Oraibi. For the sake of their religion and their ancient customs they had gone off to themselves, something man has done since the beginning of time. They were too proud to ask for help, even from their kinsmen, and so they eked out a miserable existence; and now, after the passing of more than twenty years, they have a very prosperous village, while old Oraibi is almost deserted.

THE MISHONGNOVI FLUTE DANCE OF 1908. In August, 1908, I returned to Hopiland, this time as guide for Professor H. D. Evans, owner of El Rancho Bonito, an outdoor school for boys at Mesa, Arizona. There were seven in his party, and upon my recommendation we carried all equipment on our saddles cowboy fashion, as I had done in previous years. Leaving Flagstaff on August 12, we reached Oraibi on the seventeenth, where we learned that a Flute dance would be held at Mishongnovi on the twentieth, and as the Snake dance would not take place until the twenty-first we moved camp to Sunshine mission, in the foothills below Mishongnovi. Miss McClain, the missionary in charge, gave us permission to camp in the church.

The next morning we were up before sunrise for the Flute race, which was exactly like the Snake race already described; but the dance did not take place until late in the afternoon, and during the day the author witnessed the secret ceremonies performed before the Blue Flute Altar—something that few white men had seen up to that time. It came about quite by accident. The secret rites of the Flute clans are always held in the house of the chief priest of each society instead of a kiva; and while strolling about the village I noticed a fox skin and some eagle feathers fastened to a pole on the roof of the highest house in the village. This was the sacred banner of one of the Flute societies and indicated that ceremonies were in progress in the room beneath. Climbing up the four stories I photographed it; but in returning I passed the open door of the room in which the clan was gathered, and as I looked in a moment one of the indians with whom I was acquainted invited me to enter.

Squatted around the walls were nine naked priests of the Blue Flute society engaged in council. In the end of the room to the right of the door was the altar, an elaborate and interesting affair, with reredos made of five boards, each about six inches wide and several feet long, arranged in the form of a square about four feet each way. Four boards were on each side, two joined at the top by the fifth. On each of the two outside uprights were four square rain cloud pictures, one above the other, representing clouds and falling rain, while three similar figures appeared on each of the smaller side pieces. On the slat across the top were nine rain cloud symbols, semi-circular in shape, with four zigzag sticks representing lightning and a quantity of flax in imitation of rain suspended from it. The bases of the four uprights were decorated with symbolical paintings of corn, and leaning against the wall between them were a number of small rods.

A ridge of sand across the floor, at right angles to the center of the altar, was covered with sacred meal, while four bird effigies were lying at the left side. Three small figures in front of the altar represented the Flute youth and maiden, and the Flute god. The youth held a flute, his head was ornamented with corn husks, and a necklace hung around his neck; while on the head of the maiden was a rain cloud symbol. On each side of the Flute god's body was painted an ear of corn, the Hopi staff of life. In front of this trio of deities were several small sand hills, supporting sticks with cup-shaped ends painted in various colors to represent flowers. This interesting altar was explained to me by my Hopi friend, who then obtained permission from the chief priest for me to photograph it; and I believe this was the first ever taken of the Blue Flute Altar at Mishongnovi.

I passed my tobacco and cigarette papers around, and after all had indulged in a smoke, several Flute songs were sung. My friend was the only indian present who could speak English, but with his help and some signs I managed to talk with the others; and the remainder of the morning was spent there watching them perform their strange ceremonies. Just before leaving I persuaded the chief priest, who looked almost as ancient as the village, to pose for me on the roof outside. This photograph was the first ever taken of him, and probably the last.

My Hopi friend related an interesting legend of the origin of Toreva, the Flute spring at the foot of the high mesa on which the village stands; and, as I do not think it has ever before appeared in print, I will give the story as he told it.

"Many years ago, longer than the oldest men of the tribe can remember and even beyond the memory of their fathers' fathers, when the great sea that once covered all the world was leaving them, the Hopis were afraid that they would soon be without water. They sent a runner to Nuvatikiobi (the Hopi name for the San Francisco mountains one hundred miles to the southwest), who returned with some water from the sacred fountain far up near the everlasting snows. After making much medicine and offering many prayers, the members of the Flute societies 'planted' the water and Toreva spring came forth."

This myth is especially interesting in view of the

The Hopi Flute Dance at Mishongnovi, Arizona, in 1908

Showing the complete ceremony of both the Cakwalenya, or Blue Flute, and the Macilenya, or Drab Flute societies

theory advanced by geologists that a great inland sea once covered the Painted Desert and practically all of northern Arizona. And high up on the San Francisco peaks is a large spring which now supplies the town of Flagstaff.

The public Flute ceremonies at Toreva started about the middle of the afternoon, and when we went to the spring we found a few of the clan already there. The others came in a short time, some absolutely nude except for the customary "G" string. One of the Blue Flute men was a pure albino with pinkish-white skin, light blue eyes, and blond hair.

Dressing and painting the two Flute girls of each society required considerable time; for it had to be done with great care, and they presented a picturesque appearance when this was completed. A white blanket of native weave with a black border across each end was draped around the shoulders, and each wore a white skirt, also of native manufacture, with a long girdle and white pendants around the waist; while their chins were painted black with a white stripe across the face from ear to ear. These were the maidens represented at the altars by the effigies already described. Each Flute boy, who represented the ancestral heroes of the Flute societies, had a feather fastened in his hair, and a white kilt girdled the loins; but the rest of the body was nude. During the ceremony at the spring a white kilt was the only attire worn by the priests; but before the march to the village was started they fastened white blankets around the shoulders. These had wide black borders at the top and bottom.

When all arrangements had been completed the two societies took positions on opposite sides of the spring, which has walled sides and is about twenty-five feet in diameter by three feet deep. No objections were made to the presence of white people, and we not only observed every movement closely but I was permitted to take photographs. Five men from each fraternity sat on opposite sides of the pool with their feet in the water, chanting Flute songs and keeping time with gourd rattles until a Blue Flute priest entered the spring, and after feeling around the edge brought forth a small gourd. This was repeated until six had been found when the chanting ceased.

Both societies then formed in line, the Blue Flutes first with their chief priest in the lead. Next came the three Flute children, the boy in the center, with a platoon of men behind them. The sun emblem worn by all of the Flute men at Oraibi was absent; but one of the Blue Flutes carried on his back a moisture tablet made of a piece of buckskin stretched over a rectangular frame and painted in the Hopi colors of the sun shield. At the top were eagle feathers, and the sides and bottom were adorned with horsehair stained red. This man played upon a reed flute during the march from the spring to the kisi; and another from each society carried the Flute standard. A warrior dressed in buckskin, with a quiver of arrows slung over his back, and carrying a bow and bull roarer, brought up the rear of the Blue Flutes.

The Drab Flutes formed in the same order, and their attire was similar with the exception of the bearer of the Flute standard who carried green corn stalks and wore a fox skin hanging from his waist in the rear. There was no moisture tablet carrier, or warrior, but the man who brought up the rear wore a fox skin, with green corn stalks fastened in his belt and feathers in his hair, and he played a flute, making only two flute players in the entire procession. Each of the Flute children in both societies carried one of the gourds filled with water from the spring.

With sacred meal the chief of the Blue Flutes made three rain cloud symbols joined together with long parallel lines representing rain, and upon this primitive picture the children threw their offerings, a piece of wood by the boy and a ring of twisted flag leaves by each girl. After several minutes of chanting the chief made another rain cloud picture a few feet in advance of the first and the offerings were transferred to it, the Drab Flutes using the first symbol made. This was kept up until the trail leading to the first terrace of the mesa was reached, when the ceremony was stopped and all marched up the steep path in single file. On the first terrace the same order of procession was formed, and the rites continued to the foot of the trail to the village. Across the plaza they marched in the same order, making the rain cloud symbols to the kisi, where the Blue Flutes deposited the three gourds and offerings to the gods and then went to their council chamber, followed by the Drab Flutes; and the public Flute ceremony was over.

While this performance lacked the spectacular features of the Snake dance it was equally as interesting and impressive. Each detail was carried out in the most orderly manner; and the buildings surrounding the plaza, crowded with indian spectators, added that picturesque touch characteristic of the old Southwest.

That night we sat around our campfire before the little desert mission until quite late, talking over the interesting events of the day. The brilliant Arizona moon made the night beautiful, and we could see out across the desert for miles and miles, the soft, silvery light seeming to cast a halo of mystery and enchantment around the far distant buttes and mesas; and the memory of that night will always hold a warm spot among a host of pleasant recollections of the far West. It was a wonderful night – the end of a perfect day.

THE ORAIBI SNAKE DANCE OF 1908. The next morning when we returned to Oraibi for the Snake dance we learned that it had been impossible to hold the usual Antelope dance on the afternoon of the eighth day as there were no Antelope priests left in the village. Never before in the history of that pueblo had this important ceremony been omitted; but four old Snake men stood in place of the Antelopes, and instead of the bundle of green corn and bean vines that had always been used before, a small serpent was carried by a Snake man. It was a unique performance, the first of its kind in a Hopi pueblo.

Not over five or six hundred people were left in Oraibi, and the crowd that gathered in the plaza to witness the public Snake dance on the afternoon of the ninth ceremonial day was little like that wild, picturesque assembly of desert people I had seen there two years before. A few from the Middle mesa villages and Hotevilla increased the number of spectators, and about twenty white people were there; but no Navajos appeared.

After a long wait fourteen Snake men climbed from their kiva and marched to the center of the plaza where they made the four ceremonial circuits, and then formed in two parallel lines, four standing with their backs to the kisi in place of the Antelope men. They were dressed in red kilts instead of blue as in 1906, but the rest of their attire was the same. Most of them were only novices, young men and boys between the ages of

THE LAND OF THE SNAKE DANCE

fifteen and thirty years; for the few old priests remaining with the friendlies had scoured the village for eligible men willing to be initiated.

As they lined up before the kisi with locked arms and started the droning chant, my attention was almost immediately directed to the third man from one end. He was about twenty-five years old, and beneath the black paint intense fear was plainly written upon every line of his face. Instead of looking down at the ground as is customary during the chant this man rolled his eyes from side to side in great terror and never once did his lips move. Beads of perspiration streamed down his face, and he appeared so weak from fright that I believe he would have fallen had he not been supported by the man on each side. He was the first Snake priest I ever saw who showed the least signs of fear.

When the chanting ceased they formed into groups of three, each making the circuit of the plaza before receiving a snake; but as they passed the kisi on the second round a serpent was handed out to each carrier; and the first to receive one was the man whom I have just described. The fact that it was a huge rattler about four feet long did not restore his lost courage, and he simply dragged one foot after the other as he slowly went around the circle. After the first snake was disposed of his fear vanished a little and he did fairly well during the remainder of the performance.

None of the dancers handled the serpents well, and the whole affair lacked the enthusiasm, snap and vigor of previous dances. Most of the priests were afraid, and sometimes the gatherers had to grab several times for a snake, whereas in previous performances that I had seen they never reached more than once. A very curious innovation was staged by the gatherers who went among the spectators and gave them snakes to hold, the first time that such a thing was ever known. Some refused to touch the reptiles, but a number of the more courageous took them.

At the beginning of the dance I saw the old albino Antelope priest who had been in the 1906 performance, sitting on one of the house tops, his blanket drawn over his face as a sign of disapproval and contempt. I watched closely, but not once during the entire ceremony did I see him look upon it.

This Snake dance at Oraibi in 1908 was a pitiful attempt of a few old priests to keep alive the religion and traditions of their fathers. After the last snake had been carried around the circle the gatherers hastily collected those they had distributed among the spectators, and threw them into the circle of sacred meal. When the priests plunged their hands into the wriggling mass I fully expected to see some of them bitten, but if anyone was struck he did not disclose the fact. A week later we left Hopiland with its haunting memories of old indian life that now belongs to the past.

Appendixes

I. SPANISH MISSION NAMES WITH THEIR ENGLISH EQUIVALENTS

II. ANNUAL FIESTA DATES OF THE PUEBLOS OF NEW MEXICO

III. CEREMONIES HELD BY THE HOPI INDIANS OF ARIZONA

IV. DATES OF THE SNAKE AND FLUTE DANCES AT SOME OF THE HOPI PUEBLOS

I. Spanish Mission Names with their English Equivalents

AGUA FRIA CHURCH, Cold Water.
CASTRENSE, THE, Belonging to the military profession.
CIENGA, Marshy Place.
CEBOLLETA, A Tender Onion.
CUCHILLO, Knife; gore, or a triangular piece of cloth sewed into a garment; also a piece of ground which cannot be tilled on account of a tree standing too near, or from any other impediment.
LA CONCEPCION, the Conception; refers to the Immaculate Conception.
LOS ANGELES DE GUEVAVI, the Angels of Guevavi.
NUESTRA SEÑORA DE LA ASUNCION, Our Lady of the Ascent of the Holy Virgin.
NUESTRA SEÑORA DE BELEN, Our Lady of Belen.
NUESTRA SEÑORA DE GUADALUPE, Our Lady of Guadalupe (commonly known as Guadalupe church in Santa Fé).
NUESTRA SEÑORA DE NAVIDAD, Our Lady of the Nativity.
NUESTRA SEÑORA DEL ROSARIO, Our Lady of the Rosary (commonly known as Rosario chapel in Santa Fé).
NUESTRA SEÑORA DEL SOCORRO, Our Lady of the Socorro (means succor, support).
SAN ANTONIO, Saint Anthony, a disciple of Saint Francis.

SAN AGUSTIN, Saint Augustine, or Saint Austin founder of the Augustinian Monks.
SAN BARTOLOMÉ, Saint Bartholomew.
SAN BERNARDINO, Saint Bernard.
SAN BUENAVENTURA, Saint Good Fortune, applied by Saint Francis to Giovanni de Fidanza, one of his disciples.
SAN CAYETANO, Saint Cajetan.
SAN COSME DEL TUCSON, Saint Cosme of the Tucson.
SAN CRISTÓBAL, Saint Christopher.
SAN DIEGO, Saint James, a Franciscan monk.
SAN ESTEBAN REY, Saint Stephen the King.
SAN FELIPE, Saint Philip, the happy saint.
SAN FRANCISCO, Saint Francis, founder of the Order of Franciscan Monks.
SAN GABRIEL, Saint Gabriel.
SAN GERONIMO, Saint Jerome.
SAN GREGARIO, Saint Gregory.
SAN IGNACIO, Saint Ignatius.
SAN ILDEFONSO, Saint Alphonsus, or Saint Alphonso.
SAN JOSÉ, Saint Joseph.
SAN JUAN, Saint John.
SAN LAZÁRO, Saint Lazarus.
SAN LORENZO, Saint Lawrence.
SAN LUIS OBISPO, Saint Louis the Bishop.
SAN MARCOS, Saint Mark.
SAN MIGUEL, Saint Michael.
SAN PASQUAL, Holy Easter.
SAN PEDRO, Saint Peter.
SAN SERAFIN, Holy Seraph.
SAN XAVIER DEL BAC, named for Saint Francis Xavier combined with the Piman word bac by which that locality was known, among the natives. This word bac means house, adobe house, or ruined house, and

is believed to have been given because of the ancient adobe ruins in that vicinity.

SANTA ANA, Saint Anne.

SANTA CLARA, Saint Claire.

SANTA CRUZ, Holy Cross.

SANTA GERTRUDES, Saint Gertrude.

SANTA FÉ, Holy Faith; the original Spanish name of the city was La Ciudad Real de la Santa Fé de San Francisco, meaning the True City of the Holy Faith of Saint Francis.

SANTO DOMINGO, Saint Dominick, founder of the Order of Dominicans.

II. Annual Fiesta Dates of the Pueblos of New Mexico

ACOMA,	September 1.
COCHITÌ,	July 14.
ISLETA,	August 28.
JEMEZ,	November 12.
LAGUNA,	September 19.
NAMBÉ,	October 4.
PICURIS,	August 10.
POJOAQUE,	December 12.
SANDIÁ,	June 13.
SAN FELIPE,	May 1.
SAN ILDEFONSO,	January 23.
SAN JUAN,	June 24.
SANTA ANA,	August 26.
SANTA CLARA,	August 12.
SANTO DOMINGO,	August 4.
SIA,	August 15.
TAOS,	September 30.
TESUQUE,	November 12.
ZUÑI,*	November moon.

*This is the famous Shalako, or Winter Solastice ceremony.

III. Ceremonies held by the Hopi Indians of Arizona

This list begins with the Snake dance, as it is one of the most important and best known of the Hopi ceremonies, and continues with the other ceremonies through the year from August to July.

The Kachina dances and celebrations, which are held at intervals during the year, are the most important and complicated of Hopi ceremonies. Kachina is the Hopi name for spirits, or super-natural beings, who are the intercessors between man and the gods. They are best described as the Hopi conception of angels. The first kachinas are supposed to return to Hopiland during the Soyaluña ceremony, when the Qooqoqlom Kachina dance takes place; but the Mohti or Return Kachina ceremony, held in January, celebrates the return of all of the kachinas. They remain until the latter part of July when the Niman Kachina dance is held to mark their departure for their home in the San Francisco mountains. During their stay in Hopiland the people hold a number of Kachina dances or ceremonies, in which elaborate masks are worn and the participants dress to imitate the Hopi conception of the various kachinas. No less than two hundred thirty-four different kachinas have been named and described by Doctor J. Walter Fewkes. The Hopi dolls carved from wood and dressed in various designs, which are on sale in great numbers in the curio stores of the Southwest, are kachinas, while the finest plaques, or trays, have kachina designs worked in the weave.

SNAKE DANCE; held between August 15 and September 3, rarely as late as September 6; at Hotevilla, Shipaulovi, and Shongopovi during the even years, and at Walpi and Mishongnovi in the odd years. The Snake races are held at sunrise of the same day as the public dance.

ANTELOPE DANCE; held on the evening of the day before the Snake dance and at the same village. The Antelope races take place at sunrise of this day.

FLUTE DANCE; held between August 15 and September 2, once every two years, alternating with the Snake dance; held at Walpi and Mishongnovi during the even years, and at Hotevilla, Shipaulovi, and Shongopovi in the odd years.

NUITIWA CEREMONY; held annually during the four days following the Snake and Flute dances and at the same pueblo. This is a game connected with the Snake and Flute ceremonies. Young men will appear with some object of value such as a piece of pottery, a plaque, basket, or piece of calico and hold it aloft as a challenge. The girls and women will immediately start in pursuit, and the one first overtaking the man receives the object as a prize. The author engaged in this game at Oraibi following the Flute dance in 1907, by holding up bags of candy. He was pursued by the women and the coveted sweetmeat captured.

BULITIKIBI (BUTTERFLY DANCE); held annually at Moenkapi, a small Hopi pueblo near Tuba City, on the Navajo reservation, about forty miles northwest of Oraibi. It is also held at the other Hopi villages at intervals during the year, usually following some other dance or ceremony. It generally takes place at Hano, on the First mesa, the day following the Walpi Snake dance, during the odd years.

LAGON CEREMONY; held in September during the even years at Hotevilla, Shipaulovi, and Shongopovi, and formerly Oraibi, and in the odd years at Walpi and Mishongnovi.

OöQöL CEREMONY; held in September, during the odd years at Hotevilla, Shipaulovi, and Shongopovi, and formerly Oraibi, and in the even years at Walpi and Mishongnovi.

MAMZRAUTI, OR MARAU (WOMAN'S HAND TABLET DANCE); held in September, during the odd years at Hotevilla, Shipaulovi, and Shongopovi, and formerly Oraibi, and in the even years at Walpi and Mishongnovi. Another ceremony called the Lesser Mamzrauti is held during the first part of March.

LALAKOÑTI (WOMAN'S BASKET DANCE OF THE PATKI OR RAIN CLOUD CLANS); held annually during the September moon. It has been held rarely as late as from October 23 to 29. A meeting of this clan is also held during the winter for prayer and songs.

NAACNAIYA (NEW FIRE CEREMONY); held in November, the beginning of the Hopi year. There are two New Fire ceremonies, but they are never both held the same year. The Naacnaiya is the most complicated and rarest of the two, while the other, known as the Wuwutcimti, is much more abbreviated and is the one generally held. If the Naacnaiya is held all of the other winter ceremonies which follow are more complicated than usual; but if the Naacnaiya is not held then the Powamu, Soyaluña, and Palulukoñti are only of four days duration instead of nine. As near as the author can learn Louis Akin, an artist who lived at Oraibi in 1903 and my comrade in Hopiland in 1907, was the first white man who ever witnessed the entire Naacnaiya ceremony. This was in 1903. A short ceremony called Sumaikoli is held in March during which fire is kindled by friction.

WUWUTCIMTI (NEW FIRE CEREMONY); held in November. This is the abbreviated form of the New Fire ceremony usually held. The kachinas appear in both the Wuwutcimti and Naacnaiya.

SOYALUÑA (WINTER SOLSTICE CEREMONY, COMMONLY CALLED THE SOYAL); held annually from the middle to the last of December. It is distinctly a warriors' observance, and has been called the Return Kachina, but it is more properly the return of the war god. The Momtcita War Dance of the Kalektaka, or warrior priesthood, is held in connection with the Soyaluña. The Qooqoqlom kachinas make their appearances on the eighth or ninth day.

MOMTCITA WAR DANCE OF THE KALEKTAKA OR WARRIOR PRIESTHOOD OF THE PAKAB OR REED CLANS; held annually during the Soyaluña in December. The Hopis are a peaceable people, but this is a survival of the old days when they had to fight their hereditary enemies, the Navajos and the Apaches.

QOOQOQLOM KACHINA DANCE; held annually during the eighth or ninth day of the Soyaluña ceremony in December. This marks the return of the first kachinas.

MOHTI KACHINA (RETURN KACHINA CEREMONY); held during the January moon, after the winter baho, or prayer-stick making by the Snake-Antelope or Flute societies, the organization observing it being the one that will hold either the Snake or Flute dance during the coming summer. This is a very elaborate ceremony marking the return of all of the kachinas from their home in the San Francisco mountains, whence they went after the Niman, or Farewell Kachina held during the last half of July.

POWAMU KACHINA CEREMONY (BEAN PLANTING); held annually during the last half of January. The entire ceremony, which is one of the most important in which the kachinas appear, lasts for eighteen days and continues into February. It is called bean planting because beans are planted in the kivas and forced to grow by artificial heat until the morning of the final day when they are distributed to the children with presents of dolls, rattles, and bows and arrows.

WAHIKWINEMA (WE GO THROWING), CHILDREN'S KACHINA DANCE; held annually during the middle of January by boys and girls about ten years of age, dressed and painted to represent kachinas.

PAMURTI CEREMONY; held annually in January. This is a dance dramatizing the return of the sun.

LESSER MAMZRAUTI DANCE; held annually during the first part of March.

KOHONINO BASKET DANCE; rarely held, but sometimes introduced as an episode of the Lesser Mamzrauti, from the first to the middle of March at Walpi and possibly the other pueblos.

PALULUKONTI, OR ANKWANTI KACHINA CELEBRATION; held annually during March. This very important ceremony is a theatrical performance, or mystery play to produce rain, and illustrates the growth of corn.

OWAKULTI BASKET DANCE; held by the Buli and Pakab clans in March, during the Palulukonti celebration. It has probably been discontinued.

SUMAIKOLI NEW FIRE CEREMONY; held annually in

March. This is a spring festival of short duration in which new fire is kindled by friction of fire drills on cedar bark. This new fire is then carried to the four shrines of the Fire god in the foothills, where bonfires are kindled, first to the north, then west, south and east. Another Sumaikoli of one day's duration was formerly held in the summer, but it was discontinued about twenty-five years ago.

MUCAIASTI (BUFFALO DANCE); held annually, usually during March, but occasionally as early as January. The author was told by an educated Hopi that it has been at least seventy-five years since they went on their last buffalo hunt. They had to go many miles to the buffalo country and they encountered many dangers from other tribes; yet they still hold the buffalo dance as of old in preparation for the hunt. In this dance two men wear buffalo masks, and offerings are deposited in the Buffalo shrine at the close of the ceremony.

HEMIS KACHINA DANCE; held annually in the spring usually in May. It is sometimes held as a Niman or Farewell Kachina at Oraibi, Shipaulovi, and Shongopovi. This is regarded by the Hopis as the same as the Ha-ama-ci-kwi of the Zuñis.

PAWIK KACHINA DANCE; held annually during the last half of June.

MALO KACHINA DANCE; held annually early in July. This is said by the Hopis to be a Zuñi dance.

COYOHIM KACHINA DANCE; held annually in July.

AÑA KACHINA DANCE; held annually about the middle of July, sometimes during the first days of the Niman Kachina. It has been held rarely as late as September 20, at Hano. This is similar to the Kokokoi ceremony held at Zuñi.

SHALAKO KACHINA CEREMONY; held at long intervals of time, usually in July. This is similar to the famous Zuñi Shalako, held at that pueblo in November; but its observance in Hopiland is very rare.

NIMAN KACHINA CEREMONY (FAREWELL OF THE KACHINAS); held annually from the middle to the last of July. This is one of the most important Kachina dances, and celebrates the departure or farewell to the kachinas, who are supposed to leave the pueblos and return to their home in the San Francisco mountains, known among the Hopis as *Nuvatikiobi*, the snow houses.

IV. Dates of the Snake and Flute Dances at some of the Hopi Pueblos

The following are the dates on which Snake dances have been held at some of the Hopi pueblos since 1885. These are not complete, as that is impossible. They were arranged by the author from various authentic sources.

1885: Mishongnovi on August 17; Walpi on August 18.
1891: Mishongnovi on August 20; Walpi on August 21.
1893: Mishongnovi on August 13; Walpi on August 14.
1894: Shongopovi on August 24.
1896: Oraibi on August 19; Shipaulovi on August 23; Shongopovi on August 24.
1897: Mishongnovi on August 17.
1898: Oraibi on August 22.
1900: Oraibi on August 19.
1901: Mishongnovi on August 21; Walpi on August 24.
1902: Oraibi on August 26.
1906: Oraibi on September 5; Shipaulovi on September 5; Shongopovi on September 6.
1907: Walpi on August 15; Mishongnovi on August 18.
1908: Oraibi on August 21; Hotevilla on September 2; Shongopovi on September 2.
1910: Oraibi on August 22; Hotevilla on August 23; Shongopovi on August 29; Shipaulovi on September 3.
1911: Walpi on August 22.

1912: Oraibi on August 21; Hotevilla on August 23; Shongopovi on September 1; Shipaulovi on September 5.
1913: Walpi on August 21; Mishongnovi on August 21.
1928: Hotevilla on August 23.

Some Flute Dance Dates

1896: Mishongnovi on August 15; Walpi on August 21.
1907: Oraibi on August 19.
1908: Walpi on August 19; Mishongnovi on August 20.
1911: Shipaulovi on September 2.
1912: Mishongnovi on August 19; Walpi on August 21.
1913: Oraibi on August 19; Shipaulovi on August 26; Shongopovi on August 28.

Bibliography

BANDELIER, ADOLF F., The Delight Makers, New York, 1899.

BARTLETT, JOHN RUSSELL, Personal Narrative of Explorations and Incidents in Texas, New Mexico, California, Sonora, and Chihuahua, New York, 1854.

BLACKMAR, FRANK W., Spanish Institutions of the Southwest, Baltimore, 1891.

BOLTON, HERBERT EUGENE, Spanish Explorations in the Southwest, 1542-1706, New York, 1916.

BROWN, J. ROSS, Adventures in the Apache Country, New York, 1869.

BOURKE, CAPTAIN JOHN G., On the Border with Crook, New York, 1896.

———— The Snake Dance of the Moquis of Arizona: a narrative of a journey from Santa Fé to the villages of the Moqui indians of Arizona, London, 1884.

CRANE, LEO, Indians of the Enchanted Desert, New York, 1925.

COUES, DR. ELLIOTT, On the Trail of A Spanish Pioneer: the diary and itinerary of Francisco Garcés; translated from the Spanish, 2 Vols., New York, 1900.

DELONG, SIDNEY, The History of Arizona from the Earliest Times to 1903, San Francisco, 1905.

DORSEY, GEORGE A., Indians of the Southwest, Chicago, 1903.

DORSEY, GEORGE A., and H. R. VOTH, The Mishongnovi Ceremonies of the Snake and Antelope Fraternities, Chicago, 1902.

———— The Oraibi Soyal Ceremony, Chicago, 1901.

DUELL, PRENT, Mission Architecture as exemplified in San Xavier del Bac, Tucson, Arizona, 1919.

EICKEMEYER, CARL, and LILLIAN W., Among the Pueblo Indians, New York, 1895.

EMORY, LIEUTENANT-COLONEL W. H., Notes of a Military Reconnoissance from Fort Leavenworth, in Missouri, to San Diego, in California, including part of the Arkansas, Del Norte, and Gila

Rivers; made by Emory in 1846-47, with the advance guard of the "Army of the West," Washington, 1848.

ENGELHARDT, FR. ZEPHYRIM, Franciscans in Arizona, Harbor Springs, Michigan, 1899.

―――― Franciscans in New Mexico, Harbor Springs, Michigan, 1899.

FARISH, THOMAS EDWIN, History of Arizona, 8 vols., Phoenix, Arizona, 1915.

FEWKES, DR. JESSE WALTER, A Few Summer Ceremonials at the Tusayan Pueblos in *journal of American Ethnology and Archaeology*, vol. 2, Cambridge, Massachusetts, 1892.

―――― Archaeological Expedition to Arizona in 1895 in *seventeenth annual report of the Bureau of American Ethnology*, part 2, Washington, 1898.

―――― A Reconnoissance of Ruins in or near the Zuñi Reservation in *journal of American Ethnology and Archaeology,* vol. 1, Cambridge, Mass., 1891.

―――― Hopi Kacinas: in *twenty-second annual report of the Bureau of American Ethnology*, Washington, 1903.

―――― Snake Ceremonials at Walpi in *journal of American Ethnology and Archaeology*, vol. 4, Cambridge, Mass., 1894.

―――― Tusayan Flute and Snake Ceremonies in *nineteenth annual report of Bureau of American Ethnology*, part 2, Washington, 1900.

―――― Tusayan Kacinas: in *fifteenth annual report of Bureau of American Ethnology*, Washington, 1897.

―――― Tusayan Migration Traditions: in *nineteenth annual report of the Bureau of American Ethnology*, part 2, Washington, 1900.

―――― Tusayan Snake Ceremonies: in *sixteenth annual report of Bureau of American Ethnology*, Washington, 1897.

―――― Two Summers' Work in Pueblo Ruins: in *twenty-second annual report of Bureau of American Ethnology*, part 1, Washington, 1904.

GARCÉS, PADRE FRANCISCO, On the Trail of A Spanish Pioneer: see *Coues.*

HAMBLIN, JACOB, Narrative of his Personal Experience as Frontiersman, Missionary to Indians, and Explorer, Salt Lake City, 1909.

HINTON, RICHARD J., Handbook to Arizona, New York, 1878.

HODGE, FREDERICK W., Handbook of American Indians North of

Mexico, 2 vols; bulletin 30, *Bureau of American Ethnology*. Washington, 1907.

HOUGH, WALTER, The Moki Snake Dance, Chicago, 1901.

INMAN, COLONEL HENRY, The Old Santa Fé Trail, Topeka, 1899 and 1908.

JAMES, GEORGE WHARTON, Arizona the Wonderland, Boston, 1917.

─── New Mexico, the land of the delight makers, Boston, 1920.

KIDDER, ALFRED VINCENT, Introduction to the Study of Southwestern Archaeology, with a preliminary account of the excavations at Pecos, New Haven, 1924.

KINO, FATHER EUSEBIO FRANCISCO, Historical Memoir of Pimería Alta: contemporary account of the beginnings of California, Sonora, and Arizona, 1683-1711; published for the first time from the original manuscript; translated into English, edited and annotted by Herbert Eugene Bolton: 2 vols.; this is Father Kino's Lost History, The Arthur H. Clark Company, Cleveland, 1919.

LAUT, AGNES C., Through Our Unknown Southwest, New York, 1913.

LUMMIS, CHARLES F., Mesa, Cañon and Pueblo, New York, 1925.

─── Pueblo Indian Folk-Stories, New York, 1891 and 1920.

─── Some Strange Corners of Our Country; the wonderland of the southwest, New York, 1892.

─── The Land of Poco Tiempo, New York, 1913, reprinted 1925.

McCLINTOCK, JAMES H., Arizona – The Youngest State, 2 vols., Chicago, 1916.

─── Mormon Settlement in Arizona, Phoenix, 1921.

MINDELEFF, COSMOS, Localization of Tusayan Clans: in *nineteenth annual report of Bureau of American Ethnology*, part 2, Washington, 1900.

MINDELEFF, VICTOR, A Study of Pueblo Architecture: Tusayan and Cibola: in *eighth annual report of Bureau of American Ethnology*, Washington, 1891.

PEIXOTTO, ERNEST, Our Hispanic Southwest: Arizona, Texas, and New Mexico, New York, 1916.

PRINCE, L. BRADFORD, The Spanish Mission Churches of New Mexico, Cedar Rapids, Iowa, 1915.

READ, BENJAMIN M., Illustrated History of New Mexico, Santa Fé, 1912.

RITCH, WILLIAM G., Illustrated New Mexico, Santa Fé, 1883.
SALPOINTE, BISHOP J. B., Soldiers of the Cross, Banning, California, 1898.
SALVATIERRA, FATHER JUAN MARÍA DE, S. J. Missionary in the Province of New Spain, and Apostolic Conqueror of the Californias, translated into English, edited and annotated by Marguerite Eyer Wilbur, (prepared as vol. v. of Spain in the West series published early in 1929 by the Arthur H. Clark Company, Cleveland).
SAUNDERS, CHARLES FRANCIS, Finding the Worth While in the Southwest, New York, 1924.
TWITCHELL, RALPH E., Leading Facts in New Mexican History 2 vols., Cedar Rapids, Iowa.
——— Old Santa Fé, Santa Fe.
——— Spanish Archives of New Mexico 2 vols., Cedar Rapids, Iowa, 1914.
VOTH, H. R., The Oraibi Summer Snake Ceremony, Chicago, 1903.
VOTH, H. R., and GEORGE A. DORSEY, The Mishongnovi Ceremonies of the Snake and Antelope Fraternities, Chicago, 1902.
——— The Oraibi Soyal Ceremony, Chicago, 1901.
WALLACE, SUSAN E, The Land of the Pueblos, New York, 1888.
WINSHIP, GEORGE PARKER, The Coronado Expedition, 1540-1542: in *fourteenth annual report of Bureau of American Ethnology,* part 1, Washington, 1896.

Index

Index

ABEYTA, BERNARDO: erects Santuario of Chimayó, 63
Abeytia, Ambrosio, Isleta indian: loan to federal commander, 152
Abiquiu (N. Mex.) : Penitentes strong at, 206
Abó (N. Mex.): 141, 146-147; visited by Juan and Vicente de Zaldivar, 146; mission founded, 146; headquarters of Acevedo, 146; ruins, 146; Carleton describes church, 147; abandoned to Apaches, 147; see also, *Isleta*
Accursed lakes: legend of, 142
Acevedo, Fray Antonio de: in charge of Nambé, 61
Acevedo, Fray Francisco de: founds mission at Quarai, 142; Tajique, 144; Abó, 146; Tabira, 148; death, 148
Acha: see *Picuris*
Acoma (N. Mex.): 164-167; visita of Laguna, 161; lawsuit over painting, 161; location, 161, 167; age of pueblo, 164; discovered by Alvarado, 164; battle at, 165; visited by Espejo, 165; Oñate escapes death, 165; Juan de Zaldivar's death, 165, 183, 190, 213; Oñate's return to San Gabriel, 165; Vicente de Zaldivar captures, 165; mission established, 166; Rebellion of 1680, 166; Maldonado murdered, 30, 166; De Vargas fails to capture, 166; surrender to Cubero, 166; history of present church, 166; mission selected as model building, 166; graveyard, 166; "El Camino del Padre", 167;

Ramirez's escape, 167; Enchanted mesa, 167
Acoma indians: join Jemez against De Vargas, 136
Agriculture: first Spanish colonists in New Mexico, 34; fertile lands attract Oñate's colonists, 72; irrigation by Spaniards, 134; ancient apple orchard at Tajique, 144; first grapes in New Mexico, 159; gardens and fields, 243; fruits and produce, 248; Hopi indian farming, 281; report of supposed Hopi cure for snake bite, 297
Agua Fria church (N. Mex.) : built, 57
Akin, Louis, artist: author's comrade, 301; paintings of Grand Canyon, 301
Alameda (N. Mex.): 128-129; location of ruins, 128; Santa Ana mission dedicated, 128; visita of Albuquerque, 129; pueblo abandoned, 129
Alameda station (N. Mex.): ruins of old Sandiá near, 127; Sandiá near, 128; ruins of Alameda near, 128
Alamillo (N. Mex.) : 128, 132, 158; mission established, 158; people go to El Paso, 158; burned, 158
Alarid, Juan Bautista y: erects Chapel of the Vigiles, 58
Albino Hopi indians: Antelope priest at Oraibi, 291, 330; Flute priest at Mishongnovi, 325
Albizu, Tomas de: commands avenging murder force, 174
Albuquerque (N. Mex.): 131-133; third town in New Mexico, 131;

death of De Vargas, 131; founded, 131; San Felipe church, 132
Alcalde (N. Mex.): Penitente settlement, 206
All Saints' day: Penitente rites, 199
Altar: Blue Flute at Mishongnovi, 321
Alvarado, Hernando de: visits Taos, 87; discovers Acoma, 164
Alvarez, Manuel: moves Chapel of the Vigiles to ranch, 58
American occupation of Arizona: First U. S. dragoons take possession of Tucson, 259
American occupation of New Mexico: Judge Baker tries to hold court, 46; Chapel of the Vigiles moved, 58; Taos rebellion, 88; Fernandez de Taos, during, 90; candlesticks brought from Chihuahua, 115; little attention paid to Zuñis, 184; Lewis, a Navajo trader during early years of, 192; soldiers camped at Inscription rock, 193
American inscriptions on Inscription rock (N. Mex.): 192, 193
American Museum of Natural History (New York): mural decorations, 301
American Passion play: 200
American troops: occupy Tucson, 259
Aña kachina of Hopi indians: 344
Analco (N. Mex.): occupied site of Santa Fé, 42; oldest house in United States part of, 45
Ankwanti kachina (Palulukonti) of Hopi indians: 343
Antelope dance: at Mishongnovi, 307; not held in 1908, 328; date of, 340
Antelope Spring (Ariz.): site of battle, 212
Antidote for snake bite: 296; report to author on supposed remedies, 297
Anza, Captain Juan B: commander at Tubac, 254

Apache indians: raid on Senecu, 29; raid pueblos in 1680, 80; Quartelejo, New Mexico, a Jacarilla Apache settlement, 83; raid on Taos, 91; defeated by Governor Urrizola, 91; raids on Pecos, 100; San Cristóbal, 105; Galisteo, 106; Cuchillo, 110; Salinas pueblos, 141; temporary peace with Quarai, 143; drive people from Quarai, 143; from Chililí, 145; raid on Abó, 147; force abandonment of Tabira, 149; Spaniards redeem Pueblo captives, 157; drive people out of Sevilleta, 158; raids Senecu and San Antonio, 160; raid Hawikuh in 1670, 174, 178; defense against, at Kechipauan, 180; raids Walpi, 227; raids southern Arizona missions, 229, 230; Bernave killed by, 240; raid on Guevavi in 1784, 240; almost exterminate Sobaipuri tribe, 243; raids Tumacacori, 243, 244, 247; "tigers of the desert," 243; Pete Kitchen defies, 244; raids San Xavier del Bac, 251; raid down Santa Cruz valley, 253; raids Tubac, 254, 255; Oury saves Tubac, 256; attack Tucson, 257, 258; Gandara ranch protected against, 260; James Pennington defies, 260
Apple orchards, ancient: at Tajique, 144
Architecture: Santo Domingo church, 123; faults of construction avoided, 243
Arivaca (Ariz.): visita of Guevavi, 262; camping place of rebellious Pimas, 262
Arizona: number of missions founded, 27; first headquarters of government, 37; Rebellion of 1680, 79; Casa Grande ruins, 84; Sandiá people flee to, 127; Cabeza de Vaca and companions first to cross, 170; Hopi missions of, 207-288; sheepmen use Lee's ferry, 224;

Padre Garcés journey across, 225; Hopi Snake dance, 227; southern missions of, 229-264; Father Kino's explorations, 230-232; lost Spanish mines, 234-239; Pete Kitchen, pioneer of, 243; troops withdrawn from, at outbreak of Civil war, 253, 255; first Spanish settlement, 254; cattle ranges, 278, 280; University of, 297; founding of Hotevilla, 298, 319; Mishongnovi Snake dance, 300; Oraibi Flute dance, 317; Mishongnovi Flute dance, 320; Oraibi Snake dance, 328; Spanish mission names with English equivalent, 333-335; ceremonies of Hopis, 339-345; dates of Snake and Flute dances, 347

Arizona Mining Co: at Tubac, 255

Arizonian, The: first newspaper in Ariz., 255

Arizu, Fray José de: murdered, 31, 106

Arkansas river (Kans.): Coronado follows, 148

Armijo, Antonio: trader at Oraibi, 282

Armijo, Governor Manuel: captures Texas-Santa Fé expedition, 104

Arnais, Carlos: name found in Inscription house ruin, 222

Arteaga, Fray Antonio de: founds Socorro, 159; plants first grapes in New Mexico, 159; founds mission at Senecu, 160

Arvide, Fray Martin de: in charge of Picuris, 83; resettles Patoqua and Gyusiwa, 135, 136, 139; sent to the Zipia, 173; murdered, 28, 83, 173, 183

Astialakwa (N. Mex.): 134, 139-140; escape of priest, 135, 140; San Juan de los Jemez mission at, 139; location, 140

Ati (Ariz.): named and mission founded, 262

Attempted reconquests of New Mexico: by Otermin, 115, 135, 152, 153; 158; by Posada, 132; by Cruzate, 133, 135

Avila, Fray Alonzo Gil de: murdered, 29, 160

Awatobi (Ariz.): Martinez expedition against, 192, 210-220; first Europeans, 211; Tovar opposed by Hopis, 211, 212; discovery of Grand Canyon, 211, 212; Antelope Spring identified as scene of battle, 212; Espejo's visit, 212; Oñate visits, 213; three priests go to Hopis, 213; San Bernardino mission founded, 213; Hopis belief regarding horses, 213; converts made, 213; Padre Porras restores sight, 213; Porras incurs enmity of native priests, 214; Espeleta in charge, 214; Figueroa and Santa Maria arrive, 214; Rebellion of 1680, 214; four priests murdered, 214; Figueroa murdered, 30, 214; De Vargas receives submission, 214; gain hatred of other Hopis, 214; Fray Garaycocchea visits, 214; inhabitants rebuild church, 215; destruction of, 215-219; only two men spared, 219; excavations of ruins of pueblo and mission by Dr. J. Walter Fewkes, 219; finds evidence of fire and many bones, 219

Ayala, Fray Pedro de Avila y: murdered, 29, 174, 179

Aztec Fort ruin (Ariz.): 302

Aztecs: migration, 26; tell Spaniards of Seven Cities of Cibola, 169

Aztlan: migration of Aztecs from ancient, 26

BACUANCOS (Ariz.): San Martin in charge, 234, 261, 261-262; visited by Kino, 261; mentioned as visita of Guevavi, 234, 261; abandoned, 262

Bad lands of Little Colorado river: 305

Baker, Judge: attempts to hold court, 46
Bandelier, Adolph: population of Galisteo, 107; name and population of San Marcos, 108; size of Cienega, 109; *The Delight Makers,* 111; home at Cochití, 111; says Chililí abandoned because of Apache raids, 145; discovers inscriptions on Inscription rock, 189
Barrionuevo, Francisco de: visits Taos, 87; visits Jemez pueblos, 134
Basket dances of Hopi indians: Lalakoñti, 341; Kohonino, 343; Owakulti, 343
Bean planting ceremony (Powamu): 343
Beaver City (Utah): John D. Lee's trial, 224
Belen (N. Mex.): settlement estab- and mission founded, 157
Beltran, Fray Bernardino: visits Pecos with Espejo, 98
Benavides, Fray Alonzo de: builds San Francisco church, Santa Fé, 49; builds Santa Clara mission, 71; report of indians baptized at Taos, 87; report of Pecos, 99; succeeded by Fray Perea, 172
Bent, Governor Charles: murdered, 88, 91, 92
Bernal, Fray Juan: murdered at Galisteo, 29, 107; 100
Bernave, Fray Juan Cristobomo Gil de: first Franciscan in charge of Guevavi, 240; killed, 240
Black Falls (Ariz.): ruins, 303
Black Jack mine (Ariz.): 235
Black Mesa of San Felipe: San Felipe people found by De Vargas, 124; church built, 124; ruins of old church, 124; see also, *Santa Aña pueblo*
Black Mesa of San Ildefonso: siege by De Vargas, 67; De Vargas attacks, 68

Blake, S. F: report on supposed cure for snake bite, 297
Blue Flute society of Hopi indians: ceremony at Oraibi, 317-319; altar of, at Mishongnovi, 321; secret ceremony before altar, 321; ceremony at Toreva spring, 325; description of platoon, 326; costume of performers, 326; march to village plaza, 327; ceremony in Mishongnovi plaza, 327
Bolton, Dr. Herbert E: Father Kino's lost journal, 231
Bourke, Captain John G: first account of Hopi Snake dance, 278
Bove (N. Mex.): name given San Ildefonso by Oñate, 67
Braba: name given Taos by Barrionuevo, 87
Bua, Nicholas: killed, 79
Buffalo dance of Hopi indians: 344
Buhoki: shrine of, 313
Bulitikibi (Butterfly dance) of Hopi indians: 340
Bureau of American Ethnology: Dr. J. Walter Fewkes excavates ruins for, 303
Bustamante, Governor Juan Domingo de: erects mission at Nambé, 61
Butterfly dance: see *Bulitikibi*

CAKWALEÑYA FLUTE SOCIETY: see *Blue Flute society*
Calabash clan of Cochití: kiva, 111; in Rain dance, 269, 275; dress of performers, 275
Calabazas (Ariz.): San Martin in charge, 234; on Pete Kitchen's famous road, 259; date of origin uncertain, 259; church erected, 259; old Calabazas, 259; gold discovered, 259; Ortiz grant, 259; Gandara ranch, 259, 260; military post, 260; Calabazas boom, 261; now a "ghost city," 261
California: missions founded in New Mexico and Arizona before the first in, 27; location of fabled Gran

INDEX

Quivira shifts on early maps from great plains to, 148; Panama Pacific exposition, 166; Gulf, 170, 190; first emigrant train to, 193; old Spanish trail from Santa Fé, 222; Padre Garcés at San Gabriel mission, 225; Salvatierra and Kino make plans for spiritual conquests through Sonora to, 233; no mission in California equal to San Xavier del Bac, 248; first printing press in Arizona hauled overland from, 255; Governor Gandara flees to, 260; volunteers from, garrison Fort Mason, 260

Calvario cross of Penitentes: procession, 200; crucifixion, 203

Cameron bridge: 305

Cañada de Cochití (N. Mex.): Cochití settle at Kuapa in, 112

Cañada del Oro (Ariz.): discovery of gold, 235

Cañaque dance at Zuñi (N. Mex.): 184

Canyon Diablo (Ariz.): indian trading post, 281

Carbonelli, Fray Antonio: murdered, 31, 106

Cardeñas, Don Garcia Lopez de: discovers Grand Canyon, Arizona, 171, 211, 212

Carleton, Major James H: description of Quivira, 143; of Abó, 147

Carmargo, Friar Antonio: on Hopi expedition, 192

Carson, Kit: home at Taos, 90, 91; grave, 91

Carucho, Fray José: priest at Guevavi, 234

Casa Grande ruin (Ariz.): 84; discovered by Kino, 232

Castrense church: see *Our Lady of Light*

Catholic: trail of padres, 25; first priests in New Mexico, 26, 27, 28; priests murdered, 28-30; three priests found mission at Puaray, New Mexico, 33; New Mexico divided into mission districts, 38; churches of Santa Fé, 41-58; St. Francis cathedral, 49; English speaking catholics in 1880, 53; Santuario of Chimayó, 62-67; fight between church and Señora Carmel Chavez, 63-67; Santa Cruz, New Mexico, 72-75; church at Taos, 90; ancient mission at Cochití, 111, 267; sisters of mercy, Santa Fé, present statue to Cochití, 119; paintings in Cochití mission, 119; San Felipe church, Albuquerque, 132; Jemez converts baptized, 136; Salinas missions, 141-149; success of priests among New Mexico missions, 209; Jesuits in Arizona, 229-264; expulsion of Jesuits, 239; Franciscans take charge of southern Arizona missions, 239; Franciscan college at Queretaro, Mexico, 239; see *Lamy*

Catiti: assists Popé in Rebellion of 1680, 29, 78

Cattle ranches: Gandara, Arizona, 260; San Bernardino, Arizona, 263; C O Bar, Arizona, 278, 280, 300

Catua: warns Otermin of Rebellion of 1680, 59, 79

Cavillo, Padre Battasar: starts construction of San Xavier del Bac, 252

Ceballos, Governor Francisco de la Mora: sends force to avenge murder of Letrado and Arvide, 174

Cebolleta (N. Mex.): 167-168; Navajo settlement and mission, 168

Cemetery chapel, Santa Fé (N. Mex.): 57

Center of the earth shrine, Zuñi (N. Mex.): 187

Ceremonies of Hopi indians (Ariz.): 339-345

Chamita station (N. Mex.): 34

Chamuscado, Francisco Sanchez: expedition of 1581, 28, 33, 98; visits Cibola, 171; Halona, 180

Chapel of Our Lady of Loudres, San Juan (N. Mex.): 82
Chaves, Don Fernando de: escapes from Fernandez de Taos, 91
Chavez: battle of Santa Cruz, New Mexico, 75; leader of Taos Rebellion of 1847, 75
Chavez, Señora Carmel: owner of Chimayó, 64; fight with catholic church, 64-67; leaves Chimayó to daughter at her death, 67
Chihuahua (Mexico): sick from, go to Chimayó, 63; candlesticks brought from, to Cochití, 115, 268; Lieutenant Pike taken prisoner to, 123
Children's kachina dance (Wahikwinema) of Hopi indians: 343
Chililí (N. Mex.): 141, 145; discovered by Oñate, 145; mission founded by Peinade, 145; death of Peinade, 145; abandoned, 145; converts from settle at Isleta, New Mexico, 152
Chimayó (N. Mex.): 62-67; home of famous blankets, 62; Church of Santuario, 62; shrine for sick, 62; healing powers of earth, 63; see also, *Chavez, Carmel*
Cibola: see *Seven Cities of Cibola*
Cicuye (N. Mex.): 97; see *Pecos*
Cienega (N. Mex.): 109
Cities that died of fear (N. Mex.): Quarai, 49, 142; San Cristóbal, 105; Tajique, 144; Chililí, 145; Abó, 146; Gran Quivira, or Tabira, 147; Senecu, 160
Civil war: Isleta loyal to union, 152; soldiers of, buried in Santa Fé cemetery, 54; Confederates capture Santa Fé, 41; troops withdrawn from Arizona at outbreak of, 253, 255; Fort Mason, Arizona, established during, 260
Claros, Fray Juan: missions assigned to, 38
Cochise county (Ariz.): San Bernardino ranch, 262; John Slaughter, famous fighting sheriff, 263
Cochití (N. Mex.): 111-120; location, 111; dance for rain, 111, 119, 265-275; ancient home at Tyuonyi, 112; settle at Potrero de las Vacas, 112; in Cañada de Cochití, 112; mission established, 112: escape of priest from, 112; inhabitants flee to Potrero Viejo, 115; De Vargas attacks Potrero Viejo, 115; De Vargas builds new church, 116; San Buenaventura, 116; description of present mission, 116, 119, 268; mass in old mission, 119, 267; 265-275; Marcial Quintana, governor of, 269, 270; council refuses permission to photograph Rain dance, 269-271
Colorado: sick from, go to Chimayó, 63; death of Kit Carson at Fort Lyons, 91; Lieutenant Pike, 123; Mesa Verde National park, 178; Penitentes, 196; old Spanish trail from Santa Fé to California crosses, 222
Colorado river (Texas): Coronado reaches headwaters of, 148
Comanche indians: raids on Taos, 88, 91; on Pecos, 100; ambush Pecos warriors, 100; raids on Galisteo, 106, 108; on the Salinas pueblos, 141; Spaniards redeem Pueblo captives, 157
Compostela (Mexico): starting point of Coronado expedition, 169
Concepcion, Fray Cristóbal de la: founds Hopi missions, 213
Concepcion mission, near Yuma (Ariz.): Padre Garcés murdered, 225
Conejos (N. Mex.): Apaches killed by Spaniards, 91
Confederates: capture Santa Fé, 41
Converts: number of, 27; number made by Kino, 230
Corchado, Fray Andres: missions assigned to, 38, 165, 172

Corn: indian corn from Oraibi, 282; scramble for, at Oraibi, 283; dance of Hopis, 289; scramble for, at Mishongnovi, 308, 310

Coronado, Francisco Vasquez de: expedition led by, 26, 27; Padre Juan de Padilla sets out for Gran Quivira, 28; visits Picuris, 86; in Tiguex province, 33; Puaray besieged, 33, 87; visits Pecos, 97; Galisteo, 107; at San Felipe, 124; visits Sandiá, 127; Sia, 133; Barrionuevo visits Jemez, 134; Gran Quivira myth, 147; crosses great plains, 148; executes the Turk, 148; reaches Isleta, 151; Padres Padilla and Escalona remain behind, 156; Alvarado discovers Acoma, 164; expedition leaves Mexico, 169; reaches Hawikuh, 170; captures Hawikuh after battle, 170; finds fabled seven cities only indian villages, 171; sends Tovar to Hopi country, 171, 211, 212; dispatches Cardeñas to investigate story of Grand Canyon, 171, 211, 212; Mexican indians found at Hawikuh by Espejo, 171; discovers Halona, 180; camped at Inscription rock, 189.

Cortez: searches for Seven Cities of Cibola, 169

Corvera: Fray Francisco: murdered, 30, 61

Coues, Dr. Elliott: editor of Padre Garcés Diary, 263

Coyohim kachina of Hopi indians, 344

Crane, Leo, Hopi agent: prohibits photographs of Snake dance, 209

Cristo (Christ): selection by Penitentes for crucifixion, 200; crucifixion, 203; burial, 204

Cross, Colonel Ed: published first newspaper in Arizona, 255

Cross erected by De Vargas at Sia (N. Mex.): 133

Crosses of the Penitentes: at graves, 195, 204; Calvario cross, 200, 203

Crossing of the Fathers (Utah-Ariz.): first crossing of Grand Canyon discovered by Garcés, 221; Escalante and Dominguez cross, 221, 222; known as Ute ford, 223; found by Hamblin, 223; used by Mormons, 223

Crucifixion by Penitentes (N. Mex.): 203

Cruzate, Governor Domingo de: attempted reconquest of New Mexico, 133; bloody battle at Sia, 133; Jemez flee from, 135

Cubero, Governor Pedro Rodriguez de: captures Acoma, 165, 166

Cuchillo, San Pedro del (N. Mex.): 109-110; mission established at, 110

Cuellar, Augustin de: first mission at Hawikuh, 172

Cummins, Prof. Byron (U. of Ariz.): 243

Cushing, Frank H: excavated ruins of Halona, 180; discovered names on Inscription rock, 189

DANCE FOR RAIN at Cochití: 111, 119, 265-275; see Rain Dance

Dances: see Canaque, Flute, Rain Dance, Shallako, Snake

Dates of Snake and Flute dances of Hopi indians: 347

Defouri, Rev. James H: in charge of Guadalupe church, 53

De la Llama, Fray Geronimo: bones removed to Santa Fé, 49, 143; death of, 143

Delgado, Don Simon: places third roof on San Miguel church, 42; razes the Castrense, Santa Fé, 45

Delgado, Padre: brings Sandiá people back from Arizona, 127

Del Valle, Governor: builds Castrense, 45; exhumes bones of Fray Zarate at Picuris, 49, 83; removes bones of De la Llama, 49, 143

Denver & Rio Grande railway: 34, 39; to Santa Clara pueblo, 71; built to Taos junction, 91
De Vaca, Alvar Nuñez Cabeza: survivors of Narvarez expedition, 170; wanderings across Texas, New Mexico and Arizona with Maldonado, Dorantes, and Estévan, 170
De Val, Fray Juan: murdered, 183
De Vargas, General Don Diego: captures Santa Fé, 42, 54; buried, 42, 131; restores San Miguel church, 42; builds Guadalupe church, 50; full name of, 53; builds Rosario chapel, 53; arrives before Santa Fé, 54; legend of statue of the Virgin Mary, 54; builds Agua Fria church, 57; placed Acevedo in charge of Nambé, 61; siege of Black mesa of San Ildefonso, 67-68; orders indians from Santa Cruz, 73, 106; founds villa of Santa Cruz, 73; finds Picuris deserted, 83; marches to Taos, 88; battle with Taos warriors, 88; aided by Juan Ye, 100; restores Pecos church, 100; Galisteo people fortified in old Palace, Santa Fé, 107; finds San Marcos in ruins, 109; attempts to resettle Cienega, 109; attack Cochití at Potrero Viejo, 115; builds mission at Cochití, 115; finds San Felipe people on Black mesa, 124; returns as governor of New Mexico in 1703, 131; death, 131; will, 131; induces Santa Aña people to return, 132; re-establishes mission at Sia, 133; induces Jemez to return, 135; campaign against Jemez, 135; finds skeleton at Gyusiwa, 139; fails to capture Acoma, 166; receives peaceable submission of Zuñis, 177, 183, 184; finds christian altar on Thunder mountain, 177; inscription of, 183, 191; marches to Hopi villages, 214

De Vargas procession, Santa Fé: origin of, 54
Diaz, Fray Pedro Rafael: last Jesuit in charge of Guevavi, 239
Dominguez, Fray Francisco Atanasio: 221-223; crosses Grand Canyon, 221; visits Hopi villages, 221; first over old Spanish trail from Santa Fé to California, 222; second visit to Hopi villages, 222
Doney, Benjamin: excavations at Wukoki, Arizona, ruins, 303
Dorantes, Andres: survivors of Narvarez expedition, 170; wanderings across Texas, New Mexico and Arizona with De Vaca, Maldonado, and Estévan, 170
Douglas (Ariz.): 262
Drab Flute society of Hopi indians: Oraibi Drab Flutes go to Hotevilla, 317; Mishongnovi Drab Flute ceremony at Toreva, 326; description of platoon, 326; costume of performers, 326; march to village, 327; ceremony in Mishongnovi plaza, 327
Dragoons: First U. S., take possession of Tucson, Arizona, 259; stationed at Calabazas, Arizona, 260
Durango (Mexico): see *Elizacochea*

EL CAMINO DEL PADRE: 167
Elizacochea, Don Martin de: bishop of Durango; inscription on Inscription rock, 192
El Morro: see *Inscription rock*
El Paso (Texas): Tabira people settle near, 149; Otermin's retreat to, 155, 158; Otermin establishes Isleta del Sur near, 155; Zuñiga's death, 160; Senecu del Sur near, 160
El Rancho Bonito, Mesa (Ariz.): outdoor school for boys, 320
El Tovar Hotel, Grand Canyon (Ariz.): named after Don Pedro de Tovar, 171

El Vado de los Padres: see *Crossing of the Fathers*
Enchanted mesa (N. Mex.): 167
Escalante, Fray Silvestre Velez de: 221-223; crossed Grand Canyon, 221; visits Hopi villages, 221; first over old Spanish trail from Santa Fé to California, 222; second visit to Hopi villages, 222
Escalona, Fray Juan de: builds church at Santo Domingo, 120; buried at Santo Domingo, 120
Escalona, Fray Luis de, *also called*, Juan de la Cruz: with Coronado, 28; murdered, 28, 156
Espejo, Antonio de: expedition in search of three priests, 98; visits Pecos, 98; Jemez pueblos, 134; Acoma, 165; visits Hawikuh and gives tribe name of Zuñi, 171; finds Mexican indians who accompanied Coronado, 171; Halona, 180; Awatobi, 212
Espeleta, chief of Oraibi: plots for destruction of Awatobi, 216
Espeleta, Fray José de: in charge of Hopi missions, 214; murdered, 30, 214, 220
Esquivel, Juan José: alcalde of Santa Cruz, 74; leader of Revolution of 1837, 57, 74; execution, 57
Estancia valley (N. Mex.): 141
Estévan, the negro slave: guide for Fray Marcos de Niza, 26, 170; death, 170; wanderings with De Vaca, Dorantes, and Maldonado, 170, 211
Estrada, Juan de: murdered, 88
Evans, Prof. H. D: 320

FAREWELL OF KACHINAS (Niman) of Hopi indians: 339, 345
Fernandez de Taos (N. Mex.): Gov. Bent murdered, 88, 91; 90-92; headquarters of trappers, 90; Kit Carson, 90, 91; settlement, 91; Rebellion of 1680, 91; settlement after reconquest, 91; raids by Utes and Apaches, 91; church built, 92; Padre Martinez, 92; conducts school and establishes newspaper, 92
Festival of Our Lady of Guadalupe: 53
Fewkes, Dr. J. Walter: identifies Antelope spring as site of battle, 212; excavations at Awatobi, Arizona, 219; at Wukoki ruins, Arizona, 303
Fields, The (Ariz.): old-time indian trading post, 278, 281, 305; Thanksgiving and Christmas dinner, 306; abandonment of, 306
Fiesta: dates held at Pueblos of New Mexico, 337; to San Buenaventura at Cochití, 265
Figueredo, Fray Roque de: founds first mission at Hawikuh, 172
Figueroa, Fray José de: murdered, 30, 214
Fire that never dies: in kiva at Pecos, 103; legend, 237
First: Spanish settlement in Arizona, Tubac, 20, 254; New Mexico mission, 27, 33-34; Spanish settlement in New Mexico, San Gabriel, 34-39; colonists, in New Mexico, 34-39, 98; intimation of the Rebellion of 1680, 58, 79; blood spilled in Rebellion of 1680, 59; newspaper in New Mexico, 92; Santa Fé traders, 97; baptismal in western New Mexico, 172; emigrant train across New Mexico, 193; Hopi born in christianity, 208; printing press in Arizona, 255; newspaper in Arizona, 255
Flagellantes: movement swept Europe in Middle Ages, 205; spread to New Mexico, 205
Flagstaff (Ariz.): distance to Hopi villages, 210, 279; distance to Inscription house ruin, 222; C O Bar ranch near, 278, 280, 300; distance to Black Falls ruins, 303
Florida: San Augustine founded, 37
Flute dance of Hopi indians: years

364 MISSIONS AND PUEBLOS OF OLD SOUTHWEST

held at different villages, 210, 280, 228; Oraibi Flute dance in 1907, 317-319; Flute societies, 317; costume of Oraibi performers, 317; Mishongnovi Flute dance in 1908, 320-328; Flute race in 1908, 320; secret ceremonies before Blue Flute altar at Mishongnovi, 321; description of Blue Flute altar at Mishongnovi, 321; legend of Toreva spring, 322; ceremony at Toreva in 1908, 325; dressing and painting the Flute children, 325; costumes worn by various performers, 326; procession from Toreva to Mishongnovi plaza, 327; ceremony in Mishongnovi plaza, 327; dates of dance, 340, 348

Fort Lyons (Colo.): 91

Fort Marcy (N. Mex.): 57

Fort Mason (Ariz.): 260

Fort Wingate (N. Mex.): 300

Franciscans (Order of Saint Francis): in New Mexico, 25-188; priests murdered in New Mexico, 29; San Buenaventura a fine type of early mission, 115; expelled from New Mexico, 124, 232, 252; return to New Mexico, 124; missions of the Salinas, 124; resettle Sevilleta, 158; establish Cebolleta for Navajos, 167; mission established at Hawikuh, 172; at Kechipauan, 179; at Halona, 180; Hopi missions of Arizona, 207-228; take charge of southern Arizona missions, 239; college at Queretaro, Mexico, 239; see also, *Zarata, De la Llama, Peña, Juan de la*

Freemasons: of New Mexico, erect fence around Kit Carson's grave, 91

Frijoles, Rito de los: see *Tyuonyi*

Fruit: see *Agriculture*

GADSDEN PURCHASE: adds part of Sonora to Arizona, 231; Stars and Stripes raised in Tucson, after, 259

Galdo, Fray Juan: stationed at Halona, 174; recovers remains of Ayala from Hawikuh, 174

Galisteo, Santa Cruz de (N. Mex.): Bernal and De Vera murdered, 29, 107; visita of Pecos, 100, 106-108; deserted city, 106; location, 107; visited by Coronado, 107; mission founded, 107; Rebellion of 1680, 107; village deserted, 107; return of inhabitants in 1706, 108; new mission at, 108; smallpox at, 108

Gallup (N. Mex.): 188; route to Hopi villages, 210

Gandara, Don Manuel: governor of Sonora (Mexico), 259-260; owner of Calabazas ranch, 259; establishes military post on ranch, 260; flees to California, 260

Garaycoechea, Fray: visits Awatobi, Arizona, 215

Garcés, Padre Francisco: explorations through Southwest, 220-221, 224-225; first white man to cross Grand Canyon, 221; discovers Crossing of the Fathers, 221; murdered 225, 251; in charge of southern Arizona missions, 240, 251; sick at Guevavi, 251; most beloved of all priests, 251; founder of Tucson, 254, 257; records San Serafin, 262; mentions San Bernardino, 263

Garita, the Spanish, Santa Fé: 57

Genizaros, redeemed Pueblo captives: 157

Ghost cities: San Gabriel, 39; Calabazas, 259

Gipuy (N. Mex.): Monastery built by Oñate, 112, 120; location, 120; see *Santo Domingo*

Glore, Arizona sheepman: 304

Gonzales, Padre Francisco: first resident priest at San Xavier del Bac, 248

Good Friday: Penitente rites, 199, 200; last service of Lent on, 204

INDEX 365

Granada (N. Mex.): 171

Grand Canyon of the Colorado river (Ariz.): first news of, 171, 211; Cardeñas discovers, 171, 211, 212; Garcés first white man to cross, 221; Escalante's journey to, 221; Hamblin finds new crossing, 223; Lee's ferry, 224; Louis Akin's paintings of, 301

Grand Falls of Little Colorado river (Ariz.): 305

Granjon, Bishop: restores San Xavier del Bac, 252

Gran Quivira: Padre Padilla sets out for, 28, 156; 141, 147-149; Padilla murdered, 156; see *Tabira*

Grant, President U. S: ordered loan repaid to Abeytia, 152

Grapes: see *Agriculture*

Grasshoffer, Fray Juan Baptista: death at Guevavi, 234

Guadalupe church, Santa Fé: 50-53; built, 50; change brought by railway, 53; Defouri in charge, 53

Guadalupe river (N. Mex.): ruins of Jemez pueblos, 134-140

Guadalupe, sacred spring of (Mexico): 67

Guevavi (Ariz.): 232-240; first mission in southern Arizona, 232; founded, 232, 233; San Martin, Grasshoffer, Carucho, Garcés, and Bernave, in charge, 234, 240; abandoned, 234; Pima rebellion, 234; mission plundered, 234; lost Spanish mines, 234-239; return of missionaries, 239; presidio of Tubac established, 239; Jesuits expelled, 239; name changed to Los Santos Angeles de Guevavi, 240; decline of, 240; ruins of, 240; Garcés sick at, 251

Gutierrez, Fray Andres: founds Hopi missions, 213

Gutierrez, Padre Narciso: completes San Xavier del Bac, 252

Gyusiwa (N. Mex.): abandoned, 134, 136; resettled, 135, 136; Rebellion of 1680 at, 135, 136; Maria murdered at, 135, 137; campaign of De Vargas, 135; largest of Jemez pueblos, 136; San Diego de Jemez mission founded, 136; converts baptized, 136; return to, 136; De Vargas finds remains of Padre Maria, 139; ruins of church, 139; location of ruins, 139

HAATZE (N. Mex.): ancient Cochití pueblo, 112

Halona (N. Mex.): Fray Juan de Val murdered, 30, 183; mission founded, 172, 173, 183; Arvide murdered, 173, 174; Galdo stationed at, 174; discovered, 180; visited by Chamuscado, 180; by Espejo, 180; Oñate stops, 180; Zuñis flee to Thunder mountain, 183; mission restored, 183

Hamblin, Jacob: mormon missionary explorer, 223-224; finds crossing of the Fathers, 223; discovers new crossing at mouth of Paria, 224

Hanut Cochití (N. Mex.): pueblo of Cochití in Potrero Viejo, 112

Hawikuh (N. Mex.): Fray Marcos de Niza in sight of, 26, 169, 170; Estévan murdered, 26, 170; Letrado murdered, 28, 173; murder of Ayala, 29, 174; Coronado reaches, 170; defeats Zuñis, 171; headquarters, 171; sends Tovar to Arizona, 171; Cardeñas discovers Grand Canyon, 171; Chamuscado visits Cibola, 171; Espejo names, 171; Oñate assigns province to Corchado, 171; mission established, 172, 190, 191; first mission, 172; first baptismal ceremony at, 172; Letrado goes, 173; Arvide murdered, 173; avenging force sent to, 174; Zuñis flee to Thunder mountain, 174, 184; mission work resumed at, 174; Ayala stationed, 174; Apache raid, 174; deserted, 177; tradition of priest who joined

Zuñi to escape death, 177, 178; ruins of mission excavated by Hendricks-Hodge expedition, 177-179, 184; skeleton found under main altar, 178

Hemis kachina of Hopi indians: 344

Hendricks-Hodge Hawikuh expedition: excavations at Hawikuh, New Mexico, 177-179, 184

Hep-ah-tcen-ah (N. Mex.): 187

Herrera, Cristobal de: first Spaniard killed in 1680, 59

Herrera, Sergeant Sebastian de: escapes from Fernandez de Taos, 91

Hodge, Frederick W: in charge of Hendricks-Hodge Hawikuh expedition, 178

Holbrook (Ariz.): distances to Hopi villages, 210, 279

Holland, Isaac T: inscription on Inscription rock, 193

Hopi indians: in Rebellion of 1680, 79, 207; author's theory re Hopi villages, 170, 211, 221; discovered by Tovar, 171; tell Tovar of Grand Canyon, 171; Governor Martinez marches against, 191-192; Snake dance, 208, 210, 207-228; 277-330; list of Hopi pueblos, 209; pueblos, 210, 277-330; how to reach Hopi pueblos, 210; Flute dance, 210, 280, 317, 320, 340, 348; Oraibi, 220-225, 277-298; visited by Garcés, 221, 225; by Escalante and Dominguez, 221; population, 221; farming, 281; albinos, 291, 325; founding of Hotevilla, 298-300; Aztec Fort ruin, 302; Wukoki ruins, 303; Sun emblem, 318, 326; table of ceremonies, 339-345; see *Awatobi, Flute dance, Hotevilla, Mishongnovi, Oraibi, Shipaulovi, Shongopovi, Snake dance, Walpi*

Hopi missions: 207-228; first Hopi born in christianity, 208; founding, 213; Sunshine, 208; mistakes of missionaries, 208; San Bernardino de Awatobi, 210-220; San Francisco de Oraibi, 220-225; San Bartolome de Shongopovi, 225; San Buenaventura de Mishongnovi, 226; Walpi or Kisakobi, 226-228

Hotevilla (Ariz.): founding, 209, 220, 298; trouble between friendlies and hostiles at Oraibi, 209, 298-300; outbreak of 1906, 209, 298; tug-of-war, 300; arrival of troops, 300; hostiles found new village, 300; hostile leaders sentenced to prison, 300; author's visit in 1907, 319; destitution of inhabitants, 319; description in 1907, 319

Huashpatzena (N. Mex.): 120

IMMACULATE CONCEPCION MISSION: see *Quarai*

Indian traders: see *Traders*

Indian trading-posts: Canyon Diablo, 28; The Fields, 278, 281, 306; Oraibi, 278, 281, 282; Wolfe's, 305; Ward's Tolchaco, 305

Indian tribes: see *Apache, Comanche, Hopi, Navajo, Papago, Pima, Sobaipuri*

Inscription house ruin (Ariz.): 222; location, 223

Inscription rock (El Morro) (N. Mex.): Nieto stops, 172, 190, 191; Lujan's inscription, 174, 191; De Varges' inscription, 183, 191; 188-193; location, 188; national monument, 189; Spanish inscriptions, 189-192; Oñate's inscription oldest, 189, 190, 213; lost inscription of Chamuscado's expedition, 190; Martinez inscription, 192; last of Spanish inscriptions, 192; Lewis discovers, 192; visited by Simpson and Kern, 192; inscription of first California emigrant trains, 193; inscriptions left by American soldiers, 193; ruins on top, 193

Iron Door mine (Ariz.): romance, 235-237; Frank Webber's search for, 236; Spanish record, 236-237; discovery of old shaft, 236

Irrigation: see *Agriculture*

Isleta (N. Mex.): 151-157; location, 151; not in Rebellion of 1680, 151; Spaniards take refuge, 151; deserted, 151, 152; Otermin captures, 152; loyalty in Civil war, 152; San Antonio mission founded, 152; christian converts settle, 152; San Antonio church burned, 155; used as sheep corral, 155; old church destroyed, 155; San Agustin mission founded, 155; description, 155; Isleta del Sur established by Otermin, 155; old church remodeled, 155; see *Padilla*

JAASTAD, HENRY O: finds Tumacacori erected prior to San Xavier, 243

Jaca: assists Popé in Rebellion of 1680, 29, 78

Jacarilla Apaches: 83

Jamestown (Va.): 34

Jemez missions (N. Mex.): 134-136

Jemez pueblo (N. Mex.): survivors of Pecos settle, 103; founded, 136, 140; mission founded, 140

Jemez river (N. Mex.): Sia on, 134; ruins of Jemez pueblos on, 134-140

Jemez tribe (N. Mex.): Jesus Maria murdered, 30, 135, 139; 134-140; visited by Barrionuevo, 134; seven villages, 134; visited by Espejo and Oñate, 134; consolidated into three pueblos, 134; Patoqua and Gyusiwa abandoned and later resettled, 134, 136, 139; Navajo raids, 135; Rebellion of 1680, 135, 136, 140; retreat, 135; De Vargas induces tribe to return, 135; attacked by De Vargas, 135; return to Gyusiwa, 136; Rebellion of 1696, 136; Kechipauan mission built like Jemez missions, 179; see *Astialakwa, Gyusiwa, Patoqua*

Jesuits: mission work of, in southern Arizona, 229-264; never free from Apache menace, 229; ordered out of Spain, 232, 239; laid foundation of San Xavier del Bac, 252; return to southern Arizona, 254

Jimeno, Fray: in charge of Guevavi, 239

Julian: painter of famous black pottery, 67

KACHINA DANCES of Hopi indians: see *Soyaluña, Qooqoqlom, Mohti, Powamu, Wahikwinema, Palulukonti, Ankwanti, Hemis, Pawik, Malo, Coyohim, Aña, Shalako, Niman*

Kakanatzatia (N. Mex.): ruins, 133

Kalektaka: see *Momtcita*

Kansas: Coronado crosses, 148

Katishtya (N. Mex.): name of first San Felipe, 124; see *San Felipe*

Katzimo (N. Mex.): native name of Enchanted mesa, 167

Kearney, General Stephen W: enters Santa Fé, 41, 58; camps at Pecos, 104

Kechipauan (N. Mex.); mission established, 172, 173; ruins of mission, 179, 180

Kern, R. H: inscription of, 192, 193

K'hapoo (N. Mex.): native name of Santa Clara, 71

Kiakima (N. Mex.): ruins at base of Thunder mountain, 183

Kidder, Dr. Alfred Vincent: excavations at Pecos, 105

Kino, Padre Eusebio Francisco: life, 230, 231; father of southern Arizona missions, 230; number of converts, 230; last journey to Arizona, 230; lost journal, 231, 233; arrival in Mexico, 231; founds Dolores mission, 231, 233; through Arizona, 231, 232, 233; founds San Gabriel de Guevavi, 232; holds mass in Casa Grande ruin, 232; death, 234; founds San José de Tumacacori, 243; founds San

368 MISSIONS AND PUEBLOS OF OLD SOUTHWEST

Xavier del Bac, 248; visits Sonoita, 253; visits Tucson, 256; Calabazas, 259; Bacuancos, 261; names San Francisco de Ati, 262; names San Serafin, 262
Kisakobi (Ariz.): 226; see *Walpi*
Kitchen, Pete, Arizona pioneer: builds Petrero ranch, 244; famous road, 244; Sonoita, 253; Tubac, 256; Calabazas, 259
Kohasaya (N. Mex.): ruins, 133
Kohonino basket dance of Hopi indians: 343
Koshares at Cochití Rain dance: 272
Kuapa (N. Mex.): ancient Cochití pueblo, 112
Kuchaptuvela ruins (Ariz.): see *Walpi*

La Concepcion mission: see *Hawikuh*
Lagon ceremony of Hopi indians: 341
Laguna (N. Mex.): pueblo founded, 161; mission established, 161; lawsuit over painting, 161-164
Lalakonti (Women's basket dance of Patki, or Rain Cloud clan) of Hopi indians: 341
Lamy, Bishop: to New Mexico, 50; Saint Francis cathedral, a monument to, 50; brings French priests to New Mexico, 64, 81; removes Padre Martinez from Taos, 92
Lawsuit over painting: 161
Lee, John D: in Mountain Meadows Massacre, 224; establishes Lee's ferry, 224; execution of, 224
Legend: of fire that never dies, 103; Accursed lakes, 142; Padre Padilla's coffin, 155-157; Lost Spanish mines, 235-239; Iron Door mine, 236; Padre mine, 237; Taiopa mine, 237; Tumacacori, 247; San Bernadino ranch, 264; Hopi Snake youth, 284; Toreva spring, 322
Lelande, Juan Bautista: early Santa Fé trader, 97
Lent: Penitente rites, 199; last Penitente service, 204

Lesser Mamzrauti of Hopi indians: 343
Letrado, Fray Francisco: murdered, 28, 173, 183; member of Perea's band, 173; work among Jumanos, 173; assigned to Zuñi, 173; expedition to avenge murder, 174
Lewis, an indian trader: discovers Inscription rock, 192
Little Colorado river (Ariz.): ruins on, 302-304; Black Falls, 303; lost on, 305; bad lands, 305; Grand falls, 305; Cameron bridge, 305
Little Seville (N. Mex.): 158
Lopez, Fray Francisco: founds mission at Puaray and is murdered, 33, 98; remains removed to Sandiá, 34, 127; tradition of funeral, 127
Lopez, Fray Mariano de Jesus: St. Joseph painting, 162-163
Lorenzana, Fray Francisco Antonio: murdered, 30, 120
Los Angeles (Calif.): end of old Spanish trail, 222
Los Cerrillos: discovery of minerals, 53
Los Ranchos de Taos (N. Mex.): 92-95; mission established, 92; description of today, 95
Los Santos Angeles de Guevavi mission: see *Guevavi*
Lost Spanish mines: see *Spanish mines*
Loudres, Chapel of Our Lady of: 82
Louis of Saric: leader of Pima rebellion, 234
Lugo, Fray Alonzo de: missions assigned, 38, 136; in charge of Sia, 133; established headquarters at Gyusiwa, 136
Lujan's inscription on Inscription rock (N. Mex.): 174
Lummis, Charles F: accursed lakes legend, 142; *Pueblo Indian Folk Stories*, 142; suggests origin of native name of Isleta, 151

INDEX

McCarter, Margaret Hill: *Vanguards of the Plains*, 57
Macilenya Flute society: see *Drab Flute society*
McLeod, General: leader of Texas-Santa Fé expedition, 104
Madre de Dios, Fray Francisco de la: establishes first mission at Hawikuh, 172
Maldonado, Alonzo del Castillo: survivor of Narvarez expedition, 170
Maldonado, Fray Lucas: murdered, 30, 166
Malo kachina dance: 344
Mamzrauti (Woman's hand tablet dance) of Hopi indians: 341; Lesser, 343
Manzano range, Cerro de los (N. Mex.): 141; peak, 144; near Abó, 146
Marau: see *Mamzrauti*
Maria, Fray Agustin de Santa: murdered at Oraibi, or Walpi, 214
Maria, Fray Juan de Jesus: see *Jemez tribe*
Marie: famous black pottery maker, 67
Martinez, Governor Feliz: expedition against Hopis, 192
Martinez, Padre: publishes first newspaper and books, 92; removed by Bishop Lamy, 92
Matsaki (N. Mex.): ruins, 183
Menchoro, Padre Juan Miguel: brings Sandiá people back, 127; builds church at Sandiá, 128; founds Cebolleta for Navajos, 168
Mesa (Ariz.): outdoor school for boys, 320
Mesa Verde National park (Colo.): 178
Metates: sheep corral built of, 304
Mexican war: Kearney enters Santa Fé, 41, 58; soldiers, buried at Santa Fé, 54; battle of Santa Cruz, 75; murder of Governor Bent, 88, 91; battle of San Geronimo mission, 89; Kearney camped at Pecos, 104

Mexico: mad with gold lust, 26; Coronado's expedition leaves, 26, 169; sacred spring of Guadalupe, 62; Espejo's expedition, 98, 132; bishop of Duragno, 192; Kino's work in Sonora, 230-232; Queretaro, 239; Tumacacori church, 240

Middle mesa (Ariz.): Payupki, 127; pueblos, 307

Mines: see *Spanish mines*

Miranda, Fray Pedro, de: murdered, 29, 88

Mishongnovi (Ariz.): mission founded at old, 226; church burned, 226; present village founded, 226; Snake dance, 300-317; Antelope dance, 307; Snake race, 307, 309; green corn fight, 308, 310; Flute dance, 320-328; Flute race, 320; secret ceremonies before Blue Flute altar, 321; legend of origin of Toreva spring, 322; Flute ceremony at Toreva, 325; Flute procession to village plaza, 327; Flute ceremony in village plaza, 327

Missions: number founded in Arizona, 27; number founded in New Mexico, 27; Puaray, 33; Oñate's first settlement and chapel at San Gabriel, 34; Nambé, 60; Santa Cruz church, 72; Salinas missions, 141-149; Hopi, 207-228; southern Arizona, 229-264

Missouri: 193

Mohti, or Return kachina of Hopi indians: 339, 342

Moki, or Moqui: name changed to Hopi, 207; see *Hopi indians*

Momtcita War dance of Kalektaka: 342

Montezuma mine (Ariz.): rediscovered as Black Jack, 235

Montoya, Antonio Abed: execution, 57

Montoya, Desiderio: execution, 57

Montoya, leader of Taos Rebellion of 1847: battle of Santa Cruz, 75
Mora, Fray Antonio de: murdered, 30, 88
Morada of Penitentes (N. Mex.): description, 196; officers, 199
Morales, Fray Luis de: murdered, 30, 67
Moreno, Fray Antonio: murdered, 30, 61; in charge of Nambé, 61; in charge of Santa Cruz church, 73
Mormons: old trail of emigrants from Utah to Arizona, 223; Lee's ferry, 224; Mountain Meadows massacre, 224; Lee's capture and execution, 224; Arizona sheepmen buy sheep from, 224
Mountainair (N. Mex.): railroad point, 142; distance to Tajique, 144; to Chililí, 145
Mountain Meadows massacre (Utah): 224
Mountain ranges: Cerro de los Manzano, 141; San Mateo, 166; Cebolleta, 168; Starvation peak, 196; Sangre de Cristo, 203; Santa Catalina, 235; Santa Rita, 255; Sentinel peak, 257; Sunset mountain, 301; San Francisco, 301
Mucaiasti (Buffalo dance) of Hopi indians: 344
Museum of the American Indian (New York): Hendricks-Hodge Hawikuh expedition, 177-179.

NAACNAIYA (New Fire ceremony) of Hopi indians: 341
Nafait (N. Mex.): native name of Sandiá, 127
Nambé (N. Mex.): Tomas de Torro murdered, 30, 61; Antonio Moreno murdered, 30, 61; mission established at, 60; Rebellion of 1680, 61; Bustamante erects new mission, 61; destruction of mission, 62
National monuments: Mesa Verde, Colorado, 178; Inscription rock, New Mexico, 189

Navajo canyon (Ariz.): Inscription house ruin, 222
Navajo Indians: raid Pueblos, 80; raids on Patoqua and Gyusiwa, 135, 136; plot against Spaniards, 135; join Jemez against De Vargas, 136; mission established, 167; claim raid on Hawikuh, 174, 192; raids on Walpi, 227
Navarez expedition: only survivors, 170
Nevada: route of old Spanish trail across, 222
New Fire ceremony of Hopi indians: Naacnaiya, 341; Wuwutcimti, 342; Sumaikoli, 343
New Mexico: missions of, 25-188; number of missions founded, 27; Escalona remains, 28; Chamuscado escorts priests, 28, 33; first Spanish settlement, 34; Santa Fé ,founded, 37; largest stone reredos in state, 46; Santuario of Chimayó, 62-67; Santa Cruz church, 73; Santa Cruz, 74; San Geronimo de Taos, 87; Sosa's expedition, 98; Franciscans expelled, 124; return of Franciscans, 124; Cruzate's attempted reconquest, 133; saved for Union by Abeytia's loan, 152; first grapes planted, 159; famous lawsuit over painting, 161; building at Panama Pacific exposition, 166; state museum, 166; Cabeza de Vaca and companions first to cross, 170; first baptismal in western,172; Inscription rock, 188-193; first emigrant train across, 193; Penitentes, 195-206; success of catholic priests, 209; Rain dance at Cochití, 265-275; Spanish mission names with English equivalent, 333-335; fiesta dates of Pueblos, 337; reconquest of, see *De Vargas*; see also, *Coronado, Cruzate, Oñate, Otermin, Santa Fé*
Newspapers: first in Southwest at

INDEX 371

Taos, 92; *The Arizonian*, 25;
Tombstone Nugget, 255
Nieto, Governor Manuel de Silva:
escorts three priests to Hawikuh,
172; stops at Inscription rock, 172,
190, 191; returns to Hawikuh, 172,
190, 191; inscription on Inscription rock, 190, 191
Niman kachina (Farewell to the
kachinas) of Hopi indians: 339,
345
Niza, Fray Marcos de: on trail of
Padres, 26; within sight of Hawikuh, 26, 170; reports discovery of
Seven Cities of Cibola, 26, 169;
164; through southern Arizona, 211
Nogales (Ariz.): 240, 253
Nuestra Señora de Belen mission: see
Belen
Nuestra Señora de Guadalupe mission: see *Pojoaque*
Nuestra Señora de la Asuncion mission: see *Sia*
Nuestra Señora de la Asuncion monastery: see *Gipuy*
Nuestra Señora de los Dolores mission: founded by Kino, 231, 233;
location, 231
Nuestra Señora de los Dolores y San
Antonio de Sandia mission: see
Sandiá
Nuestra Señora de los Remedios:
founded by Kino, 233
Nuestra Señora de los Remedios de
Galisteo: see *Galisteo*
Nuestra Señora del Socorro mission:
see *Socorro*
Nuestra Señora de Navidad mission:
see *Chililí*
Nueva Seville, 158; see *Sevilleta*
Nuitiwa ceremony of Hopi indians:
340
Nusbaum, Jesse L: in charge of
field work at Hawikuh, 178-179
Nuvatikiobi: Hopi name for San
Francisco mountains, Arizona, 322-345

OCA, FRAY JOSÉ MONTES DE: murdered, 30, 120
Ohio: 193
Oldest house in U. S., Santa Fé: 45
Omtau: warns Otermin of Rebellion
of 1680, 59, 79
Oñate, Don Juan de: discovers native painting, 33; founds San Gabriel, 34, 77; names San Juan de
los Caballeros, 37, 77; San Gabriel
chapel built, 37, 78; founds Santa
Fé, 37, 41; mission districts assigned to padres, 38, 127, 132, 171;
builds San Miguel church, 41;
visits San Ildefonso, 67; visits
Taos, 87; Pecos, 99; Cochití, 112;
builds Nuestra Señora de la Asuncion monastery at old Gipuy, 120;
visits San Felipe, 124; Tamayo,
132; Jemez pueblos, 134; discovers Chililí, 146; Abó, 146; names
Sevilleta, 158; names Socorro, 158;
plot to murder, 165, 180; turns
back from Halona, 165, 190; inscription on Inscription rock, 190,
213; discovers the Sea of South,
190, 213; visits Hopi villages, 213
Oöqöl ceremony of Hopi indians: 341
Oracle (Ariz.): 236
Oraibi (Ariz.): priests murdered, 30,
214, 220; outbreak of 1906, 209,
298; site, 209; founding of Hotevilla, 209, 290-300; De Vargas does
not attempt to enter, 214; Espeleta,
chief of, 215, 216; warriors attack
Awatobi, 216; known as "place of
the peaches," 219; mission founded,
220; mission destroyed, 220; Garcés reaches, 220, 225; population,
221; visit of Escalante, 221, 222;
last old-time Snake dance at, 277-298, 290; founding of Hotevilla,
209, 290-300; Flute dance, 317-319;
Snake dance, 328-330; Antelope
dance, 328; dance in 1908 a burlesque of former performances, 329
Ortiz grant at Calabazas (Ariz.):
259

Ortizea chapel, Santa Fé: erected, 57
Otermin, Governor Antonio de: warned of Rebellion of 1680, 29, 79; besieged, 79, 83; hangs forty-seven indians in plaza, 80; retreat to Mexico, 80; attempted reconquest of 1681, 115; Cochití flee from, 115; finds three priests murdered at Santo Domingo, 120; burns Sandiá, 127; Jemez flee from, 135; finds Isleta deserted, 151; captures Isleta, 152; Isleta church used as sheep corral, 155; people of Sevilleta accompany, on retreat, 158; burns Alamillo, 158; people of Socorro accompany, on retreat, 159; founds Socorro del Sur, 159
Our Lady of Guadalupe church: see *Guadalupe church*
Our Lady of Light church: 45-49; built by Governor Del Valle, 45; great stone reredos, 46; Judge Baker tries to hold court in, 46; razed by Delgado, 49
Our Lady of Loudres: chapel of, 82
Our Lady of the Rosary: chapel, 53-57
Oury, Granville R: leads rescue party to Tubac, 256
Outlaws: camp in San Xavier del Bac mission, 252; Mexican, attack Tubac, 256; Tumacacori burned by Mexican, 256; of Tombstone country, 263
Owakulti basket dance of Hopi indians: 343

PACHECO, LUIS: murdered, 88
Padilla, Padre Juan de: with Coronado, 28; first christian martyr, 28; legend of his coffin, 28, 155-157; accompanies Tovar to Hopi country, 212
Padre mine (Ariz.): legend, 237
Painted Desert (Ariz.): Hopi missions, 207-228; original Cibola possibly the, 212; great tragedy of, 215; Garcés journey across, 225;

Hopi villages, 277-330; gathering of desert indians for last big Snake dance at Oraibi, 289; sunrise on, 308
Pakab, or Reed clan of Hopi indians: see *Momtcita*
Palace of the Governors, Santa Fé: first American court held in, 49; De Vargas attacks indians in, 54; Spaniards besieged in, 79; Galisteo people take possession, 107
Palulukonti: see *Ankwanti kachina*
Pamurti of Hopi indians: 343
Panama Pacific exposition: New Mexico building, 166
Panguitch (Utah): John D. Lee captured, 224
Papago indians: join Pimas in Rebellion, 234; San Xavier del Bac mission, 248; care for San Xavier del Bac, 251, 252; Tucson derives name from, 256
Paria river (Ariz.): Hamblin discovers crossing at mouth of, 224
Patki, or Rain Cloud clan of Hopi indians: Lalakoñti, 341
Patoqua (N. Mex.): San José de los Jemez mission, 130; abandoned, 134, 139; resettled by Arvide, 139
Paver, Fray Francisco: in charge of San Xavier del Bac, 251
Pawik kachina of Hopi indians: 344
Payupki (Ariz.): built, 127
Pecos (N. Mex.): Velasco murdered, 29; early missionaries, 38; landmark on Santa Fé trail, 97; Lelande and Pursley, 97; native name, 97; population and size, 97, 98; visited by Coronado, 97; by Espejo and Beltran, 98; captured by Sosa, 98; visited by Oñate, 99; Padre San Miguel founds mission, 99; present church built, 99; Benavides' report of church, 99; Juan Ye warns Valasco, 99; Valasco murdered, 100; Pecos warriors march against Santa Fé, 100; De Vargas unopposed, 100; Juan Ye

joins De Vargas, 100; church restored by De Vargas, 100; decline, 100; last survivors abandon, 103; picture of the Virgin, 103; Agustin Pecos, the last survivor, 103; José Miguel Pecos, 103; statue of Virgin, 104; sacred cave, 104; Texas-Santa Fé prisoners confined in ruins, 104; Kearney camped, 104; Dr. Kidder's excavations, 105; arched doorway of mission, 105; ruins today, 105

Pecos, Agustin: 103

Pecos, José Miguel: death, 103

Pedroza: Juan de la: murdered, 88

Peinade, Fray Alonzo: founds mission at Chililí, 145; death, 145

Peña, Fray Juan de la: head of Franciscans in New Mexico, 152; resettles indians at Isleta, 152, 155

Peña Blanca (N. Mex.): priest from in charge of Cochití, 111; priest holds mass at Cochití, 119, 267, 269; priest from, in charge of San Felipe, Cochití, and Santo Domingo, 124; priest from, witnesses Rain dance at Cochití, 275

Penitente, Venerable Third Order of: founded in Santa Fé and Santa Cruz, 205

Penitentes: chapel in Santa Cruz church, 74; wayside crosses, 195; season of ceremonies, 196; where found, 196; morada, 196; officers, 199; principal ceremony, 199; procession of self-whippers, 199, 200; selection of Cristo, 200; American Passion play, 200; procession to Calvario, 203; crucifixion, 203; burial of victims of self-punishment, 204; last service, 204; Flagellantes of Europe, 205; in New Mexico from early date, 205; origin of, 205; Alcalde, 206; Taos, 206; Abiquiu, 206

Pennington, James: settles at Calabazas ranch, 260; killed by Apaches, 261

Peñuela, Marquis of: rebuilds San Miguel church, 42

Perea, Fray Estevan de: removes remains of Friar Ruiz to Sandiá, 127; at Quarai, 143; succeeds Benavides as mission custodian, 172; reaches Santa Fé with thirty priests, 172; sends priests to Hawikuh, 172; Letrado with, 173

Perez, Governor: defeated by rebels, 74; assassinated and head cut off, 74

Perez, Ignacio: receives grant for San Bernardino ranch, Arizona, 263

Petrero ranch (Ariz.): established, 243

Pfefferkorn, Fray Ignacio: in charge of Guevavi, Arizona, 239; establishes San Francisco de Ati, 262

Phillips Academy, Andover (Mass.): expedition of, to Pecos, New Mexico, 104, 105

Picuris (N. Mex.): 83-84; Fray Mathias Rendon murdered, 30; Del Valle exhumes bones of Fray Zarate, 49, 50, 83; Tupatu, 78, 83; first visited by Coronado, 83; priests in charge, 83; an important mission, 83; Rebellion of 1680, 83; Rendon murdered, 83; inhabitants march against Santa Fé, 83; De Vargas finds ruins, 83; the old church, 84; the scalp house, 84

Pike, Lieutenant Zebulon M: discoverer of Pike's peak, 123; visits Santo Domingo, 123; taken prisoner to Chihuahua, Mexico, 123

Pima indians: 234; Bacuancos, a rancheria, 261

Pima Rebellion of 1751; see *Rebellion of 1751*

Pimeria Alta (Mexico): extent, 231; Bacuancos, 261

Pino, Padre: brings Sandiá people from Arizona, 127

Pio, Fray Juan Bautista: murdered, 29, 59

Pioge (N. Mex.): name of first San Juan settlement, 77
Pioneer Historical Society, Tucson (Ariz.): 255
Plymouth Rock (Mass.): 34
Pojiuuingge (N. Mex.): name of third San Juan settlement, 77
Pojoaque (N. Mex.): San Francisco mission founded, 60; original church destroyed, 60
Ponce de Leon, General Don Diego de Vargas Zapata Lujon: see *De Vargas*
Popé, leader of Rebellion of 1680 (N. Mex.): native of San Juan, 78; tries to save forty-seven indians from execution, 78; secretly preaches doctrine of revolt, 78, 88; kills brother-in-law, 79; success of rebellion, 79; elected ruler of Pueblos, 80; deposed and Tupatu elected ruler, 80; re-elected, 80; death, 81
Porras, Fray Francisco: murdered, 29, 214, 227; founds Hopi missions, 213, 220; makes many converts, 213; restores sight of son of a chief, 213
Posada, Governor Pedro Reneros de: attempted reconquest of New Mexico, 132; burns old Santa Ana, 132
Posten, Colonel Charles D: rehabilitates Tubac, Arizona, 255
Potrero de las Vacas (N. Mex.): ancient home of Cochití, 112
Potrero Viejo, the Gibraltar of Cochití: Cochití people settle, 112; build strong fort, 115; attacked by De Vargas, 115
Powamu kachina of Hopi indians: 343
Price, Colonel Sterling: battle of Santa Cruz, 75; marches against Taos, 89; battle of San Geronimo mission, 89; executes leaders of Taos rebellion, 89
Priests: list of those murdered before Rebellion of 1680, 28-29; list of those murdered during Rebellion of 1680, 29-30; list of those murdered after Rebellion of 1680, 30-31
Prince, Hon. L. Bradford: buys painting of Virgin from Pecos, 103; description of ruins of Quarai, 144
Printing press: first in Arizona, 255
Pro, Fray Antonio Sanchez de: murdered, 30, 67
Procession of Penitentes (N. Mex.): self-whippers, 200; to Calvario, 203
Puaray (N. Mex.): San Bartolomé mission founded at, 27, 33; first priests murdered, 28, 33, 98, 127; Oñate discovers painting, 33; Friar Lopez's remains discovered, 34; location, 34
Purisima Concepcion de Halona mission: see *Halona*
Pursley, James: Santa Fé trader, 97
Puye (N. Mex.): Santa Clara people claim descent from inhabitants, 71

Qooqoqlom kachina of Hopi indians: 339, 342
Quarai (N. Mex.): 141, 142-144; location, 142; Immaculate Conception mission established, 142; Perea, 142; De la Llama, 49, 143; peace with Apaches, 143; Apache raids, 143; Carleton's description of mission ruins, 143; Prince's description, 144; communal dwelling, 144; converts settle at Isleta, 152
Quartelejo (N. Mex.): Picuris flee to, 83
Queretaro (Mexico): Franciscan college of Santa Cruz, 239
Quiñones, Fray Cristobal de: builds church at San Felipe, 124; death, 124
Quintana, Marcial, governor of Cochití: letter, 269; favors photographs of Rain dance, 270

INDEX 375

RAIN DANCE at Cochití: 111, 119, 265-275; fiesta of San Buenaventura, 265; held by Turquoise and Calabash clans, 265; mass in old mission, 268; council with Turquoise clan, 269; permission to take photographs refused, 271; Turquoise clan starts dance, 271; attire of dancers, 271; koshares, 272; reverence paid to statue of San Buenaventura, 272, 275; ceremony of Calabash clan, 275; dress of Calabash dancers, 275

Rainbow Natural bridge (Utah): Inscription house on trail, 223

Ramirez, Fray Juan: takes painting of Saint Joseph to Acoma, 162; builds first church at Acoma, 166; saved from shower of arrows, 167

Ranches: Petrero, 244; Gandara, 260; Calabazas, 260; San Bernardino, 262, 264; Slaughter's, 263; C O Bar, 278, 300

Ranchos de Taos (N. Mex.): see *Los Ranchos de Taos*

Read, Hon. Benjamin M: theory of site of San Gabriel settlement, 38

Rebellion of 1680: priests murdered, 29; leaders, 29, 78, 83; Maldonado murdered, 30, 166; San Miguel church, 41-45; plot revealed to Otermin, 59; first blood, 59; old Tesuque, 59-60; Pojoaque abandoned, 60; Torres murdered, 61; Morales and Pro murdered, 67; Santa Clara church destroyed, 71; Spaniards driven from Santa Cruz valley, 72; execution of forty-seven indians, 78; no plot in all history its equal, 78; Popé, the leader, 78, 81, 88; Pueblo indians worked into state of revolt, 78; Piros not included, 79; Catua and Omtua warn Spaniards, 79; date changed, 79; Santa Fé saved by warning, 79; Spaniards besieged in old Palace, 79; Otermin hangs forty-seven indians, 80; Otermin's retreat to Mexico, 80; old Pueblo order restored, 80; Popé, the monarch of Pueblo empire, 80; raids by Navajo, Utes and Apaches, 80; Popé deposed and Tupatu elected, 80; Popé again elected, 80; Popé's death, 80; Taos used by Popé as central point, 88; Padres Mora and Pedroza murdered, 88; Spaniards driven from Taos valley, 88; Pecos, 99, 100; Juan Ye warns Valasco, 99; Galisteo inhabitants move into old Palace at Santa Fé, 107; Tinoco murdered, 109; priest escapes from Cochití, 112; Cochití take part in, 112; Santo Domingo, 120; San Felipe, 124; Sandiá, 127; Tamayo, 132; Sia, 133; Jemez take part in, 135, 136, 139, 140; Padre Jesus Maria murdered, 139; escape of priest, alcalde, and three soldiers from Astialakwa, 140; Spaniards gather at Isleta, 151; Otermin reaches Isleta, 151; tradition of priest who joined Zuñi to escape death, 177, 178, 179; Zuñis take part in, 177, 183; Juan de Val murdered, 183; priests murdered at Hopi villages, 214, 220, 225, 226, 227

Rebellion of 1696 (N. Mex.): priests murdered, 30; Friar Acevedo murdered, 61; five priests and twenty-one Spaniards murdered, 88; Padres Carbonelli and Arizu murdered, 106

Rebellion of 1751 (Ariz.): Guevavi plundered, 234; Ruen murdered, 234, 253; uprising of Pimas, 234; Luis, of Saric, the leader, 234; Spaniards driven from southern Arizona, 234; priests murdered, 234; all trace of mines destroyed, 235; legends of lost Spanish mines, 235-239; San Xaxier del Bac plundered, 248; rebellious Pimas camp at Arivaca, 262

Rebellion of 1847 at Taos (N. Mex):

battle of Santa Cruz, 75; battle of San Geronimo mission, 87, 89; Governor Charles Bent murdered, 88; battle of Thurley's mill, 89; Colonel Price's army, 89; leaders executed, 89

Reconquest of New Mexico: see *Attempted reconquests, De Vargas*

Reed clan of Hopi indians: see *Momtcita*

Rendon, Fray Mathias: murdered, 30

Return kachinas of Hopi indians: Mohti, 339, 342; Soyaluña, 339, 342

Revolt of 1910, Taos (N. Mex.): cause, 89

Revolution of 1837 (N. Mex.): 57; battle of Santa Cruz, 74; four leaders executed, 57

Rio, Fray Jose del: with Garcés at San Xavier del Bac, 251

Rio Grande river (N. Mex.): mission at old Puaray, 27, 33; site of San Gabriel, 34; Santa Clara, 71; Cochití, in valley, 111; washes two Gipuy pueblos away, 120; flood destroys Santo Domingo mission, 123; ruins of old Sandiá, 127; ruins of Alameda, 128; Isleta, 151; disturbance of, causes rising of Padre Padilla's coffin, 156; ruins of Belen, 157; Sevilleta, 158; Alamillo, 158; San Pascual, 159; Senecu, 159

Rito de los Frijoles (N. Mex.): see *Tyuonyi*

Rodriguez, Fray Agustin: 28, 33, 98; body at Isleta, 157

Rosario chapel: built, 53; story of founding, 54; legend of statue of Virgin Mary, 54; De Vargas procession, 54; present chapel built in 1807, 57

Rosas, Fray Juan de: missions assigned to, 38; in charge of San Felipe and Santa Ana, 124, 132

Ruen, Padre Enrique: murdered, 234, 253

Ruins of: Abó (N. Mex.) 146-147; Alameda (N. Mex.) 128; Alamillo (N. Mex.) 158; Astialakwa (N. Mex.) 139; Awatobi (Ariz.) 210-220; Aztec Fort (Ariz.) 302; Belen (N. Mex.) 157; Black Falls group (Ariz.) 303; Black mesa of San Felipe (N. Mex.) 124, 132; Chililí (N. Mex.) 145; Cienega (N. Mex.) 109; Cuchillo (N. Mex.) 110; Frijoles canyon (N. Mex.) 112; Galisteo (N. Mex.) 107; Gipuy (N. Mex.) 120; Glore Spring group (Ariz.) 303-304; Gran Quivira (N. Mex.) 147-149; Gyusiwa (N. Mex.) 136; Haatze (N. Mex.) 112; Halona (N. Mex.) 180-183; Hanut Cochití (N. Mex.) 112; Hawikuh (N. Mex.) 170-179; Homolobi (Ariz.) 226; Inscription house (Ariz.) 222; Inscription rock (N. Mex.) 193; Kakanatzatia (N. Mex.) 133; Katishtya (N. Mex.) 124; Kechipauan (N. Mex.) 179; Kiakima (N. Mex.) 183; Kisakobi (Ariz.) 227; Kohasaya (N. Mex.) 133; Kuapa (N. Mex.) 112; Kuchaptuvela (Ariz.) 227; Matsaki (N. Mex.) 183; Mishongnovi (old) (Ariz.) 226; Nafiat (N. Mex.) 127; Patoqua of the Jemez (N. Mex.) 139; Payupki (N. Mex.) 127; Pecos (N. Mex.) 97-105; Pioge (N. Mex.) 77; Pojiuuingge (N. Mex.) 77; Potrero de las Vacas (N. Mex.) 112; Puaray (old) (N. Mex.) 33-34; Quarai (N. Mex.) 142-144; Rito de los Frijoles (N. Mex.) 112; Sajiuwingge (N. Mex.) 77; San Cristóbal (N. Mex.) 105; Sandiá (old) (N. Mex.) 127; San Felipe (old) (N. Mex.) 124; San Gabriel (N. Mex.) 34-39; San Geronimo de Taos (N. Mex.) 84-90; San Lazaro (N. Mex.) 106; San Marcos (N. Mex.) 108; San Pascual (N. Mex.) 159; Santa Ana de Alamillo (N. Mex.) 158; Senecu (N. Mex.)

159-160; Sevilleta (N. Mex.) 157-158; Shongopovi (old) (Ariz.) 225; Socorro (N. Mex.) 158-159; Tabira (N. Mex.) 147-149; Tajique (N. Mex.) 144-145; Tamayo on Black Mesa of San Felipe (N. Mex.) 124, 132; Tesuque (old) (N. Mex.) 59; Tyuonyi (N. Mex.) 112; Walpi (old) (Ariz.) 227; Wukoki (Ariz.) 303-304; Yugeuingge (N. Mex.) 34, 37, 77
Ruiz, Friar: see *Rodriguez*

SACRED SPRING OF GUADALUPE (Mexico): 67
Saeta, Padre Francisco Xavier: murdered, 234
Saint Francis, Third Order of: Penitentes descended from, 205
Saint Francis cathedral, Santa Fé: 49-50; cornerstone laid, 50; reredos removed from the Castrense, 46
Saint Joseph: lawsuit over painting, 161
St. Vrain, Ceran: old-time trapper and trader, 90
Sajiuwingge (N. Mex.): name of second San Juan settlement, 77
Salazar, Fray Cristobal de: missions assigned, 38; founded mission at Nambé, 60
Salemeron, Fray Zarate: baptizes converts at Jemez, 136
Salinas lakes (N. Mex.): Accursed lakes, 141; mission of Kechipauan built like missions of the, 179
Salinas pueblos (N. Mex.): Quarai, 49, 142; cities that died of fear, 141-149; Tajique, 144; Chililí, 145; Abó 146; Gran Quivira, or Tabira, 147
Salpointe, Rev. A. B: gives date of founding of Guevavi, 232
Salt Lake City (Utah): railroad projected to Arizona, 224
Salvatierra, Padre Juan Mariá de: arrival at Dolores, 232, 233; appointed superior of missions, 233;

plans for conquest of Pimeria Alta, 233; he and Kino found Guevavi, 233
San Agustin de Isleta mission (N. Mex.): see *Isleta*
San Agustin del Tucson (Ariz.): see *Tucson*
San Agustin Oiaur (Ariz.): Kino named indian village near Tucson, 256
San Antonio de Awatobi mission: see *Awatobi*
San Antonio de Isleta mission: see *Isleta*
San Antonio de Senecu mission: see *Senecu*
San Augustine (Fla.): founded, 37
San Bartolome de Shongopovi mission: see *Shongopovi*
San Bartolome mission at Puaray: see *Puaray*
San Bernardino ranch (Ariz.): 262-264; treasure, 262: Mexican grant to Perez, 263; purchased by Slaughter, 263; famous cattle ranch, 263; supposed treasure in ruins of old mission, 264
San Buenaventura, Fray Juan de: missions assigned, 38
San Buenaventura de Cochití: see *Cochití*
San Buenaventura de Mishongnovi mission: see *Mishongnovi*
San Cayetano de Calabazas mission: see *Calabazas*
San Cosme del Tucson: visita of San Xavier del Bac, 257
San Cristobal (N. Mex.): Carbonelli and Arizu murdered, 31, 106; inhabitants settle at Vera Cruz, 73, 106: one of cities that died of fear, 105; location, 105; date of mission unknown, 105; Apaches drive inhabitants out, 105; inhabitants flee to Hopi country, 106
Sandiá (N. Mex.): location, 127; mission established, 127; abandoned, 127; new pueblo founded,

127; new church built at, 128; ruins of old mission, 128
San Diego (Calif.): Panama Pacific exposition, 166
San Diego de Alcala mission: founded, 27
San Diego de Jemez mission: see *Gyusiwa*
San Diego river (N. Mex.): ruins of Jemez pueblos on, 136-140
Sandoval county (N. Mex.): mission at old Puaray, 27
San Estévan Ray de Acoma mission: see *Acoma*
San Felipe (N. Mex.): 123-127; founded by Cochití people, 112; flee with Cochití to Potrero Viejo, 115; warriors join De Vargas against Cochití, 115; three villages of this name, 123; 123-127; first called Katishtya, 124; Oñate visits, 124; church built, 124; Rebellion of 1680, 124; ruins of old church, 124; present church erected, 124
San Felipe church: 132
San Francisco de Ati: see *Ati*
San Francisco de los Españoles (N. Mex.): founded by Oñate, 37; name changed to San Gabriel, 37
San Francisco de Oraibi mission: see *Oraibi*
San Francisco de Pojoaque mission: see *Pojoaque*
San Francisco de Sandiá mission: see *Sandiá*
San Francisco mountains (Ariz.): 301; sacred mountains of Hopi indians, 322; Hopi name of, 322, 345; Hopi kachinas return to their homes, 339, 345
San Francisco, parish church of Santa Fé (N. Mex.): burial place of De Vargas, 42, 131; 49-50; first built by Benavides, 49; destroyed and rebuilt, 49; Zarate's bones moved to, 49, 83
San Francisco Xavier (N. Mex.): name given San Felipe church, 132

San Gabriel (N. Mex.): 34-39; Oñate's first settlement, 34, 131; first chapel, 37; abandoned, 37; headquarters of mission work, 38; ghost city, 38; dispute over location, 38; location identified, 39; ruins of chapel found, 39; Oñate's return to, 165
San Gabriel de Guevavi mission: see *Guevavi*
San Gabriel mission: Padre Garcés reaches, 225
San Geronimo de Taos mission: see *Taos*
Sangre de Cristo range (N. Mex.): 203
San Gregorio de Abó mission: see *Abó*
San Ignacio de Sonoita mission: see *Sonoita*
San Ignacio mission at Caborca, Sonora (Mexico): founded by Kino, 233
San Ildefonso (N. Mex.): 67-71; Oñate's first visit, 67; date of founding of mission uncertain, 67; Santa Clara and San Juan visitas of, 67; home of Julian and Marie, 67; Morales and Pro murdered, 30, 67; Black mesa, 67; siege by De Vargas, 68; mission re-established, 68; Corvera and Moreno murdered, 68; mission burned, 68; De Vargas again assaults the Black mesa, 68; new church built, 68
San José de Himeris mission: founded by Kino, 233
San José de Laguna mission: see *Laguna*
San José de los Jemez mission: see *Patoqua*
San José del Tucson mission: see *Tucson*
San José de Tumacacori mission: see *Tumacacori*
San Juan (N. Mex.): Oñates reaches, 34, 77; former sites, 34, 77; named, 37, 77; visita of San Ildefonso, 67,

77-83; date of first church unknown, 78; home of Popé, 78; Rebellion of 1680, 78; plans kept secret, 79; Popé kills brother-in-law, 79; plans betrayed, 79; uprising date changed, 79; Santa Fé saved, 79; Spaniards besieged, 79; retreat of Spaniards, 80; Pueblos reign supreme, 80; Popé becomes monarch, 80; raids by Navajos, Utes and Apaches, 80; Popé deposed, 80; church built after reconquest, 81; old church destroyed, 81; pestilence of 1782, 81; Rev. Camilo Seux, 81; Padre Seux erects statue of Virgin Mary, 81; Chapel of Our Lady of Loudres, 82; present brick church, 82

San Juan de los Jemez mission: see *Astialakwa*

San Lazáro (N. Mex.): 78; visita of San Marcos, 106; mission established, 106; driven out by Pecos, 106

San Lorenzo de Picuris: see *Picuris*

San Luis de Bacuancos mission: see *Bacuancos*

San Luis Obispo de Sevilleta mission: see *Sevilleta*

San Marcelo (Ariz.): first name given Sonoita by Kino, 253

San Marcos (N. Mex.): Tinoco murdered, 30, 107; once a large pueblo, 108; native names, 108; named by Sosa, 108; little known of mission, 108; San Lazaro and Cienega visitas, 109; abandoned, 109; people flee with Cochití to Potrero Viejo, 115

San Martin, Padre Juan de: in charge of Guevavi, Calabazas and Bacuancos, 234, 261

San Mateo mountains (N. Mex.): 166

San Miguel: Taos mission first named, 87

San Miguel, Fray Francisco de: missions assigned, 38; founds Pecos church, 99

San Miguel church, Santa Fé (N. Mex.): 41-45; built, 41; bloody history, 41; roof burned, 42; restored by De Vargas, 42; tower blown down, 42; De Vargas believed buried under floor, 42, 131; bell of San Miguel, 42; oldest house in United States, 45

San Miguel de Tajique mission: see *Tajique*

San Pascual (N. Mex.): 159; mission established at, 159

San Pedro de Cuchillo: see *Cuchillo*

San Serafin (Ariz.): 262; named by Kino, 262; little known of its history, 262

San Serafino del Napcub (Ariz.): 262

San Serapin Actum (Ariz.): 262

Santa Ana (N. Mex.): Saraoz murdered, 29

Santa Ana de Alamedo mission: see *Alamedo*

Santa Ana de Alamillo mission: see *Alamillo*

Santa Ana pueblo (N. Mex.): 128; ruins of old mission, 132; called Tamayo, 132; burned by Posada, 132; present church, 133; visita of Sia, 133; location, 133

Santa Catalina mountains (Ariz.): Iron Door mine, 235, 236

Santa Clara (N. Mex.): visita of San Ildefonso, 67; first mission, 71; church destroyed, 71; new church and monastery built, 71; from visita to mission, 71; description of church, 71; destruction of old church, 72

Santa Cruz (N. Mex.): colonists settle, 72, 73, 106; ordered out by De Vargas, 73; third settlement, 73, 131; present church erected, 73; an important town, 74; battle of 1837, 74; battle during Mexican war, 75

Santa Cruz de Galisteo mission: see *Galisteo*

Santa Cruz river (Ariz.): Guevavi

ruins, 240; Pete Kitchen's road, 244; Tumacacori, 244; San Xavier del Bac, 253; Sonoita, 253; Apache raid, 253; Tubac, 256; Calabazas, 259, 261; Bacuancos, 261

Santa Fé (N. Mex.): 41-58; founded, 37, 131; San Miguel church, 41, 131; oldest house in U. S., 45; the Castrense, 45; San Francisco, the parish church, 49, 131; St. Francis cathedral, 49-50; Guadalupe church, 50; Rosario chapel, 53; De Vargas procession, 54; Agua Fria church, 57; old cemetery chapel, 57; Spanish garita, 57; Ortizea chapel, 57; Chapel of the Vigiles, 58; forty-seven indians executed, 78; saved from destruction, 79; besieged in old Palace, 79; Otermin hangs forty-seven indians in plaza, 80; Otermin's retreat to Mexico, 80; Picuris warriors march against, 83; Galisteo people take possession of old Palace, 107; De Vargas' burial place, 131, 172; Venerable Third Order of Penitentes founded at, 205; old Spanish trail to California, 222

Santa Fé railway (Atchison, Topeka & Santa Fé): Bernalillo near Puaray ruins, 24; San Cristóbal ruins, 105; Thornton near ruins of Gipuy, 120; to Santo Domingo, 123; to San Felipe, 124; to Sandiá, 128; to ruins of Alameda, 129; Belen Cut-off to cities that died of fear, 142; Abó station on Belen Cut-off, 147; San Agustin de Isleta church, 155; ruins of Belen mission, 157; Alamillo, 158; Laguna, 161; Gallup, 188; Holbrook, Winslow and Flagstaff, Arizona, nearest railroad points to Hopi villages, 210

Santa Fé river (N. Mex.): Cienega, 109

Santa Fé trail: 41-58; *Vanguards of the Plains*, 57; ruins of Pecos church, 97; Lelande and Pursley, early traders, 97

Santa Gertrudes de Tubac: see *Tubac*

Santa Maria de Galisteo misson: see *Galisteo*

Santa Rita mountains (Ariz.): old Spanish mines, 255

Santo Domingo (N. Mex.): priests murdered, 30; Catiti, 78; Galisteo survivors settle, 106; founded, 120; Huashpatzena, 120; church built by Escalona, 120; Rebellion of 1680, 120; Lorenzazana, Talaban and Oca murdered, 120; damaged by floods, 123; present pueblo built, 123; present church erected, 123; Lieutenant Pike visited old church, 123

Santuario of Chimayó: see *Chimayó*

San Xavier del Bac Mission (Ariz.): rehabilitated, 234, 248; Garcés takes charge, 240, 251; 248-253; founded by Kino, 248; Gonzales, first priest, 248; plundered in Pima Rebellion, 248; Apache raid, 251; Del Rio at the mission, 251; decline sets in, 251; foundation laid by Jesuits, 251; Papagos secrete sacred articles, 251, 252; construction work started, 252; end of the missions, 252; camping place for outlaws, 252; romance of one tower, 252; restoration, 252; Garcés reaches after long journey, 255; Paver's escape, 256

Saraoz, Fray Domingo de: murdered, 29

Sea of the South: 165, 180; Oñate discovers, 190, 213

Segesser, Fray Felipe: in charge of San Xavier del Bac, 234, 248

Senecu (N. Mex.): Apache raid, 29, 160; Fray Avila murdered, 29, 160; 159; mission founded, 160; Zuñiga buried, 160; pueblo abandoned, 160; Senecu del Sur founded, 160

INDEX 381

Sentinel peak (Ariz.): 257
Seri indians: join Pimas in Rebellion, 234
Serra, Fray Junipero: founder of San Diego de Alcala mission, 27
Seux, Rev. Camilo: sent to San Juan, 81; erects statue of Virgin Mary, 81; erects Chapel of Our Lady of Loudres, 82; erects present San Juan church, 82
Seven Cities of Cibola (N. Mex.): De Niza reaches, 26, 170; Estevan murdered, 26, 170; Coronado fails to find wealth, 147; Aztecs tell Spaniards of, 169; Cortez leads an expedition in search of, 169; De Niza reports discovery, 169; Coronado in search, 169; Hawikuh, the first city, 170-179; author's theory re, 170, 211, 221; Coronado captures Hawikuh, 171; Tovar goes to Hopi country, 171; Cardeñas discovers Grand Canyon, 171; Chamuscado visits Cibola, 171; mission work in Cibola, 171; see *Hawikuh, Halona, Kechipauan, Zuñi*
Sevilleta (N. Mex.): 157; named by Oñate, 158; deserted, resettled and mission established, 158
Shalako kachina of Hopi indians, 345
Shallako, or Winter solstice of Zuñis, 184
Shiewhibak: native name of Isleta, 151
Shipaulovi (Ariz.): founded, 226
Shongopovi (Ariz.): priest murdered, 30, 214, 225; mission founded, 225; ruins of mission, 225
Shrines (indian): "center of the earth" at Zuñi, 187; Buhoki at Mishongnovi, 313
Shufino (N. Mex.): 71
Sia (N. Mex.): mission founded, 133; location, 134
Simpson, Lieut. J. H: first description of Inscription rock, 192
Sisters of Mercy, Santa Fé: present statue to Cochití, 119; witness Rain dance, 275
Slaughter, John: establishes San Bernardino ranch, 263
Snake dance of Hopi indians: photographs prohibited, 209; years held at different villages, 209, 280, 340, 347; how to reach Hopi villages, 210, 279; last old-time Snake dance at Oraibi, 277-298; Capt. Bourke gives first description, 278; outfit for journey to, 278, 301; origin of, 280, 284; Snake race at Oraibi, 283; Snake legend, 284; nine days' ceremony, 286; gathering of indians for last Snake dance at Oraibi, 289; Oraibi dance, 290; antidote for snake bite, 296; Mishongnovi Snake dance, 300-317; Wukoki built by Snake clan, 303; Mishongnovi Snake race, 307, 309; Mishongnovi Antelope dance, 307; 313-317; Oraibi Snake dance, 328-330; kilts different from those in 1906, 328; dance in 1908 a burlesque of former performances, 329
Sobaipuri indians (Ariz.): ask for priest, 233; Tumacacori, a settlement of, 243; rancheria of, 253; Jamac, 254
Socorro (N. Mex.): 128, 132; named by Oñate, 158; mission established, 159; natives join Otermin, 159; settle at Socorro del Sur, 159; first grapes, 159
Solstice, Shallako, or Winter, of Zuñis (N. Mex.): 184
Sonoita (Ariz.): Ruen murdered, 234, 253; visited by Kino, 253; abandoned, 253; on Pete Kitchen's road, 253; 254
Sonora (Mexico): explored by Kino, 230, 231; Dolores mission, 231; Magdalena, 232; missions founded by Kino, 233; Salvatierra appointed superior of missions, 233; Pete Kitchen's road, 244; Manuel Gandara, governor, 259

382 MISSIONS AND PUEBLOS OF OLD SOUTHWEST

Sosa, Castaño de: leads colonists to New Mexico, 98; visits Pecos, 98; captures Pecos, 98; visits Taos, 99; arrested, 99; names Cuaka, San Marcos, 108; visits Gipuy, 120; names San Felipe, 124
Southern Pacific railway: starts Calabazas boom, 261
Soyaluña, or Soyal (Winter solstice ceremony) of Hopi indians: 339, 342
Spain: slow in colonizing New Mexico, 26
Spanish cemetery chapel: see *cemetery chapel*
Spanish inscriptions on Inscription rock (N. Mex.): 189-192
Spanish mines: legends of lost Spanish mines, 234-239; Montezuma mine rediscovered, 235; long search for Iron Door mine, 235-237; Padre mine, 237; lost Taiopa, 237-239; mines near Tumacacori and Tubac, 247, 255; Calabazas, 259
Spanish mission names with their English equivalent: 333
Spanish settlement at Tubac (Ariz.): 255
Spanish soldiers killed at Zuñi (N. Mex.): 184
Spanish trail from Santa Fé to California: 222
Spring: sacred spring of Guadalupe, Mexico, 62; Glore, 304; Toreva, 307, 322; Oraibi Flute, 317
Starvation peak (N. Mex.): Penitente cross, 196
Statues of San Buenaventura: 116
Stein, Major: in command of Calabazas, 260
Stokes, William: captures John D. Lee, 224
Styook-zone: Papago name from which Tucson derived, 256
Sumaikoli New Fire ceremony of Hopi indians: 343
Sun emblem of Hopi indians, 318, 326

Sunset mountain (Ariz.); an extinct volcano, 301
Sunshine mission (Ariz.): 208, 320, 327

TAAIYALONE MOUNTAIN: see *Thunder mountain*
Tabira (N. Mex.): 141, 147-149; myth of Gran Quivira, 147; Turk guides Coronado, 147; Coronado in search of Gran Quivira, 148; kills the Turk, 148; myth persists to present time, 148; churches built by Acevedo, 148; description of ruins, 149; abandoned, 149; converts flee to Isleta, 152
Tabla dance at Cochití: see *Rain dance*
Tacu: assists Popé in Rebellion, 29
Tafoya, leader of Taos Rebellion of 1847: battle of Santa Cruz, 75; battle of San Geronimo mission, 87, 89
Taiopa mine (Sonora): 237-239; story, 237; legend of the fire that never dies, 237; search for, 238; no record of, 238; indians bring in rich ore, 238; Mexican woman guided to, 238
Tajique (N. Mex.): 141: ancient apple orchards, 144; San Miguel mission, 144; last of cities that died of fear, 145; converts settle at Isleta, 152
Talaban, Fray Juan de: murdered, 30, 120
Tamayo (N. Mex.): see *Santa Ana pueblo*
Tamita mesa (N. Mex.): 124
Taos (N. Mex.): 84-90; Miranda murdered, 29; De Mora murdered, 30; Carbonelli, 31, 106; Jaca, 78; previous names, 87; largest communal dwelling in U. S., 87; visited by Alvarado, Oñate and Barrionuevo, 87; by Sosa, 99; Benavides' report of baptisms, 87; Miranda and two soldiers mur-

dered, 88; Mora and Pedroza murdered, 88; attacked by De Vargas, 88; revolt of 1696, 88; surrender to De Vargas, 88; raids by Utes and Comanches, 88; Rebellion of 1847, 88; Governor Bent murdered, 88; battle of Thurley's mill, 89; Colonel Price's army, 89; battle of Santa Cruz, 75; battle of San Geronimo mission, 87, 89; leaders executed, 89; revolt of 1910, cause, 89; ruins of old mission, 89; picturesque pueblo, 90; Penitentes strong at, 206; see *Fernandez de Taos, Los Ranchos de Taos*

Tapolo: chief of Awatobi, Arizona, 215; plots destruction of people, 216

Ta-wa-quap-te-wa: chief of friendlies at Oraibi, plot to assassinate, 299

Tello, Padre Tomas: murdered, 234

Tesuque (N. Mex.): Catua and Omtua warn Otermin, 29, 59, 79; Fray Juan Bautista Pio murdered, 29, 59; location, 59; old mission, 59; old pueblo abandoned, 59; modern pueblo founded, 59; visita of Pojoaque, 60

Texas: western formerly part of New Mexico, 37; Texas-Santa Fé expedition prisoners, 104; Coronado reaches Rio Colorado, 148; Tabira people settle near El Paso, 149; Socorro del Sur, 159; Narvarez expedition wrecked on coast, 170; Cabeza de Vaca and companions first to cross, 170; see *El Paso*

Texas-Santa Fé expedition: 104

Thoma, Frank de: 157

Thornber, Dr. J. J: report on supposed Hopi snake bite antidote, 297

Thornton, Sandoval county (N. Mex.): ruins of Gipuy near, 120; near San Felipe, 124

Thunder mountain (N. Mex.): Zuñis go to, 171, 174, 177, 183, 184; peaceable submissioon to De Vargas, 177, 183; De Vargas finds christian altar, 177; Matsaki and Kiakima at base, 183; view of, across housetops of Zuñi, 188

Tigua (N. Mex.): Puaray principal settlement, 33

Tiguex, province of (N. Mex.): Escalona murdered, 28; Coronado spends winter in, 33; Sandiá, 127

Tinoco, Fray Manuel: murdered, 30, 107, 109

Tolchaco mission (Ariz.): founded, 301; Ward's trading post, 305

Tombstone (Ariz.): *Tombstone Nugget* published at, 255; outlaws of, 263

Toreva Spring (Ariz.): 307; legend of origin, 322; Flute ceremony at, 325

Torres, Fray Tomas de: murdered, 30, 61

Tovar, Don Pedro de: discovers Hopi villages in Arizona, 171, 211, 212; brings Coronado news of Grand Canyon, 171, 211; battle at Awatobi, 212

Towih (N. Mex.): Tewa name of Taos, 87

Town crier: of Zuñis, 187; of Hopis, 286

Traders: see *Bent, Carson, Le Lande, Lewis, Pursley, St. Vrain*

Trading posts: see *indian trading posts*

Trail of the Padres: beginning, 25; first European on, 26

Trappers: headquarters of, at Taos, 90; see *traders*

Treasure: of Gran Quivira, 148; of San Bernardino ranch, 262, 264; of Tumacacori, legend of the, 247; see *Spanish mines*

Truxillo, Fray José de: murdered, 30, 214, 225

384 MISSIONS AND PUEBLOS OF OLD SOUTHWEST

Tshiquite (N. Mex.): native name of Pecos, 97
Tubac (Ariz.): Garcés leaves on journey through Southwest, 224; presidio established, 239, 254; Pete Kitchen's road, 244, 253; first Spanish settlement in Arizona, 254; garrison removed to Tucson, 254; garrisoned by Pimas, 254; decline of mission, 254; mission abandoned, 255; rehabilitated by Posten, 255; old Spanish mines, 255; first newspaper in Arizona published at, 255; federal garrison withdrawn, 255; Americans attacked by Apaches, 256; Oury brings rescue force, 256; Mexican bandits repulsed, 256; town abandoned, 256
Tucson (Ariz.): record of Iron Door mine, 236; Pete Kitchen's road, 244; founded by Garcés, 254, 257; not an ancient city, 256; Kino named indian village San Agustin Oiaur, 256; name derived, 256; San Cosme del Tucson, 257; San José del Tucson mission, 257; Garcés builds a pueblo and church, 257; description of church, 257; bloody history, 257; Apache raids, 257; description of fortification, 258; name of mission changed, 258; American occupation, 259
Tumacacori (Ariz.): 240-247; founded by Kino, 243; present church erected, 243; Apache raids, 243, 244; an independent mission, 244; last Apache raids, 247; legend of buried treasure, 247; present ruins, 247; location, 247; burned by Mexican outlaws, 256
Tupatu: aids Popé in Rebellion, 78, 83; leads Picuris against Santa Fé, 83
Turk (The): Coronado's guide, 147; executed by Coronado, 148
Turner, William: 187
Turquoise clan of Cochití (N. Mex.): kiva, 111; council, 269; in Rain dance, 269, 271; dress, 271; permission to photograph Rain dance refused, 271
Tusayan (Ariz.): Spanish province, 171, 207, 211, 214, 220
Twin cities of Painted desert (Ariz.): 208, 226; see *Mishongnovi, Shipaulovi*
Twitchell, Col. Ralph E: 38
Tyuonyi (N. Mex.): San Ildefonso on ·oad to, 67; discovered by Bandelier, 112; location, 112; communal house at Quarai similar to, 144
Tziguma (N. Mex.): native name of Cienega, 109

UDELL, JOHN: 193
United States: military cemetery, Santa Fé, 54; Taos, largest communal dwelling, 87
Urrizola, Governor Manual: surprises Apaches at Conejos, 91
Utah: route of old Spanish trail across, 222; Rainbow Natural bridge, 223; Mormon trail, 223; John D. Lee, 224; Mountain Meadows massacre, 224; railroad projected from Salt Lake City, 224
Ute indians: raid pueblos, 80; raids on Taos, 88, 91; ford across Grand Canyon, 223; raids on Walpi, 227

VAL, FRAY JUAN DE: murdered, 30, 183
Valdez, Governor Francisco Cuervo y: founds Albuquerque, 131
Valladolid (N. Mex.): name given Taos by early Spaniards, 87
Velasco, Fray Fernando de: murdered, 30, 99, 107
Venerable Third Order of Penitentes (N. Mex.): founded, 205
Vera, Fray Domingo de: murdered, 29, 107
Vergara, Fray Pedro: missions assigned, 38
Vetancurt: 177

Vigil, Donaciano: 46
Vigil, José: execution, 57
Vigiles, chapel of: erected, 58
Virgin Mary: statue brought by De Vargas, 54; Agua Fria church built for statue, 57; painting of, 103
Vogt, Evon Z: 189
Volz, Fred: indian trader, The Fields, 278, 281, 306; Oraibi, 278, 281, 282; gives Thanksgiving and Christmas dinner to indians at the Fields, 306; abandons the Fields, 306
Voth, Rev. H. R: Hopi missionary, 297

WAHIKWINEMA (we go throwing), children's kachina dance of Hopi indians: 343
Walatoa (N. Mex.): native name of Jemez pueblo, 136
Walled town: Tucson, Arizona, only one in U. S., 258
Walpi (Ariz.): 226-228; mission founded at old Kisakobi, 226; Kuchaptuvela, 227; murder of Padre Porras, 29, 214, 227; priest murdered and church destroyed, 214; Kisakobi abandoned and modern Walpi built, 227; see *Snake dance*
War dance of Hopi indians: see *Momtcita*
Ward, David: indian trader, 305
Warrior priesthood of Hopi indians: see *Momtcita*
Water House clan of Hopi indians: 313
Webber, Frank: search for Iron Door mine, 236-237
Williamson, P. H: 193
Winslow (Ariz.): distances to Hopi villages, 210, 279; ruins of Homolobi near, 226
Winter solstice ceremony: Shallako of Zuñis, New Mexico, 184; Soya-luña of Hopi indians, Arizona, 339, 342
Witchcraft: execution of indians, 78
Wolfe's trading post (Ariz.): ruins, 305
Woman's basket dance of Patki or Rain Cloud clan (Lalakoñti) of Hopi indians: 341
Woman's hand tablet dance (Mamzrauti or Marau) of Hopi indians: 341
Wright, Harold Bell: *The Mine With the Iron Door*, 235
Wukoki ruins (Ariz.): built by Hopi Snake clan, 303; excavations by Doney and Fewkes, 303; discovered by Glore, 304; sheep corral built of metates, 304

XIMENA (N. Mex.): name given Galisteo by Coronado, 107

YE, JUAN: warns Velasco of Rebellion of 1680, 99; joins De Vargas, 100
Ysopete: guides Coronado in Kansas, 148
Yugeuingge (N. Mex.): Oñate stops, 34, 77; natives give up village to Spaniards, 34, 37, 77; San Gabriel built, 37
Yu-ke-o-ma: chief of hostiles at Oraibi, 299; 300

ZALDIVAR, JUAN DE: discovers Abó, 146; death, 165, 183, 190, 213
Zaldivar, Vicente de: discovers Abó, 146; captures Acoma, 165
Zamora, Fray Francisco de: missions assigned, 38, 83; builds mission at Taos, 87
Zarata, Fray Ascencion: bones exhumed, 49, 50, 83
Zipia indians: Arvide murdered, 28, 173, 183
Zuñi N. Mex.): Fray Marcos de Niza reaches, 26, 170; Estévan killed, 26, 170; Arvide murdered, 28, 83,

173, 183; join Jemez against De Vargas, 136; first named, 171; flee to Thunder mountain, 174; return from Thunder mountain, 174, 184; tradition of priest who joined tribe to escape death in 1680, 177, 178; 183-188; modern Zuñi, 184; mission founded, 184; Spanish soldiers killed, 184; garrison kept, 184; mission permanently abandoned, 184-187; ancient rites still observed, 184, 187; Shallako, 184; Cañaque, 184; sacred shrine of center of earth, 187; town crier, 187; ruins of the mission today, 187; Escalante's journey from Zuñi to Tusayan, 221

Zuñiga, Fray Garcia de: founds Socorro, 159; plants first grapes, 159; founds mission at Senecu, 160; death, 160

Zutucapan, chief of Acoma: plots to murder Oñate, 165